Bonsai school

Bonsai school

Craig Coussins

STERLING

New York / London
www.sterlingpublishing.com

Creative Director: Sarah King
Editor: Clare Haworth-Maden
Project editor: Sally MacEachern
Designer: Axis Design Editions

Library of Congress Cataloging-in-Publication Data available

10   9   8   7   6   5   4   3   2

Published in 2003 by Sterling Publishing Company, Inc
387 Park Avenue South, New York, N.Y. 10016

First published in the U.K. by D&S Books Limited
Kerswell, Parkham Ash, Bideford, EX39 5PR

© 2002 D&S Books Ltd
© 2008 Kerswell Books Ltd

Distributed in Canada by Sterling Publishing
C/o Canadian Manda Group
165 Dufferin St.,
Toronto, Ontario, Canada M6K 3H6

Every effort has been made to ensure that all the information in this book is accurate.
However, due to differing conditions, tools, and individual skills. the publisher cannot
be responsible for any injuries, losses, and other damages which may result from the
use of the information in this book.

Printed in Singapore

Sterling ISBN 978-1-4027-3560-8

Contents

introduction

introduction

It is strange that we often turn to the most complicated things to relax us when the simplest things usually succeed in doing the job. My grandfather Louis, who was blinded during World War I, became a wonderful gardener as he tried build a life bereft of the sense of sight. He used to say to me, "Always stop and look at the flowers along the way, but if you can't see them, at least immerse yourself in their scent, for that will create in your mind a memory, a moment of reflection."

We sometimes do not even know, or are unaware of, the things that we love. Perhaps you enjoy a walk through the park or woods on a spring morning as you breathe in the heady scent of damp soil, grass, and wild flowers floating in the air. Some of the things that I enjoy are the fun of throwing snow-balls; sitting under the spreading boughs of an ancient tree; a drink of ice-cold mountain-stream water; picking wild berries on a hot summer's day, popping the warm fruits into my mouth with my eyes closed and feeling my tastebuds well up for a minute in response to the sweet, sharp taste. Photographing wonderful landscapes with my wife is always a pleasure, and the images that we develop are reminders of our lovely experiences. In short, uncomplicated memories relax me and fill me with peace.

Shortly after taking up bonsai, I discovered that when I was working with my little potted trees, my sense of time, as well as my awareness of the outside world, simply disappeared. That feeling of being separated from the spinning world and all of its stresses can be very addictive. Although there are many things that you can do to relax, working with an ongoing project such as a bonsai will enable your mind, soul, and heart to develop. Nor will you have to learn a new language, just the names of the trees that you want to work with and those of the techniques and styles that you want to try out. Bonsai focuses the mind and, as you will discover for yourself, encourages natural meditation, so that while your body remains on the ground, your mind will soon be carried away as you work on your little trees.

Learning bonsai

When starting to learn bonsai, it's important not to become disheartened and to despair of ever achieving success. You will: your learning will gradually grow and develop, a process that will never stop.

Remember that it's not about being the best, but being the best that you can be. So do not be depressed if success seems to elude you, and instead applaud the fact that you are discovering new things, even when you think that you know it all.

Offering a lifelong path to enlightenment, bonsai can be as challenging to an old hand as to a newcomer. After thirty years of practicing bonsai, I now realize that what I thought I knew was fact fifteen years ago has changed, developed, and grown. Over that time I, too, have changed, and although I teach bonsai, my students also teach me: as they improve, they discover new things, which they share with me. So as you achieve knowledge, do not be impatient with others who do not seem to be able to learn as fast as you. Crawl, walk, jog, or run to your destination, but try to remain tolerant as you progress through your journey.

When you reach the level of bonsai or penjing that you are comfortable with, do not be lazy and remain there for too long. If you do not forge on, you will become idle and tired and will never learn all that there is to know, so keep looking for answers and stretch yourself as much as you can. Thinking that you know everything is a disease of the ego, and remember that teachers and artists are always experimenting, in a sense making them perpetual students.

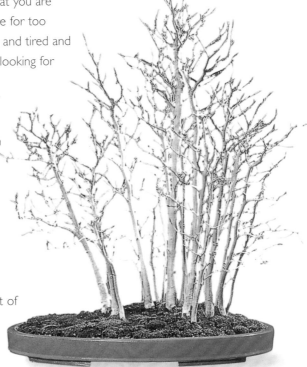

The following quotation, dated September 10, 1716, is taken from Yamamoto Tsunetomo's *The Hagakure—The Way of the Samurai*, a three-hundred-year-old manual of samurai strategy that illustrates how we should learn:
"In one's life there are certain levels in the pursuit of study. In the lowest level, a person studies, but nothing comes of it, and he feels that both he and others are unskillful.

At this point, he is worthless. In the middle level, he is still useless, but is aware of his own insufficiencies and can also see the insufficiencies of others. In a higher level, he has pride concerning his own ability, rejoices in praise from others, and then laments the lack of ability in his fellows. This man has worth. In the highest level, a man has the look of knowing nothing.

These are the levels in general. But there is one transcending level, and this is the most excellent of all. This person is aware of the endlessness of entering deeply into a certain 'Way,' never thinking of himself as having finished. He truly knows his own insufficiencies and never in his whole life thinks that he has succeeded. He has no thoughts of pride, but with self-abasement knows the 'Way' to the end."

It is said that Master Yagyu, a famous teacher, once remarked, "I do not know the way to defeat others, but the way to defeat myself."

Throughout your life advance daily, becoming more skillful than yesterday, more skillful than today. This is never-ending.

A brief guide to *Bonsai school*

In this book, I have approached the teaching of bonsai in a new way. When I was going through my education in school and college, I had a number of teachers who imparted the information necessary for me to pass my exams. Some of these teachers made a deep impression on me, but I have forgotten many others. I became a teacher of fencing, and eventually of bonsai, and when planning *Bonsai school* I decided to go back to my educational roots: I would ask a number of learned teachers for their input in creating a book that would act as a bonsai school. My bonsai faculty includes teachers of all levels of expertise to enable you to form a balanced view of subjects that could prove valuable in your development as a bonsai artist. Just like a school, we have teachers, professors, and some experts in special subjects who will discuss their particular forte. Everyone who has written for *Bonsai school* is a dedicated educationalist who not only loves what he or she does, but also enjoys sharing their knowledge. I am sure that they will make a deep impression on you in your quest for answers. I would like to thank all of the artists (whose names are listed on page 255—256) who gave their time and expended considerable effort in writing illuminating sections and supplying excellent images for inclusion in *Bonsai school*.

At the basic level, *Bonsai school* presents a course on how to make bonsai. Featured throughout the book are excellent images of classical bonsai created by artists who teach in the United States, Canada, South Africa, New Zealand, China, and Europe. Indeed, I have tried to show that good bonsai and penjing can be created in any country as long as you have developed the necessary skills. In other words, if shown the correct "Way," anyone can make a miniature tree, as well as excel in artistic areas associated with bonsai, such as pots and stones.

Each part of *Bonsai school* examines the techniques required to create a bonsai in depth.

Part 1

Lau Chung Ming, *Celtis sinensis*, 35in (90cm).

An outdoor penjing display in China.

The two opening chapters explain the history of the art of miniaturizing trees. Bonsai historian Robert Baran and I have worked together to tell the true history of bonsai, thereby clearing up some of the myths and misinformation that are occasionally put forward. This absorbing part of the book will help you to understand why bonsai is popular in today's culture.

Introduction

Part 2

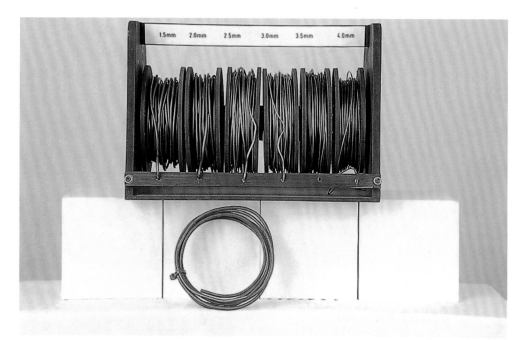

Part 2 will teach you bonsai techniques and how to take care of bonsai trees.

The second part of the book consists of four chapters that together form a structured course in how to create bonsai, covering popular methods and techniques, as well as trees suitable for bonsai culture.

Part 3

The third part of the book builds on an explanation of bonsai techniques and styles with a series of photo essays that systematically cover many bonsai-creating techniques. Working with material of the highest quality, bonsai masters from around the world demonstrate their art in a way that is both inspiring and easy to understand.

A bonsai that was brought to to the United States during President Lincoln's time is now in the care of the Golden State Bonsai Federation Collection in San Francisco, California.

Part 4

A miniature red maple measuring 8in (20cm), in a Korean pot with a miniature suiseki mountain range and waterfall.

The final part of the book explores those areas of interest that are associated with bonsai, namely suiseki, Chinese viewing stones, pots, and tools. Apart from the trees themselves, pots, which, because they are designed to frame the bonsai artwork, stand unassumingly in the background, are perhaps one of the most interesting facets of bonsai culture. Gordon Duffett, a well-known British potter, creates bonsai pots of such high-quality form and glaze that they can compete with the finest of ancient Chinese pots, and *Bonsai school* traces Duffett's development from his first pot to his most recent. In addition, Alan Harriman, the respected English creator of elegant pots with whom I work closely, discusses the design process. Joshua Roth, an outstanding bonsai toolmaker, wrote the tool section, while the viewing-stone sections were contributed by two of the United States' most respected authorities, Felix Rivera and stand-maker Sean Smith.

Bonsai and penjing

When reading *Bonsai school*, you will notice references to penjing, as the Chinese school of bonsai is called outside China. The reason for this is that huge numbers of non-Japanese tree-growers in Asia and the Pacific Rim follow penjing. In addition, references are made to other Asian styles of creating miniature trees and landscape plantings, including the Vietnamese Hon Non Bo. In the images (many of which have never before been seen in the West) and lessons presented in *Bonsai school* by some of the most respected growers of penjing in China, you will see similarities to bonsai in subject matter, but a different way of practising the art of creating miniature trees. And understanding some of these ancient and modern techniques will help you to develop as a student of the art of growing miniature trees.

Liang Run Jia, *Bougainvillea glabra*, 45 x 43in (115 x 110cm).

Part 1
Getting into bonsai

If you are interested in growing bonsai, you may want to know more about the history and development of the art, which is why this part of *Bonsai school* looks at how bonsai and penjing, its Chinese form, evolved.

The author at work.

During the past thirty years, bonsai and penjing have become one of the most popular horticultural interests. In the United States, for example, you can visit the National Arboretum (in Washington DC) that houses the National Bonsai and Penjing Pavilions. American presidents, dating as far back as Abraham Lincoln, have been given bonsai and penjing artworks (indeed, the Golden State Bonsai Federation Collection in San Francisco, California, looks after a tree from that early period). As you read these words, cities the world over either already host collections of bonsai and penjing or else are preparing to house them. Along with collections that are open to the public all over Europe and North America, you can see major exhibitions in Singapore, China, and Japan. In addition, private collections exist in virtually every world city, many of which are open by arrangement. Bonsai really is a worldwide hobby.

A bonsai that was brought to the United States in President Lincoln's time is now in the care of the Golden State Bonsai Federation Collection in San Francisco, California.

Bonsai can make beautiful additions to the home.

Who keeps bonsai?

Bonsai have become very trendy over the past ten years. Reflecting our current lifestyle and interests, garden centers, hardware stores, and even modern furnishing emporiums have all started to sell bonsai, while bonsai clubs are attracting an ever-increasing number of young people eager to learn the intricacies of growing miniature trees. Easy to care for, bonsai trees can be grown in windows that are neither too sunny nor too hot, as well as in other light environments or even bathrooms. And depending whether you live in a cold or temperate climate, bonsai can thrive both inside and outside.

Depending on the climate, bonsai can be either indoor or outdoor trees.

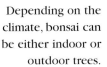

Getting into bonsai

classic gardens of Europe's palaces and castles, such as Versailles in France, it is not just the very rich who can enjoy a wonderful garden today. For thousands of years people have tried to become closer to nature by creating gardens, and now we are all trying to discover (or should that be rediscover?) the art of relaxing in our own backyards or personal spaces. And with Oriental-style gardens having become increasingly popular, the peace and tranquillity of a well-designed minimalist Oriental garden can be enhanced by the judicious placement of a bonsai or three.

Tenth-century garden in Suzhou, China, with large areas of water forming lakes and ponds.

In a world in which gardeners have become television stars in the West, everyone now seems to want to have water features or stone arrangements in their garden to help them to chill out and recover from the stresses of modern life. Decks and backyards are increasingly being designed to act as outdoor rooms, and with their architectural simplicity, bonsai or pen-jing trees often form part of these designs.

Beautifying the garden with pools, water features, and follies is not a new con-cept, however: the ancient Egyptians created gardens of beauty, as did the Islamic culture that succeeded that of ancient Egypt. Many "gardens of delight" and "gardens of Allah" were added to wealthy homes and palaces throughout the vast Moorish empire, traces of which can still be seen in the Spanish region of Granada. In England, knot gardens were created during the sixteenth century (and, indeed, are still being made today) with little hedges made of such trees as box (*Buxus sempervirens*). And in contrast to the wealth that was needed to create the great

There is no particular type of person who wants to have a real tree in miniature, but it is precisely this desire that defines bonsai-growers. The idea of holding the miniature image of a huge tree in your hand somehow appeals to all of us, perhaps reminding us of our childhoods, when we played with toys that represented bigger things, such as toy trains, cars, action figures, dolls and dollhouses.

Although anyone can keep bonsai, it is how you keep them that makes the difference. If you have just one bonsai or penjing, you could tend to this tree as you would a houseplant, giving it just enough care to keep it alive. If you move beyond this houseplant concept, however, you will find yourself on a wonderful journey of discovery, a journey that may even awaken something that you did not realize you had lost.

Manyeshnaya Square, Moscow—a twenty-first-century water garden in nineteenth-century style.

The sixteenth-century Generaliffe water gardens in the Alhambra, Granada, Spain.

Frequently asked questions

Here are the answers to some frequently asked questions about looking after indoor bonsai.

Q. Is keeping an indoor bonsai easy?

A. Yes. Simply acquire the best species for your environment and then follow the simple instructions for caring for it (see pages 69 to 101).

Q. Do bonsai need water?

A. Yes, but just enough to keep the soil damp and not swimming in mud. Mist your bonsai with a fine spray of water twice a day if it is housed in an air-conditioned office, but only three times a week in most other situations.

Q. Do bonsai need food?

A. Only during the growing season, when you should feed your bonsai with houseplant fertilizer once every two weeks.

Q. Where in the home or office should a bonsai not be kept?

A. It's important to remember that any plant that needs to be watered should not be kept near any electrical units or sockets or televisions, computers, radios, and other types of electrical appliance. In addition, don't place a bonsai near a working fireplace or radiator because the heat would cause it to dry up very quickly.

Q. Can a bonsai be kept in a window?

A. Before placing a bonsai in a window, note the following three pieces of advice.

1. Is the window very sunny? If so, the sunshine could fry the bonsai's small soil area, as well as its leaves.

2. It's best to keep your bonsai in a window that receives only a little sun, but a lot of natural light. Remember to turn the bonsai once a week so that it receives light evenly. Place a little marker on one of the edges of the pot and make sure that the marked side is facing you one week and pointing away from you the next.

3. Don't draw the drapes over a bonsai at night because the heat level surrounding it will suddenly drop, causing potentially serious damage to the tree in cold weather. It's best either to leave the drapes open or to remove the bonsai from the window area at night.

Mister spray.

Your bonsai will
thrive in a light, but
not sunny, window.

Q. Do bonsai need repotting?

A. If it is a young bonsai, it will need repotting once every year or two years, but a mature bonsai should be repotted once every three years.

Q. Is repotting a bonsai complicated?

A. No more complicated than repotting a houseplant. See pages 74 to 77 for full instructions.

Wu Yee-Sun
Pinus aspera.

Checklist

To sum up, keeping an indoor bonsai is easy as long as you follow some really basic instructions:

- keep it in a light position
- turn it regularly
- give it just enough water to keep the soil damp
- feed it a little every week
- if it is an indoor bonsai, mist it lightly every day
- repot your bonsai when necessary.

The origins of bonsai

Traditional Chinese gardens in Suzhou.

When I was writing this book, I came to realize that bonsai, penjing, Oriental gardens, landscapes in miniature, and the appreciation of viewing stones were inextricably linked over the centuries that predate our modern understanding of bonsai.

When the coliseum was being built by the Romans, others in the Far East were creating miniature landscapes in their gardens. I have always enjoyed studying the history of bonsai and have shared our general understanding of this art and its venerable history with my classes. The history that you are about to read is probably the most comprehensive ever written for a Western bonsai book. When you have read it, I hope that you will have a better understanding of the background of what has now become a hobby (but remember that it was not always classed as a pastime).

The evolution of bonsai

It is clear that the art of Chinese bonsai, or penjing (or pentsai, as it was also called), was the precursor of modern Japanese bonsai, its various styles having been practiced in the Far East for many centuries prior to its introduction to Japan. Other names are also used in Pacific Asia for the growing of miniature trees or the making of miniature landscapes, but most people are familiar with penjing, which can mean a tree or plant in a container with rocks or sand, and pentsai, which means a tree or arrangement of trees that may include a rock or rocks.

When pentsai was introduced to Japan through trade, the Japanese changed the name pentsai to bonsai, which essentially means a tree (bon) in a tray (sai). And although bonsai may not have meant a tree in a container in precise Japanese terminology, it became the generic word commonly used to describe the little landscapes and trees that the Chinese were exporting at that time. Today, the Japanese also have other names for tray landscapes, such as bonkei and bonseki, which are differentiations of the generic title bonsai (pronounced "bone-sigh").

The historical aspects of bonsai make a compelling study in themselves. Ancient drawings on Egyptian tombs showing small trees in containers placed around temples seem to suggest that there was a religious element uniting trees and worship. Alternatively, these plants may have been medicinal, which may have been why Egyptian priests kept them near their temples. Indeed, in Indian religious culture many plants and trees were used for medicinal purposes, and physicians, medicine men, or shamans could therefore have grown these plants in containers to make it easier to transport them.

Ancient records tell of traveling Hindus using Ayurvedic medicine, a system of treatment dating back to about 3000 B.C. that focuses on keeping the body free of disease. Regarding the human body as a microcosm of the universe, Ayurvedic medicine considers that if the prana, or life force, within us is unbalanced, ill-health will result. To explain further, three doshas (forces) determine the correct balance needed for the health of the human organism: kapha (water and tides), pitta (heat and energy), and vata (connected with the wind). Finding a person's balance through Ayurvedic medicine sometimes requires a dietary change, meditation, praying aloud, treatment with herbs, plant leaves or barks, massage, and special exercises based on a type of yoga.

The origins of bonsai

Chinese gardens
in Suzhou.

Ayurvedic medicine had a great influence on traditional Chinese medicine, the basis of which can be traced back to this point of reference, and if they were to have the right plants to hand to restore the balance of the person being treated, traveling Chinese medicine men, shamans, and monks (disciples of Buddha, or lohans) had to carry living plants with them. In order to make their transportation easier, these plants were constantly trimmed, and it is thought that the medicine men eventually realized that this treatment reduced the plants' leaf size, as well as encouraging them to develop dense twigs, so that they reflected the image of a much larger tree in miniature. Such miniaturized trees were so fascinating to look at that it is assumed that some were sold and others propagated to achieve a similar appearance.

Early evidence of bonsai was discovered in the tomb of Prince Zhang Huai, who died in 706 during the Tang Dynasty (618–907), in the form of two wall paintings (copies of which hang in China's Shanghai Botanic Gardens) showing servants carrying what we believe to be bonsai. One of these paintings depicts a miniature landscape being carried and the other a pot with a tree in it.

The design and arrangement of plants and stones in this way could date back around 1,800 years, but apart from a few references during the Jin Dynasty (265–420), very little material predates the Tang

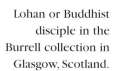

Lohan or Buddhist
disciple in the
Burrell collection in
Glasgow, Scotland.

An example of Hon Bon No, created by Lit Van Phan.

Today viewing stones, called suiseki in the West, are enthusiastically collected in such countries as Indonesia, China, Japan, and Korea.

Dynasty. By the time of the Sung Dynasty (960–1279), however, the art of arranging trees in pots was becoming popular, with many artists vying with each other to procure interesting little trees and unique stones. The development of this interest in penjing was based on the belief that such tree images would simulate the natural environment and assist meditation.

At this point you'll need to try to switch from a Western to an Eastern mind-set. Stones, for example, were thought of in an almost religious manner in the East as parts of nature that held an internal, sometimes significant, power. In those far-off days, stones were not thought of as being spirits in themselves, but places within which a spirit could stay. In both Japanese and Chinese mythology and indeed religion, forests, cliffs, waterfalls, mountains, and valleys were similarly believed to be the homes of Kami spirits, such places being both

venerated and treated carefully so that nothing would upset the spirits in residence, for whom offerings were left in the hope of appeasing them. Local Japanese communities who followed the Shinto religion all had their own Kami spirits and protected their special places in order to avoid incurring a poor harvest or a spring so bad that the crops were ruined.

The history of miniaturizing trees therefore has a multitude of beginnings and, in many cases, dead ends, too. Korea, China, and Japan in the Far East certainly developed the art of growing mini-trees, but was this the result of commerce between Indian and Chinese itinerant traders? (I have seen amazing trees in Singapore styled into Chinese characters denoting good-luck symbols or words.)

A painted- and gilded-marble, Buddha-like figure from Sri Lanka.

Buddhism, meditation, and bonsai

Religious beliefs were certainly being spread from India to China through Buddhism, a system of religious belief taught by Prince Siddhartha Gautama. Born in Nepal, Buddha taught in the valley of the Ganges, in India, from 544 B.C., the date of his enlightenment, until his death in 489 B.C. In China, his followers, or disciples, were called lohans. Buddha adjusted his teaching according to his students' level of advancement. In some cases, he would teach at the highest level, not speaking, but pointing at both reality and the Buddha nature within each of us to show us that we can all be part of the whole. The realization of our Buddha-nature is called illumination, or Buddhahood, and Buddha taught that the way to attain illumination is through meditation or, to use a more popular expression, "Meditation is the road to enlightenment."

While religious beliefs developed along their own lines in China and other places, in Japan it was Buddhism, and subsequently Shintoism, that became the stronger element of religious focus over the following centuries. Traders from China traveled through Korea across the sea to Japan, a country that they called "The Floating

This fifteenth-century figure of a lohan (a disciple of Buddhism) is part of the Burrell Collection in Glasgow, Scotland. About 4ft (1.2m) in height, the figure is made from polychrome (gilding and colored paint) on biscuit glaze with traces of gilding.

Islands." Buddhism was already the main religion of Korea, and the Koreans introduced Buddhist concepts to Japan from around the sixth century A.D. This period of Japan history is known as the Suiko (or Asuka) period, dating from A.D. 522 to 646. The Empress Suiko, after whom the period is named (a highly intelligent and exceptionally good ruler for those times) was instrumental in persuading her people to take up this new religion. The introduction of Korean Buddhism to Japan was an extremely quick process. The Buddhist element of

Buddhas and suiseki in a home—not for religious reasons, but for decora

simplicity and minimalism appealed to the Japanese, a very intellectual society, and their rapid understanding of the concepts of Buddhism is testament to that intelligence. Not only did the Japanese accept the religious ideas of Buddhism, but also adopted many other elements of the cultures of Korea and China over the next five hundred years.

Chinese gardens in Suzhou.

The figure of the lohan is inscribed with the words "The 20th year of Chenghua," dating it to A.D. 1484.

The art of creating miniature trees reached Japan around nine hundred years ago. The sale of goods by Chinese and Korean traders to Japan prompted an increasing desire among the Japanese to study the artistic and manufacturing methods of the Chinese. Japan therefore dispatched representatives to China and Korea to learn about the making of materials, art, architecture, and even the legal aspects of central and local government. This hunger for knowledge really got into gear during the time of the later Sung period, that of the Southern Sung Dynasty (1127–1279), when the Japanese stepped up their importation of aspects of Chinese culture, calligraphy, ceremonies, and the arts. And although the Chinese form of Buddhism, known as Chan, which specializes in teaching and practicing meditation ("Chan" is derived from the Sanskrit word "Dyana," which means "meditation," and the Japanese translation of Chan is Zen), had been introduced to Japan from Korea more than five hundred years previously, during this period its cultural aspects now came into their own. Chan trains the mind, for example, through the "Way of the Brush," using ink, paper, ink stones, and brushes (the source of Sumi-e brush-painting). The Chinese had already mastered the art of growing little trees and now taught this art to Japanese enthusiasts, notably the Japanese aristocracy.

The study and enjoyment of penjing and bonsai are therefore partly based on the teachings of Buddhism and partly on the simple enjoyment of nature. Perhaps we should now look at some of the teachings that developed from meditation and the attempt to attain self-awareness.

The origins of bonsai

An example of Hon Non Bo created by Lit Van Phan from Vietnam.

In an attempt to find the key to meditation, some followers of Buddhism used stones and miniature landscapes, with or without trees, with which to focus their minds. Acting like Russian or Greek icons, these tiny representations of the world around them encouraged meditation. Again like icons, they were not objects of worship, but channels for the meditator's devotion and focus, for through concentration comes meditation.

In China, when people, be they ordinary people, scholars or priests, made small natural images of mountainscapes in

The amazing limestone mountains in the Gweilin (Guilin) region of China are often referred to in Chinese art.

Stone in Chinese gardens forms part of the design as a home for spirits.

their homes or gardens, they sometimes used them as incense-burners and called them boshanlu, "magic mountain braziers." This practice can be dated back to the Han Dynasty (202 B.C.–A.D. 220), and there are also references to it during the preceding Ch'in Dynasty when the association was with finding a home for the spirits. The practice, which had a religious significance that has a strong association with Daoism, was passed down through the centuries in China, taking on the mantle of other subsequent religions in the process.

Some boshanlu were created in the shape of the Three Isles

of the Blessed – Yingzhou, Fangzhang, and Penglai—where the Chinese Immortals were thought to live, as well in the mystical, cloud-covered Western Mountains. Among the myths surrounding the islands and mountains between which the Immortals moved was the belief that the islands could vanish into mist or a cloud, just as the Immortals could when mortals approached them. A boshanlu consisting of rocks and plants or three small islands on a marble slab incorporating an incense-burner thus created an image of the mysterious, mist-enshrouded places inhabited by the Immortals. And if a boshanlu did not bring you good luck, at the very least it would help you to meditate.

The Chinese also created wonderful gardens from limestone lifted from lakes. Ling bi stones (usually limestone rocks) incorporated water channels and holes, making them appear imbued with character. This mountain imagery was enhanced by the addition of very old, small trees taken from mountainsides, a practice that can be traced back to the Tang Dynasty. (See the section on Vietnamese rock-plantings, pages 179 to 181, for further information.) Given the Japanese interest in all things Chinese, it is not surprising that these stones and trees made their way to Japan, and that the trade and purchase of Chinese products, culture, and art, started during the Sung period, would continue for many centuries.

Perhaps it was the Chinese love of nature that brought such arrangements of stones and trees into the home, not only for meditation or focusing, but to give your spirit a home within your home so that you could make offerings to it whenever you wanted to please it. Indeed, one needs only to appreciate the popularity of the Chinese system of feng shui, whose history is documented over the course of five thousand years, to understand how important it is for people in the Far East to try to improve their home and family lives by living in harmony with the Earth.

Unfortunately, many of the ancient arts of China were considered irrelevant by China's communist régime during the twentieth century, and it is only during the past thirty years that penjing has again become popular in China. Rather ironically, it was the Japanese who helped to introduce bonsai to some parts of China during the latter half of the twentieth century, the Chinese in turn now having redeveloped the ancient art of penjing. Today, penjing is quickly becoming as popular as bonsai throughout the world, in reflection of which I have blended bonsai and penjing in *Bonsai school*.

Many enthusiasts who keep bonsai or penjing say that they find great peace when they work on their trees: as the time passes, their worries and stresses seem to float away on a cloud. If that isn't meditation, what is?

A twenty-year-old penjing Chinese elm (*Ulmus parvifolia*) measuring 19in (50cm).

Chinese landscapes typified by Gweilin JR.

This penjing *Bougainvillea glabra* on a rock, which was created by Wong Kee Mein, measures 53in (135cm).

Development of bonsai,
by Robert J. Baran
(United States)

Robert J. Baran, a bonsai historian from Phoenix, Arizona, now gives us his views on the development of bonsai.

This penjing Chinese elm (*Ulmus parvifolia*) was created by Qing Quan Zhao.

Chinese schools of penjing

From the sixteenth through to the late nineteenth century, certain rigid styles developed throughout China. While most of these regional styles are no longer practiced, some have been revived. There were six penjing schools based on these regional variations which emerged during this period. Many of these various styles identified not only a regional master

and his school, but used local material. There was another group of people who created penjing that were less rigid in style. Creating miniature trees was, for some masters, like painting and styles of penjing were often imitated from Chinese traditional painting. In addition, many Chinese officials retired to the garden city of Suzhou and not only built their own garden, (indeed many thousands were built although less than 30 survive), but also designed penjing in whatever style they wished.

Categories of penjing

Penjing have traditionally been divided into two categories: shansui and shumu. Shansui are the "mountain and water," or landscape, penjing that feature mostly rocks and depict mountain scenes. Trees may or may not appear; if they are included, they play a minor role in the overall composition. Shumu, or "tree" penjing (also known as pentsai), are the close cousins of the Japanese bonsai, depicting the image of one or several trees, those being the main material and dominant element in the composition.

A penjing *Podocarpus macrophyllus* measuring 82in (210cm), from the Yuen Yuen Institute in Hong Kong.

A penjing Chinese elm (*Ulmus parvifolia*) created by He Shi Chuang.

When creating a shumu penjing—or a traditional painting, for that matter—the Chinese artist pays much attention to variation inherent in contrast, seeking to generate opposites (upright versus slanting, solid versus void, dense versus sparse and so on) that will successfully unite in a harmonious fashion. Although nursery-grown stock is now the source of most material, shuzhuang (literally "tree stump"), or collected penjing, was the traditional beginning for a composition. The six basic forms in China are the straight trunk, slanting trunk, curved trunk, cliff-hanging, vine, and forest styles. Literati penjing form a category of their own, which is imbued with the characteristics of aloofness, sparseness, refined elegance, and plainness.

27

A penjing white pine (Pinus parviflora) created by Liu Rong Sen.

Regional styles and schools in China

Because penjing seeks to recapture real scenery and the characters and moods of natural trees, it is not surprising that this ancient art form displays as much variation as the Chinese regions (which differ in their geography, climate, and the appearance of their trees) in which it has developed and is practiced. The materials chosen by artists in different regions are not alike—styling techniques vary as well —and each has its merits. Further variables include the artist's personality, philosophy, and artistic training.

The Su school or Northern group

Over the centuries, different penjing schools have emerged in China. At present, there are two main groups of regional style with regard to shumu penjing. The first is the Su school or Northern group from the area of the Yangtze River Valley, whose trees—predominantly conifers—show the presence of distinctly shaped foliage layers or clusters. In addition, because of a shorter growing season, the tree shapes need to be established using wiring. Apart from these common traits, however, styles differ significantly, although in general Northern landscape penjing are noted for their grand, fantastic appearance. The Northern school is subdivided into the Eastern Su and Western Su schools.

An example of Yangzhou garden penjing.

EASTERN SU:
The Eastern Su school
The Yangzhou school

The Yangzhou school has a long tradition of training penjing featuring neat, distinctive foliage layers. Limbs trained into thin, flat, oval-shaped foliage, horizontally placed and usually of equal or similar size, are traditionally known as "cloud layers" and are the product of artistic exaggeration. A tree usually features an odd number of these richly decorative layers. Penjing with one to three levels represent the "platform style," and those with over three levels are of the "ingenious or delicate cloud style." Most of the trunks are trained into a spiraling shape known as "roaming dragon curves."

Yangzhou artists are highly skilled at bending the trunk, heavy branches, and shorter branches with palm-fiber strings. Trained from an early age, the trees undergo meticulous bending and pruning. This style requires a high level of skill and is very time-consuming. Scrupulous attention is paid to every detail, and their meticulous work has earned the artists universal respect. The traditional, conventional, and standardized styles, with their unique features, have been preserved to this day. Material used includes species of pine, juniper, elm, and boxwood.

Introducing Qing Quan Zhao

Qing Quan Zhao is the vice president of the Association of Penjing Artists of China, a third-generation penjing enthusiast and a penjing master at Hong Yuan in Yangzhou. During the 1970s, Zhao began developing what has become a third category of penjing, shuihan ("water-and-land" style). Inspired by Yangzhou's classical garden art and the great landscape paintings of the south-western provinces, he has created garden scenes of inextricably linked water, rocks, and trees in miniature on very shallow containers (usually marble slabs).

that are typical of an aged specimen.

Some Anhui bonsai (Anhui Province is situated in the north-west of East China across the basins of the Yangtze River and the Huaihe River) are characterized by their screen-like, horizontal extensions. At an early stage of cultivation, their branches are trained sideways. Sometimes several trees are combined by means of grafting to achieve a multi-dimensional, geometric shape.

The Penjing gardens in Yangzhou.

A chastetree (*Negundo*) created by Zhou Guo Liang.

The Tung, or T'ung school

The Tung, or T'ung, school is based in Anhui. Similar to the method of the Yangzhou school, the Tung uses as a guideline for the styling of "plum penjing in She county" the ancient saying that "a plum tree is beautiful when twisted and devoid of appeal when straight." Beginning with a circular bend starting from the plant's roots in the container, the upper trunk is curved with two half-bends into a smooth "S" configuration. The trees, positioned so that they incline forward, gradually reach upward in a form known as "coiled dragon," named for its resemblance to a roaming dragon.

When training the Chinese cypress or Sargent juniper, Anhui artists twist the trunk into a spiraling shape when the tree is still young to create the striations in bark

A twenty-year-old penjing Celtis sinensis measuring 44in (86cm), Man Lung Penjing.

WESTERN SU:
The Western Su school
The Suzhou school

Trees trained by members of the Suzhou school are known for the aged appearance of their trunks and their curved branches. Pure and beautiful, they impart a feeling of classical elegance. Traditional forms were fairly standardized, one major style calling for the trunk to be twisted from one side to the other into a total of six curves; three branch arrangements extending from the bole to the right and three to the left. These branches were called "six platforms."

Three more were trained toward the back, being the "three bases." Another cluster crowned the top, and the entire design was named "six platforms, three bases and one top."

The area around the town of Guangfu (near Suzhou) has certain formulae for training plum penjing. These include the "tree branches overhanging a cliff" style, "split-trunk" style, "screen" style, and "following the wind" style. The latter form is similar to the "slanted-trunk" form, but the angle of the trunk is extreme and an overly extended branch protrudes abruptly from the top. Pine trees are often used, and they can then be placed in living rooms because they mimic a beckoning gesture that is easily observed by guests. Such creations are called "guest-welcoming pines."

The "basic shaping through bending" and "fine shaping through pruning" techniques are used for style development. The bole and branches are first bent into "S" configurations with the help of palm-fiber strings. Over the ensuing years, this elementary shape is refined by meticulous pruning. Cutting is viewed as the chief styling method, assisted by trunk- and limb-bending. Special features of Suzhou penjing are an old-looking trunk with a large number of branches, sharp contrasts between dead wood and lush sections and a plump, smooth foliage layer rounding out the top. Deciduous species such as the hedge sageretia, Chinese elm, trident maple, plum, and pomegranate are extensively used. Conifers like the Chinese juniper and five-needle pine are a common sight in Suzhou penjing as well.

A penjing white five-needle pine (*Pinus parviflora*) created by Wu Yee-Sun.

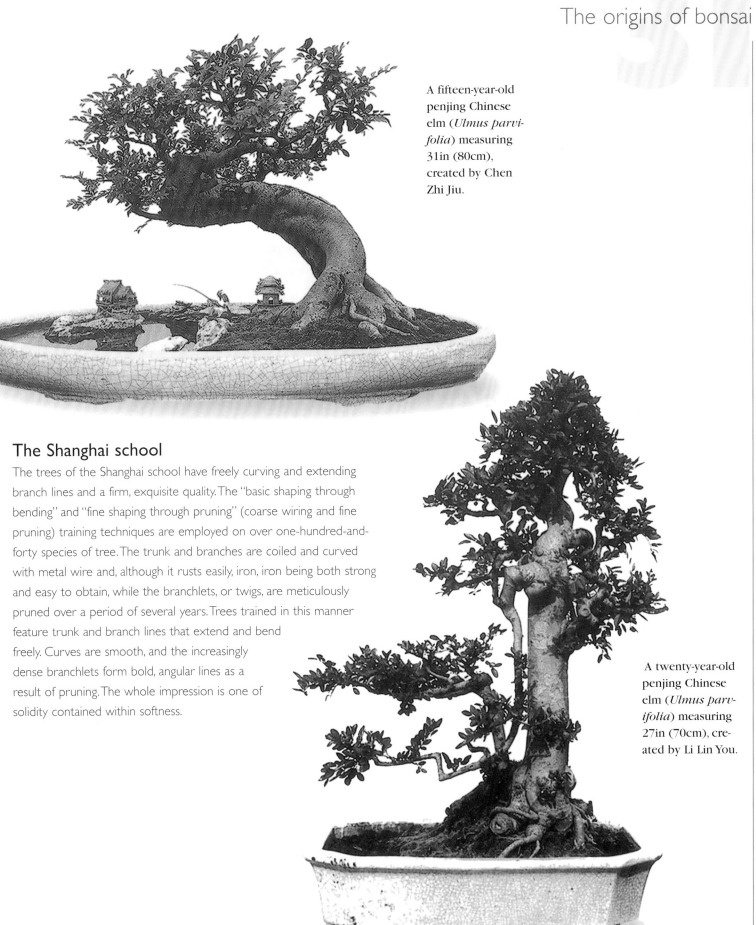

A fifteen-year-old penjing Chinese elm (*Ulmus parvifolia*) measuring 31in (80cm), created by Chen Zhi Jiu.

The Shanghai school

The trees of the Shanghai school have freely curving and extending branch lines and a firm, exquisite quality. The "basic shaping through bending" and "fine shaping through pruning" (coarse wiring and fine pruning) training techniques are employed on over one-hundred-and-forty species of tree. The trunk and branches are coiled and curved with metal wire and, although it rusts easily, iron, iron being both strong and easy to obtain, while the branchlets, or twigs, are meticulously pruned over a period of several years. Trees trained in this manner feature trunk and branch lines that extend and bend freely. Curves are smooth, and the increasingly dense branchlets form bold, angular lines as a result of pruning. The whole impression is one of solidity contained within softness.

A twenty-year-old penjing Chinese elm (*Ulmus parvifolia*) measuring 27in (70cm), created by Li Lin You.

Here you can see how stones used in Suzhou give the impression of distant mountains.

2. Those made from soft rock, such as coral rock, pumice, and sedimentary sandstone. The rocks are meticulously carved to bring out the outlines and grain. Small grasses are cultivated on the rocks and trays typically feature a wide expanse of water. Artists employ a "flat distance" or "deep distance" composition to recreate the countryside south of the Yangtze river, a region of rivers and lakes.

The Shanghai Botanic Garden, the largest and most famous in China, is undoubtedly the center of dwarf-tree culture in that country. Growing in the garden are eight to nine hundred penjing from all parts of China. The collection includes a large number of old trees inherited from the Guomintang

Shanghai rock plantings

Rock plantings were used extensively by the artists of the Shanghai school. Eagerly tapping the rich local reservoir of hard rocks for use as penjing material, landscapes were created from what were called axe-cut rock, stone bamboo-shoot rock, ying rock, xuancheng rock, and others. These masters also pioneered the cultivation of miniature trees and other plants on these rocks.

At present, miniature landscapes from Shanghai may be further divided into two rough categories.

1. Those made from hard rock that recreate a near scene by combining rocks and trees in an ingenious manner. It appears that enormous peaks scrape the sky, while beautiful plants grow luxuriantly further down the mountains.

In perfect harmony with its surrounding, this Suzhou stone graces a Chinese garden.

Many gardens in China recreate images from the country's many mountain regions. This waterfall, in Yosemite, shows how water and stone can come together to produce an amazingly balanced image of natural art.

A penjing *Podocarpus macrophyllus* measuring 51in (130cm), created by Ng Yau Yuen.

government, while some were given to the garden by Japan in 1930. During the domestic turmoil within China, these trees were protected and spared. Containing one hundred-and twenty varieties of tree and twenty different kinds of rock, the Shanghai Botanic Garden is managed by a production brigade of fifty experienced workers. In addition to the main collection, a large number of miniature landscapes and trees are created for export. The production of penjing has been increasing: in 1980, some twenty thousand were sold from here (most of these going to Japan), and by 1988 the number exported had doubled.

The Nantong school

The specialty of the Nantong school is the *Podocarpus*, whose trunk is trained with palm-fiber strings into two-and-a-half forward-leaning curves. The foliage layers are arranged on either side, making the whole a unique design.

The Moon Gate in Suzhou Gardens, China.

The Zhejiang school

A newcomer to penjing, the Zhejiang school uses the same species as the Shanghai school, training its foliage into distinctly shaped layers. To treat the trees, the artists use metal wire and palm-fiber strings combined with meticulous pruning, such as pruning back buds and shoots and removing terminal buds. Much attention is paid to rhythmic change as the artists strive for dynamic beauty. Artists in Zhejiang province do not always seek to curve a tree's trunk, however, when training the five-needle pine in particular, often aiming for an erect bole and striving to highlight such features as venerability, a lean, strong frame and a majestic, tall appearance. The most common styles are thus the "tall trunk" and "forest" styles.

A rock landscape
in a tray from
China.

A mountain scene like this
in the Yosemite Valley in
the United States can
suggest source material
for a mountain landscape
in your own garden.

The Hunan school

The Hunan school is notable for training *Sabina chinensis* cv. *Procumbans* (juniper) penjing into the "hanging cliff" style.

The Hubei school

The Hubei school effected a breakthrough in styling techniques with a penjing named "autumn melancholy." As a result of pruning, the branches and foliage appear to be fluttering off to one side, the artist thus sculpting a penjing that vividly portrays a tree being attacked by high winds.

The Henan school

The specialty of the Henan school is training the tamarisk.

The Shandong school

In the city of Shandong can be found landscape penjing made with tortoise-vein rock and green laoshan rock, both of which are known for their bold, yet unpretentious, character and the imposing and rugged nature of their contours. These rocks are often used to depict Peng Lai, the magical abode of the Immortals, or the majestic grandeur of Mount Tai.

The Beijing school

The collection of potted trees at the Beijing Botanic Garden was only established during the late 1970s, the art of pentsai having been almost obliterated as a result of China's modern political upheavals, which is why most of the young trees here lack the vigor and appearance of age.

A twenty-five-year-old penjing *Sageretia theezans* measuring 6in (16cm).

The Sichuan, Chuan or Ch'uan school

The trees of the Sichuan, Chuan, or Ch'uan school, which are twisted into a multitude of shapes, are characterized by their many flowing curves and upward-moving spirals, so that they appear old, grand, and dignified, also displaying a touch of the unusual.

Based on strict patterns, the boles and branches of most of the traditional penjing of this school are curved into a variety of shapes, with palm-fiber strings being used for training. Each has a focal point, poetically referred to as a "pearl embraced by a cavorting dragon." Popular formulae for trunk-coiling include "square turns" (corner bends), "curves with paired branches," "reversing curves," "large curves with drooping branches," "straight trunk with crown," "coiling dragon embracing a staff or pillar," "old woman combing her hair," or "wife applying make-up." Branches may also be twisted to appear as "flat," "spiraling," or "coiled," "half-flat," "half-spiraling," and so on. These shapes are collectively referred to as "earthworm curves."

Sichuan landscape penjing artists use mostly sedimentary sandstone.

The Liaoning school

Landscape penjing from the Liaoning school are made from petrified wood to represent the steep mountain scenery of China's northern region.

The Jilin school

Pumice penjing are also created by the Jilin school, again in an attempt to capture the appearance of the steep mountain scenery of northern China.

A twenty-year-old penjing Chinese elm (*Ulmus parvifolia*) measuring 37in (95cm), created by Ye De Jin.

Craig Coussins and Luigi Crespi pictured by the huge fig (*Ficus*) in the Crespi Nurseries' bonsai gallery.

The Lingnan school or Southern group

The second main group of regional style with regard to shumu penjing is the Lingnan school or Southern group, whose miniature landscapes reflect the warm climate and plentiful rainfall that is enjoyed throughout the year in the southern regions of China. The penjing created here frequently feature an erect, majestic posture and exuberant growth, also reflecting the prevalent environment.

Artists of the Lingnan school, in Guangdong province, select species of tree for their ability to shoot from old wood and their compatibility with the "grow and clip" training technique. Hedge sageretia, orange jasmine, Fukien tea, Chinese elm, Japanese zelkova, and fig—particularly banyan—are the most common materials used.

It is only during the past few decades that there has been a gradual development toward more natural styles. Today, the shape of a penjing is largely determined by the tree's natural growth pattern, the artists no longer being bound by any formula. The artists have attained a high level of proficiency in pruning: trees taper from base to apex, while the proportions between trunk, limbs, and branchlets are highly developed. If one were to cut off any branch at random, that branch itself would display the shape of a grown tree, highlighting the exquisite results that can be achieved with the "grow and clip" method. Bending using wires, weights, and other artificial means of training is not utilized by the artists of the Lingnan school, only selective pruning techniques. The Lingnan artist strives to reveal, not control, the nature of a specimen (a goal that is very much in line with Daoism), with spontaneity and whimsy being encouraged.

In Guangdong province, landscapes made from ying rock are common. Pieces of rock are piled in an ingenious manner to create an appearance of both grandeur and elegance or to effect rock formations that either seem to thrust into the sky and pierce the clouds or lie across the container apparently stretching toward the horizon.

Other members of the Lingnan school include the artists of Fujian province, who are known for their pentsai figs, which are of a jade-like green color throughout the year and possess aerial roots drooping from the trunks. The limbs and exposed roots are coiled into bizarre shapes on the container surfaces to convey a sense of the southern region of China.

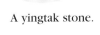

A yingtak stone.

The Li river that runs through Guilin's (Gweilin's) limestone cliffs has inspired Chinese poets for over three thousand years.

Southern landscape penjing are renowned for their elegance and beauty. Those created in Guangxi province, for example, are frequently made from local sedimentary sandstone or reed-pipe rock and depict the landscape around Guilin. The essence of the scenery along the Li river, with its jade-like peaks, elegant waters, bizarre caves, and gorgeous rocks, is fully captured.

Buddhist sects blended with elements of nature-honoring Shinto on Japanese soil and Zen Buddhism emerged. The core of Zen philosophy could be summed up as "beauty in severe austerity," with all non-essentials being stripped away to reveal the true Buddha nature of a thing.

Bonsai and its development in Japan

Around the time of the introduction of penjing from China, Japanese contemplative gardens were called shima ("islands"). These were scaled-down models of sea and island scenery, some faithfully copying particular locations using the basic form of a pond with a central island. (This native design would be applied to gardens until the twentieth century.) Some of these landscapes would be "dry," in that they consisted of sand and stones only. A blend of the Japanese contracting of nature with the new Chinese ideas resulted in bonseki ("tray rocks"), dry mountain-landscape gardens reduced to the size of a box or tray.

Attempts to work with plants similar to those used in China gave way to compositions that made use of native plants and rocks. Because the Japanese natural landscape had relatively less diversity when compared with that of China, Japanese gardens and tray landscapes tended to be more plant-oriented. In addition, some Chan

Gweilin's limestone cliffs.

37

The origins of bonsai

In Japan, the epitome of dwarf-potted landscapes representing the interplay of the natural with the supernatural became those that were distilled into a single, ideal tree. The same expression of the concept of compressing the universe into a smaller space is mirrored in ikebana ("dancing flowers"), the art of focusing on nature-contracted beauty in an overall arrangement of varied plant parts rather than on the blooms themselves. Another example is haiku, the minimalist,

A maple (*Acer palmatum*), measuring 32in (81.25cm), created by P. Chan.

seventeen-syllable poetry of Japan, as is seen in this haiku poem by Jessie Edwards of South Africa:

Five stories up
Optimistic fig
Sends forth roots
To reach the ground.

As in China, monks, scholars and aristocrats were the first Japanese people to design and care for these dwarves. Although the image of a potted miniature tree was eventually adopted by everyone, from shoguns to merchants and other common folk, who delighted in the seasonal changes of these

portable trees, the ideal faded somewhat as hachinoki ("trees in bowls") became a commodity that almost anyone could afford. While the best specimens still were those gathered from the wild, many more were available through the equivalent of nursery propagation. Scrolls, and later woodblock prints, occasionally included one as a decorative feature or even the subject of a still-life.

At the turn of the twentieth century, a group of Japanese students of traditional Chinese culture and philosophy decided that they needed to create a specific version of these artistic pot plants, one that was perhaps "purer" and closer to its Chinese roots. Having studied the classic painter's manual and adopted much of its terminology, they named their trees bonsai, the Japanese pronunciation of the Chinese characters that make up the word pentsai. A handful of Japanese works on the creation of bonsai were then published. At the end of the twentieth century, bonsai specialty magazines, organizations of bonsai enthusiasts, national exhibitions of bonsai, the importation of Chinese pots, the fabrication of Japanese containers, and the use of copper wire for the shaping of branches and trunks could all be seen in Japan.

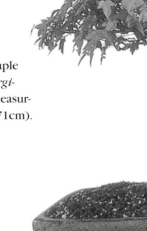

Trident maple (*Acer buergi-ranum*) measuring 28in (71cm).

Over the intervening generations, there has been at least three distinct stages of the art's development into so-called "modern bonsai." One specialty side branch saw the ultimate reduction in size, the greatest condensing by the Japanese of hundreds of years of natural growth and vast amounts of space. Many different varieties of tree were now being cultured as mame ("bean") bonsai. Growing in thimble-sized planters, these were, and continue to be, small enough to enable a representation or two of the universe to fit into the palm of one's hand.

During the 1920s, tools specifically designed for use on bonsai, including the concave-cutter, were becoming available in Japan. And, two years after the great earthquake of 1923, thirty families of professional bonsai-growers from Tokyo re-established themselves to the north-east, in a forest clearing on the northern edge of the town of Omiya. The bonsai village of Omiya would become the center of the world of bonsai visited by enthusiasts from all over the world, especially after World War II.

The Kokufu Exhibition, which was first held in Tokyo in 1934 by the Kokofu Bonsai Society, became an annual event and the most prestigious show in the art of bonsai. In addition, by the late-1930s, the principles for the display of bonsai were being altered as attitudes changed and trees were being shaped by more people than ever before. The individual beauty of the tree was at last recognized as being more important than any spiritual or symbolic significance that it might hold. The Kokofu Bonsai Society, which had become the Nippon Bonsai Association in 1934, was formally authorized by the Japanese Ministry of Education in 1965. It is the only incorporated bonsai organization in Japan.

After the widespread devastation caused during World War II and the depression that followed, the remnants of the art of bonsai were slowly revitalized in Japan as the seeds of interest that had been planted around the world began to take root. Because of a dearth of mature raw material, young plants had to be utilized more often than before, and the art of saikei is an offshoot of this historical necessity.

Robert Baran.
.

A mame ("bean") bonsai created by I. Murray.

A Scots pine (*Pinus sylvestris*) created by M. Bradder.

Bonsai in Vietnam

Finally, I'd like to look at the development of bonsai and its associated disciplines in Vietnam. Despite war and political upheaval, the Vietnamese nevertheless managed—through perseverance and secrecy—to keep their arts alive, including their unique form of miniature landscapes and bonsai. I first came across Vietnamese plantings when I taught in Russia and worked with the leader of Moscow's bonsai club, Tamara Belousova, who had studied in Vietnam. Also a teacher and one of the principal curators of the Moscow Botanic Gardens, Tamara understood many of the concepts of Vietnamese bonsai, as well as of Vietnamese landscape and rock arrangements.

Examples of Hon Non Bo created by Lit Van Phan. These arrangements of stones or plants represent the natural landscapes of Vietnam.

A Vietnamese grower who has settled in the U.S. state of California, Lit Van Phan has recently published a book on the Vietnamese form of rock landscape planting called Hon Non Bo. Lew Buller, his co-author, and his publisher, Timber Press, were kind enough to give permission for the following extract, adapted with permission from *Mountains in the sea: the Vietnamese miniature landscape art of Hon Non Bo*, Timber Press, Portland, Oregon, 2001, to appear in *Bonsai school*.

Hon Non Bo: Vietnamese miniature landscape art

Hon Non Bo, which is quite distinct from Vietnamese bonsai, was developing in Viet Nam about the same time that penjing was developing in China, and perhaps before the Japanese learned about the living art of bonsai. Early written records about Hon Non Bo are non-existent; Viet Nam was dominated by the Chinese for a thousand years and invaded periodically after that, and each time it was invaded, all the written and cultural history was destroyed. Not until A.D. 939 did the Vietnamese people enjoy full independence, and even that was interrupted and threatened in later centuries. The struggle to unite North and South Viet Nam and to remain independent continued more than a thousand years after freedom from foreign control was first achieved.

With independence in 939, people resumed writing books, and miniature landscapes were described in them, so there is evidence that Hon Non Bo have been around for at least a thousand years. Long before 939, the ancient Vietnamese worshiped trees, rivers, and stones, and although there are no books from that period, bronze drums dating from the seventh to the second century B.C. were incised with designs representing the mystical powers of mountains and water. These early Vietnamese believed that caves in the mountains were the homes of the immortals and that anyone who could join these immortals in the caves would live for eternity with them.

Unable to live in the caves, the people began to place stones in their gardens to gain some of the protective powers associated with trees, rivers, and stones. While it is not certain, it is probable that people began placing rocks and plants in shallow containers and calling them Hon Non Bo in about A.D. 1000. Royalty—kings, high-ranking generals, and mandarins—built the largest Hon Non Bo, usually including one or more in the grounds of their palaces.

The widespread existence of Hon Non Bo demonstrates the existence of a long tradition of belief in the power of rocks, an appreciation of the beauty of mountains and plants, and a recognition of the importance of water in all of its forms in our world.

Part 2
Trees suitable for bonsai

This part of *Bonsai school* tells you every-thing you need to know about how to grow and care for bonsai, as well as introducing you to the most common bonsai techniques.

A penjing *Ficus microcarpa* meas-uring 47in (120cm), grown by Luk Hok Ming.

A penjing *Carmona micro-phylla* created by Wu Yee-Sun.

Trees suitable for bonsai

This chapter covers the most popular trees suitable for bonsai (see also the section on bonsai styles, pages 121 to 124).

Indoor or outdoor bonsai?

In many climates, a number of species and varieties of tree are suitable for bonsai. If you live in a cold climate, however, you should grow a warm-climate tree inside because exposure to cold conditions outside, particularly during winter, could damage it. (As long as you water them well and give them some shade or other-wise protect them from the sun, most indoor trees will enjoy a bit of fresh air during the summer.) The basic-care section (see pages 69 to 89) covers many of the salient points to note when looking after indoor trees.

(I have illustrated many of these trees in pages throughout the book.)

Indoor bonsai

I shall now look at some of the more com-mon species of tree that are suitable for growing inside in colder climates.

Figs (*Ficus*)

Most figs fall into the category of indoor trees in colder climates. Many are suitable for bonsai culture, including *Ficus benjamina*, *F. nerifolia*, *F. carica*, *F. retusa*, *F. microcarpa* and *F. salicifolia*. All have oval leaves and exude latex when cut. None like draughts or being moved from one room to another, which prompts them to drop their leaves. (See also the section on shohin figs page 190.)

A penjing *Podocarpus macrophyllus* created by Wu Yee-Sun.

A penjing *Ulmus parviflora* created by Wu Yee-Sun.

A Fukien tea tree measuring 30in (76.2cm).

Fukien tea trees (*Ehretia*)

Formerly called *Carmona microphylla*, and now known as *Ehretia buxifolia*, the Fukien tea tree, which has small, oval leaves similar to those of the box tree (*Buxus*, hence *buxifolia*), is very popular among bonsai-growers in many areas. Other species of *Ehretia* that are suitable for bonsai include *E. dicksoni* and *E. thrysiflora*, both of which are hardier than *E. buxifolia*.

Although Fukien tea trees can be grown outside in warmer climates, they should still be protected from winter frosts or cold. In colder climates, Fukien tea trees should be grown inside for most of the year. They can, however, be placed outside on sunny summer days and may even be left outside for as long as the weather remains warm.

Satinwood, orange jasmine or cosmetic bark trees (*Murraya paniculata*)

Originating from China, the *Murraya* genus comprises five species known by various common names, such as satinwood, cosmetic bark tree and orange jasmine, while Mary Millar, one of the most experienced growers of bonsai in the United States, informs me that *Murraya* is also known as orange jesamine in America. (This problem with identification illustrates why you'd be well advised to learn and use the Latin name of any tree, which is universal.)

These trees grow happily outside in warm areas, such as Florida and the hotter regions of the Far East. They are not the easiest of trees for a beginner to grow as indoor bonsai, however. Requiring a bright, draft-free position, *Murraya* should be watered with distilled water and will only flourish when in slightly damp soil. I have grown them for years simply because I enjoy the challenge that they present in my own, cold climate. Having bought an import over twenty-five years ago, all of my orange jasmines have been grown from cuttings.

A penjing *Sageretia theezans* grown by Chen Rong Sen.

Pomegranates (*Punica granatum*)

The pomegranate (*Punica granatum*) has two principal forms: the normal-sized pomegranate and the dwarf pomegranate. A very attractive tree for bonsai, even young *Punica* quickly establish a tree shape. The *Punica* needs a warm climate or indoor conditions if it is to flourish, but because it is a deciduous tree, it is best to place it in a cool spot during the winter to enable it to go into dormancy.

My first pomegranate was a tree measuring about 10in (25cm) in height, which looked as though a few trees had been twisted together, with the tops spurred off to create a foliage pad. It was lovely, but sadly could not tolerate damp conditions. Indeed, no tree likes very wet soil apart from some *Salix* and *Taxodium*, so mist a *Punica* in summer and keep the soil damp, but not sodden. A *Punica* will like being fed, which can encourage flowers to grow on any unpruned shoots, but note that supporting too many flowers will exhaust the tree. Fruits should not be encouraged for the same reason, unless the *Punica* is very large.

A penjing *Murraya paniculata* measuring nearly 70in (180cm), created by Pong Wai Kwong.

獨坐幽篁裏
彈琴復長嘯
深林人不知
明月來相照

A penjing *Serissa foetida* grown by Wu Yee-Sun.

Sagretia (*Sageretia theezans*)

Many different varieties of sagretia are now available, including very tiny-leaved ones, such as *Sageretia microphylla*. They tend to be grown in an informal upright style, their initial attraction lying in their old-looking trunks and exposed roots. Essentially evergreen, like all evergreens, a sageretia sheds its leaves as it grows, replacing old leaves with new ones.

Sageretia need regular misting if kept indoors, and although they like warm conditions, this doesn't include full sun or close proximity to radiators. During periods of warmer weather, sageretia can be kept outdoors. If you want the tree to flower, do not prune it until it has finished flowering, and only then prune it back to the first or second new leaf growth.

Trees of a thousand stars (*Serissa foetida*)

One of the most popular indoor trees, the *Serissa foetida* grows into a tree-like form almost effortlessly. The Latin species name may give you a hint of one of its characteristics: when cut, the roots and branches give off a slight fetid smell, a little like rotting meat. And like all bonsai, the roots need to be cut at least every two years at repotting time, and the branches also need pruning so that their shape can be developed. Don't worry: the smell's not that bad!

You will need to prune it as tightly as a hedge, as a result of which its foliage will quickly assume a structured mass. *Serissa foetida* lose their leaves during the colder period of the year, but these are replenished soon afterward. If the tree is allowed to become waterlogged, is positioned in a drafty place or not fed, its leaves will turn yellow, however.

A penjing Chinese elm (*Ulmus parvifolia*) created by Zhong Ji Nan.

Chinese elm (*Ulmus parvifolia*)

Chinese elms can be deciduous or evergreen. In warmer climates or inside, they will remain evergreens that create new leaves. A hugely popular indoor tree, *Ulmus chinensis* can also be grown outside as long as it is protected from frost.

You can prune a Chinese elm to form a tree image over two years by cutting back to the first set of new leaves in the top third section, to the second set in the middle and to the third set in the lower area. It will need to be fed well, so use a houseplant fertilizer on an indoor plant every week to encourage growth. Keep the soil moist, mist the leaves once a day and, if the tree is kept inside, turn it regularly to ensure that it receives light evenly.

Outdoor bonsai

There are many species of tree suitable for outdoor bonsai, but space prevents me from covering them all. The same general guidelines given for the two categories of tree outlined here, conifers and broadleaf (both deciduous and evergreen), apply to a number of the species that I haven't included, however.

Popular outdoor bonsai: conifers

Pine (Pinus)	Styling notes	Soil/repot	Feeding	Notes	Pests and diseases
Two-, three- and five-needle pines are all popular. Choose a small-needle species. The most popular pines are Scots pine, Japanese white pine and red pine. Collected throughout the cooler areas of the world, there is probably a species that is best for your area. Only a few species like warm climates. Many pines are unsuitable for indoor bonsai, however.	Pines can be grown into most shapes, although formal, informal and literati-bunjin (similar to sumi-e ink-and-pen drawings or Japanese woodblock prints showing trees clinging to mountains having lost many branches), windswept, cascade and group styles are popular. Dead-wood areas and jinns are used.	**Soil:** Higher levels of grit are required for free draining: 70% grit to 30% organic. Young trees can be 60% Kiriyu™ to 40% Akadama™. (See soil section, pages 69 to 77.) **Repot:** every three years or up to every five years for very old specimens. Look for root aphids every year, not just when repotting, by carefully lifting the root mass and replacing it after examination.	Feed low nitrogen 0-10-10 at the start of the growing season and in late summer; high nitrogen in the spring; and balanced feed in early summer. Feed older trees once a month and younger trees either every two weeks or give them a half-strength feed every week.	Leave one or two buds on new growth. Trim long candles by half, starting at the bottom of the tree for two-needle pines and working from the top down for five-needle pines. Work on one level per week.	Black aphids and root aphids. Assorted soil larvae, adelgids and woolly aphids. Loph, a fungus, seen as yellow horizontal stripes. Rust, a fungal mold, on bark and needles (small orange lumps).

Yew (Taxus)	Styling notes	Soil/repot	Feeding	Notes	Pests and diseases
Taxus baccata and *T. cuspidata*.	Yews can be grown into most shapes, but I prefer the formal upright and contorted shapes derived from collected specimens.	**Soil:** 60% grit to 40% organic. However, yews will grow in 70% grit to 30% organic in wet climates. **Repot:** every three years, although because yews are slow-growing, you can possibly leave it longer for older bonsai. Look for root aphids when repotting.	Feed low nitrogen at the start of growing season and in the late summer; high nitrogen in spring; and balanced feed in early summer. Feed older trees once a month and younger trees either every two weeks or give them a half-strength feed every week.	Arrange yew foliage on flat planes. Yews can take heavy carving. Trunk growth is very slow once a yew tree has been planted in a bonsai pot.	Very few pests or diseases attack yews. Yellowing of needles indicates the need for a dose of Miracid™.

Larch (Larix)	Styling notes	Soil/repot	Feeding	Notes	Pests and diseases
Many varieties of larch grow in cooler parts of the world. Larches do not grow in warm climates, however.	Larches can be grown into most shapes apart from broom. They make good formal uprights and groups.	**Soil:** Larches grow equally well in 60% grit to 40% organic and 70% organic to 30% grit. The former is more suitable for wet climates and the latter for dry climates, the higher organic content helping moisture retention. These deciduous, fleshy trees need a lot of moisture during the growing season and then require a semi-dry soil condition. **Repot:** repot these fast-growing trees every two years. Be careful when removing large roots because this could cause dieback on the opposite branch supported by the root. Always seal cuts.	Feed a half-strength feed every week in spring; high nitrogen for young trees; nothing in mid-summer; low nitrogen in late summer. Feed older specimens as you would a pine (see pages 81–82).	It is pointless making shari on larch trunks because the bark grows so quickly. You can, however, jinn the branches. Prune to the last set of new buds in winter, but well before the buds swell. Do not prune during the growing season because this will slow the development of buds and twigs (ramification).	Larches are fairly resistant to most pests and diseases. Aphids and adelgids on new shoots in early to mid-summer. Scale on the needles. Cones may indicate that the tree is struggling and should be removed before giving the tree and soil a thorough check.

Juniper (Juniperus)	Styling notes	Soil/repot	Feeding	Notes	Pests and diseases
Popular junipers include: Chinese, *J. argentii* (shimpaku), blauws, (*J. blaauw*) *J. prostrata*, *J. recurva*, *J. virginiana*, *J. rigida* and *J. sabina*. There are a number of varieties in North America, including: California, Arizona, Rocky Mountain and Utah junipers. All can be used for bonsai.	Junipers can be grown into most shapes apart from broom. They make good formal uprights and groups.	**Soil:** At least 60% grit to 40% organic, but 70% grit can be used if the bonsai is mature. **Repot:** every two years when young and every three to four years when mature. Junipers have slow-growing roots.	Feed low nitrogen in early spring; a little high nitrogen in early summer; and low nitrogen in late summer. Feed young trees once every two weeks and older trees once a month. Junipers prefer pellet cake feed. This can be left on soil surface so removing the need to use liquid fertilizers.	Pluck junipers throughout the growing season. Reduce the foliage mass in early autumn to prevent the tree from developing foliage pads that are too heavy and out of proportion.	Scale insects may be a problem in some areas. Red spider mites are the main problem and the dense foliage should be checked throughout the growing season. Discoloration is an indication of infestation, but by the time you've noticed it it may be too late. So shake the pads over your hand regularly and the small, dust-like mites will drop out. Treat the tree with a systemic insecticide designed to combat red spider mites. Vine weevils can also be a problem.

Cedar (Cedrus)	Styling notes	Soil/repot	Feeding	Notes	Pests and diseases
Four species comprising many varieties and types are used for bonsai, including: *Cedrus brevifolia* (Cyprian cedar), *C. atlantica* (Atlas cedar), *C. atlantica glauca* (blue Atlas cedar), *C. libani* (cedar of Lebanon), and *C. deodara*, which may be difficult to train due to its pendulous nature, although keeping the branches short usually helps. There are a number of cedars throughout the world suitable for bonsai.	I find that it's best to use larger specimens when styling cedars. Suitable styles include formal upright, slanting, groups and windswept, but not cascade, unless the tree already has a cascade or prostrate form. To thicken a cedar, grow it in the ground and feed it heavily.	**Soil:** Like all conifers, cedars need a free-draining mix, although they need slightly dryer soil conditions than many conifers, making a mix of 35% organic to 65% grit advisable. In clay soil, use 40% Akadama™ to a minimum 60% Kiriyu™. **Repot:** cedars don't like being transplanted, having their roots cut or being disturbed. They have slow-growing roots, so it's usual to repot them every three to four years. They may drop their needles after being repotted, but if they are healthy a new crop of needles will quickly grow, with little or no loss of twigs.	I feed cedars heavily when they're young and use surface feeder pellets when they're mature. Feed standard high nitrogen in spring; balanced food in early summer; and low nitrogen from late summer to early winter.	My one problem with cedars is that their branches have an initial tendency to grow upward. Scarring (making some sharp cuts) under a branch a few times prior to wiring will injure the cambium (inner bark), causing it to heal along the cut lines so that the branch hardens into the required shape. This is a useful technique for similar problem species. Cuts made to cedars heal very slowly.	Most scale and needle foliage suffers from attacks at the base of the needles by red spider mites, aphids and sometimes adelgids. Although needle drop may occur during repotting, unless the tree is unhealthy, the needles should recover. Check for root aphids when repotting. Treat with a systemic and spray the foliage with insecticide.

Japanese cedar (*Cryptomeria japonica*)	Styling notes	Soil/repot	Feeding	Notes	Pests and diseases
Cryptomeria japonica is the central *Cryptomeria* species. Note that some of the hybrids do not have the same compact growth habit. Slow-growing varieties include *C. vilmoriniana*, which is compact, but grows less than 1/16in (25mm) a year. All *Cryptomeria* are easy to grow from cuttings, making pruning a bonus. These trees are unhappy in warm climates.	Styles for *Cryptomeria* include the formal and informal upright styles, groups and most of the styles that emulate a pine.	**Soil:** *Cryptomeria* do well in most soil mixes, but do not like soggy soil conditions. The normal mix is 50% grit to 50% organic. The same proportions apply if you are using Akadama™ and Kiriyu™ or clay granules. **Repot:** when repotting, use 50% grit to 50% organic or even 40% grit to 60% organic in dryer climes.	Feed low nitrogen in early spring; a little high nitrogen in early summer; and low nitrogen in late summer. Feed young trees once every two weeks and older trees once a month. *Cryptomeria* prefer pellet cake feed.	*Cryptomeria* need nipping out throughout the growing season. They do not like damp conditions, so allow air to circulate freely. When planted in groups, the inner branches may die off as the group fills in. Protect these trees from frost during the winter as soon as it becomes cold to encourage their foliage to change to their bronze-green winter color.	Red spider mites can be a problem, so spray *Cryptomeria* with a systemic and also drench the soil with it. They can also be attacked by adelgids. Mildew and dieback can be caused by a lack of light and poor air circulation. Treat with a fungicide and protect soil.

Popular outdoor bonsai: broadleaf trees

Cotoneaster (*Cotoneaster*)	Styling notes	Soil/repot	Feeding	Notes	Pests and diseases
Cotoneasters mainly originate from cooler northern climates, but because this genus comprises nearly four-hundred species, there will probably be one that suits your climate, wherever you live. Their glossy leaves and bright-red berries are very attractive. Popular species include *C. horizontalis*, *C. microphyllus* and the tiny *C. congestus*.	You can grow cotoneasters in almost any style. I prefer them in groups, and if you use one of the smaller species, such as *C. conspicuous decorus*, they will give you a wonderful show in spring.	**Soil:** Cotoneasters do well in most soil mixes, but do not like soggy soil conditions. The normal mix is 50% grit to 50% organic. The same proportions apply if you are using Akadama™ and Kiriyu™ or clay granules. **Repot:** use 50% grit to 50% organic or even 40% grit to 60% organic in dryer climes.	Feed low nitrogen in early spring until flowering, then stop until flowering has finished. Then feed a little high nitrogen in early summer and low nitrogen in late summer. Feed young trees every two weeks and older trees once a month. When developing, cotoneasters feed voraciously, but also develop lots of suckers, which you should nip out.	To encourage dense twig growth (ramification), keep cutting back new shoots to either the first or second set of leaves. At the top of the tree, cut back to the first set of new leaves, leaving them in place, from which point two new buds will grow. Repeat throughout the growing season. Prune back to the second set of new leaves at the sides throughout the season. Cut out or wire any wayward branches. Do not prune during the flowering period.	Scale is a pest, but mostly the only one that attacks cotoneasters. Root aphids can sometimes be a problem, however, so look out for them. Don't allow weeds (such as pearlwort, which looks like grass) to take hold on the surface because they will damage the cotoneaster's growth structure. Treat scale by removing one at a time. Use a general systemic to clear out most pests. Spray with Malathion for others but read the instructions. Treat fungal with a fungicide but protect soil.

Oak (*Quercus*)	Styling notes	Soil/repot	Feeding	Notes	Pests and diseases
The *Quercus* genus consists of around six-hundred species world-wide, both evergreen and deciduous. I have worked on many, from mountain oaks in Italy to huge wide oaks in Britain and the United States. In North America, I also worked on forming large box-woods into oak images and visited the famous Oak Alley Plantation in Louisiana, returning with some great images. Outside my home town, Glasgow, are many enormous ancient oaks in every possible shape. I have included images of some of these beautiful trees in *Bonsai school*.	The main bonsai style for oaks still emulates a mature tree, with a broad trunk, and perhaps a little crack developing to a hollow trunk, excellent ramification and perhaps some shari or a few jinn. One can't just state that oaks grow in formal or informal upright shapes, however: I have seen a superb cascade, huge groups, multi-trunked oaks and so on, the point being that there are many different styles of wonderful mature specimens all over the world. In Italy, for example, heavily fissured oaks of many shapes and sizes are collected.	**Soil:** Oaks do well in most soil mixes, but do not like soggy soil conditions. The normal mix is 50% grit to 50% organic. The same proportions apply if you are using Akadama™ and Kiriyu™ or clay granules. **Repot:** when repotting, use 50% grit to 50% organic or even 40% grit to 60% organic in dryer climes.	Feed low nitrogen in early spring; a little high nitrogen in early summer; and low nitrogen in late summer. Feed young trees once every two weeks and older trees once a month. Oaks also prefer pellet cake feed.	If it is a deciduous oak, prune back to the first or second new buds after the leaves have opened. Otherwise, prune back to the first or second set of leaves on new wood.	Although oak wood is very acid, and therefore usually insect-free, aphids (rarely) and thrips in the soil sometimes cause problems. Mildew (Botrytis) can result if the air around the tree is turgid. Oaks like breezy conditions so that their leaves do not grow too tightly. This can cause humidity and mildew, so if you have a mature tree, carefully tease out the leaves a little once a day.

Maple (*Acer*)	Styling notes	Soil/repot	Feeding	Notes	Pests and diseases
Although the *Acer* genus includes many species, the two that are generally used for bonsai are *A. palmatum* and *A. buergirianum* (trident maple). Although Chinese tridents are sometimes *A. buergirianum*, they can also be *A. maximowiczianum* or *A. triflorum*. The labels of imported trees are often vague about the exact species, but Chinese tridents are softer in leaf and have a distinct roundness about the leaf base. Comprising around a hundred species and hundreds of varieties, the variations of *A. palmatum* are too numerous to cover here. *A. dissectum*, the lace-leaf maple, is a shrubby tree with a distinct growth form, while *A. koreanum* or var. *coreanum* can also be used.	The most popular styles for maples include the formal or informal upright, raft, group and root over rock.	**Soil:** Maples do well in most soil mixes, but do not like soggy soil conditions. The normal mix is 50% grit to 50% organic. The same proportions apply if you are using Akadama™ and Kiriyu™ or clay granules. **Repot:** when repotting, use 50% grit to 50% organic or even 40% grit to 60% organic in dryer climes.	Feed low nitrogen in early spring to harden off the leaves and increase the nitrogen thereafter. (Feeding will not encourage good fall color, but this is not a problem in the early stages of a maple's development. When feeding mature specimens, however, reduce the feed to pellet feed. For developing trees, follow the low-nitrogen feed with a little high nitrogen in early summer, don't feed in midsummer, and feed low nitrogen in late summer. Feed young trees once every two weeks and older trees once a month (mature trees prefer pellet cake feed).	Leaves tend to reduce in size when the tree is growing in a pot. You should, however, nip out the new leaves in early spring as they start opening, but before they have done so completely. This forces a second flush of smaller leaves. Maples can be leaf-pruned in late spring after the leaves have hardened off. This means cutting off all of the leaves, leaving the leaf stalk to die back. This will prevent the secondary buds at the base of the leaf from being torn. In warmer areas, do this twice or three times during the growing season. Only use this technique if you have planned the ramification of new twigs.	Pretty much everything attacks maples: black aphids will destroy the tender young branches overnight, while scale will develop on the young stalks. Protect maples by applying systemic to the soil to alleviate these attacks. Although spraying the leaves with insecticide will probably damage their fine structure, the leaves will soon be replaced. Don't remove the leaves for at least three weeks after spraying, however, to give the tree time to feed the systemic to the bugs.

Hawthorn (*Crataegus*)	Styling notes	Soil/repot	Feeding	Notes	Pests and diseases
There are around two-hundred species and over a thousand varieties of *Crataegus* world-wide. *Crataegus monogyna* is the common hawthorn, while *C. cuneata* is the Japanese hawthorn. Most species are very thorny and bear thick bunches of flowers in a number of colors. (*C. monogyna* has white, pink and red flowers.) *Crataegus* form attractive trees, and bonsai versions are created in the wild by grazing deer and sheep.	*Crataegus* can be grown in most bonsai styles. Collecting yamadori (trees from the hills or mountains) hawthorns will, in many cases, indicate what style you will be able to create because the wood is very hard and not easy to bend. Young trees with thin branches are therefore your only option if you want to create your own style. Just go with the flow, as they say. When working with a collected hawthorn, make sure that you protect it from wind, frost and inclement weather while its root system is developing, which usually takes three years.	**Soil:** Hawthorns do well in most soil mixes, but do not like soggy soil conditions. The normal mix is 50% grit to 50% organic. The same proportions apply if you are using Akadama™ and Kiriyu™ or clay granules. I have also used pure Akadama™ when the roots of collected trees are developing, which works perfectly. **Repot:** when repotting, use 50% grit to 50% organic or even 40% grit to 60% organic in dryer climes. Hawthorns like moist soil. When the tree is young, you may have to repot it every year, but only every three or four years as the tree matures.	Feed low nitrogen in early spring; a little high nitrogen in early summer; and low nitrogen in late summer. Feed young trees once every two weeks and older trees once a month. Mature hawthorns prefer pellet cake feed.	Remove any suckers from the base, from under the branches and from the trunk. Wire the new shoots into shape as soon as you can because they will quickly harden up. Prune branches in fall, after the leaves have fallen, and seal all cuts. After the terminal buds have grown, pluck them to force secondary growth. Keep the branch length as short as your style will allow. Remember that healthy hawthorns grow quickly.	Hawthorns may be susceptible to scale, mildew and occasional aphid attack, but this occurs rarely. Treat scale by removing one at a time. Use a general systemic to clear out most pests. Spray with Malathion for others but read the instructions. Treat fungal attacks with a fungicide but protect soil.

57

Crape myrtle (*Lagerstroemia indica*)	Styling notes	Soil/repot	Feeding	Notes	Pests and diseases
Lagerstroemia comprises about fifty species, both evergreen and deciduous, many of which are suitable for bonsai. Originating mainly from warm countries, like China and Korea, *Lagerstroemia* will flower after a hot, or very warm, summer, producing red, white, lavender, or purple blooms. There has been a recent surge in the popularity of miniature crape myrtle offering a number of different-colored flowers, particularly in the United States, and these make almost instant bonsai. (Specialist dealers sell them over the Internet.) *Lagerstroemia* can be grown indoors in cooler climes.	*Lagerstroemia* take well to broom styles because this is the tree's normal growth pattern. Let young shoots grow until late spring and then cut them back to the second or third set of new leaves. Don't prune or pinch until late summer or early fall because flowers develop within the shoots during the summer.	**Soil:** *Lagerstroemia* does well in most soils, including 50% grit to 50% organic. **Repot:** transplant *Lagerstroemia* every two years because the tree grows quickly.	Feed high nitrogen in spring; a balanced feed in early summer; and low nitrogen in late summer, just before the fall. This tree requires an intense feeding regime in the early period of its development, but when it is mature feeding can be reduced to once a month.	The crape myrtle will flourish in full sun or partial shade. If it is grown as an indoor tree in a cooler climate, make sure that it enjoys a cool, moist (not wet) and light position over the winter. Like all indoor trees, *Lagerstroemia* can be placed outside during the summer.	Very few pests attack the crape myrtle apart from aphids specific to it, Tinocallis kahawalu-okalani, in southern areas of the United States and in other warm climates. Attacks start in early to late summer, peaking in mid-summer. The crape myrtle occasionally suffers from powdery mildew, which you should treat with a fungicide to protect soil.

Stewartia (*Stuartia*)	Styling notes	Soil/repot	Feeding	Notes	Pests and diseases
The *Stuartia* genus is related to the *Camellia* family. Although the most popular bonsai species is *S. monadelpha*, others of the *Stuartia* genus are also possible contenders, such as *S. pseudo-camellia*, *S. kore-ana*, and *S. sinensis*, which have large leaves, although their size can be reduced *S. pteropetiolata* and *S. serrata* are also alternatives for bonsai. The advantage of *S. monadelpha* is that it has a smaller leaf and axel: up to two-thirds smaller than those of the other species.	*Stuartia* are traditionally styled in an upright form because the tree is grown for its beautiful cinnamon color. Grow it as a single bonsai or in a group, that is, if you can obtain the necessary material, which may be difficult, depending on where you live.	**Soil:** Use 50% grit to 50% organic (or, in warmer areas, 60% organic). Because *Stuartia* prefer a moist soil, you could also use a water-retentive lime-free medium. **Repot:** once it has been planted, the tree does not like its roots being disturbed, so transplant it every two years. However, check the growth on younger trees for the first six years in case it decides to grow faster because of your water quality, placement and feeding. Thereafter, as the tree grows older, repot it every three years.	Feed Miracid™ or ericaceous fertiliser. Follow an intense feeding regime every two weeks in the tree's early period of development, then reduce feeding to once a month once it has become mature. After its form has developed, use pellet feed (you want to retain the shape rather than develop it further).	This tree needs a semi-shaded position out of direct sun because its roots must remain cool. It also likes slightly moist conditions. In the fall, however, you can expose it to as much sun as you like to assist the development of good leaf color, but make sure that the roots are in the shade. Prune back new growth throughout the growing period to suit your design. Because wire damage is very easy to inflict, make sure that you remove any wire after three or four weeks. Finally, only give it lime-free water.	Few pests attack *Stuartia* apart from scale, but watch for aphids never-theless. Treat scale by removing one at a time. Use a general systemic to clear out most pests.

Beech (*Fagus*)	Styling notes	Soil/repot	Feeding	Notes	Pests and diseases
About ten species of the *Fagus* genus are used in bonsai, of which the European beech, *F. sylvatica*, and the Japanese beech, *F. crenata*, are the most popular. *F. grandifolia* is native to the United States, although many other species have also been introduced. Most species can be treated in the same way for bonsai. As a child, my garden was full of mature beeches, including a copper beech, *F. sylvatica atropurpurea*, which I called 'the black tree' because no light seemed to permeate its branches, unlike the green beech *F. sylvatica* next to it, which seemed to dance with lime-green color when the sun was shining.	Although formal upright or informal upright are the usual choices for styling beeches, they also make great groups, and if the tree is the right shape, the windswept style is also an option. I am sure that other styles are possible, too, although they may not be quite so suitable. Try to design a typical beech shape, with a wide trunk and sweeping branches.	**Soil:** *Fagus* do well in most soil mixes, but prefer a shallow, moist soil. Interestingly, although the bulk grows outward in shallow soil, the feeder roots stretch deep, so that young trees develop good surface roots, or nebari, which act as a support. 50% grit to 50% organic is the usual mix, and the same proportions apply if you are using Akadama™ and Kiriyu™ or clay granules. **Repot:** when repotting, use 50% grit to 50% organic, or even 40% grit to 60% organic in dryer climes. Repot young trees every two years, and mature trees every four or five years, as necessary.	Give a balanced feed in late spring, after the leaves have hardened off, and also in early summer. Do not feed in mid-summer or when it is hot because beeches enter a dormant period in hot weather. Start feeding low nitrogen in late summer, twice or three times only before the fall. When the tree has reached maturity, reduce feeding to once a month. Give beeches pellet feed once they are mature, which will retain their shape rather than develop it.	A reduction of leaves happens almost naturally in most beeches over about four or five years. It is easy to rescue the leaves, however, by waiting until the new leaves start to unfurl. Pluck those on the strongest branches. The next flush will be slightly smaller. This should be done every year for up to seven years, after which the leaves will be enormously reduced in size and will then stay small. If you want to create fine ramification, you will have to undertake this technique to encourage the necessary twig formation. Remove the winter leaves as the spike buds begin to grow.	In warmer areas, infestations of whitefly may take hold under the leaves. This area is also targeted by aphids, who will feed on the sap. Scale is sometimes a problem, too. Prevent insect infestations by spraying a systemic under the leaves twice a year, in early spring and mid-summer.\n\nIf the tree's position does not enable fresh air to flow freely, the build up of humidity may result in mildew or Botrytis, both fungal conditions. Although these can be treated, it's better to address the underlying cause by placing the tree in a position where air can circulate through the thick leaves.

Honeysuckle (*Lonicera nitida*)	Styling notes	Soil/repot	Feeding	Notes	Pests and diseases
Although there are around one-hundred-and-eighty species in the *Lonicera* genus, *L. nitida*, (hedging honeysuckle), which has very small leaves, is commonly used for bonsai. There are also a number of varieties of *L. nitida*. Honeysuckles are so easily grown that one of our faculty, Koos Le Roux, once told me that after pruning them he leaves the cuttings lying on the soil because they usually take root. He does, however, live in a part of South Africa that enjoys warm springs, hot summers, warm falls and cool winters. In colder climates, you can emulate these conditions by growing Lonicera in a greenhouse.	Lonicera don't like wire, but then these small trees are easily pruned into any style. They are particularly good for training into regular tree shapes.	**Soil:** Honeysuckles do well in most soil mixes, but do not like soggy soil conditions. 50% grit to 50% organic is the normal mix. The same proportions apply with Akadama™ and Kiriyu™ or clay granules. You could also use 30% grit to 70% organic in dryer climes. That having been said, this tree is exceptional inasmuch as it will grow in most soils. **Repot:** repot young trees every year and mature trees every two years. Prune a group's root mass by cutting into it in 'V' shapes to allow new roots to grow into these areas.	Feed high nitrogen in spring; a balanced feed in early summer; and low nitrogen in late summer, before the onset of fall. Maintain an intense feeding regime in the early period of the tree's development, but reduce feeding to once a month when it is mature. Giving a foliar feed will help the structure to grow, whether singly or in groups. Like privet, honeysuckle is a voracious feeder.	This tree requires some basic protection from frost and wind. The pruning regime should be the same as for elms (see page 62). Cut back to the first set of new leaves at the top, to the second set at the sides, and to the third set on the lower areas to form a 'traditional' tree shape (although you can, of course, create other forms). Immediately after flowering, thin out and cut back to the last set of new leaves to force tighter growth. After the structure has developed, prune it as you would a hedge.	Honeysuckles are subject to very few pests and diseases. Watch for root rot, however, because they don't like soggy conditions. (Because they have fibrous trunks, they can store more water than many other trees, however.)

Elm (*Ulmus*)	Styling notes	Soil/repot	Feeding	Notes	Pests and diseases
Many evergreen and deciduous species of *Ulmus* are used for bonsai all over the world, in just about every climate. Depending on the species, *Ulmus* can be both grown indoors and outdoors. *Ulmus* is one of the easiest species to turn into bonsai.	Formal, informal or broom shapes are popular styles for *Ulmus*, and groups can be grown in all sizes.	**Soil:** *Ulmus* does well in most soil mixes, but does not like soggy soil conditions. A mix of 50% grit to 50% organic is normal. The same proportions apply if you are using Akadama™ and Kiriyu™ or clay granules. **Repot:** When repotting, in early spring use 50% grit to 50% organic or even 40% grit to 60% organic in dryer climes.	Feed high nitrogen in spring; a balanced feed in early summer; and low nitrogen in late summer, before the onset of fall. Maintain an intense feeding regime in the early period of the tree's development, but reduce feeding to once a month when it is mature. Give elms pellet feed once they are mature, which will retain their shape rather than develop it.	Elms require protection from the frost and wind and need partial shade in mid-summer. When pruning, cut back to the first set of new leaves at the top, to the second set at the sides, and to the third set in lower areas to form a 'traditional' tree shape. (You can also create other forms, of course.)	Elms may be attacked by aphids, scale and soil flies. Treat scale by removing one at a time. Use a general systemic to clear out most pests. Spray with Malathion for others but read the instructions. Treat fungal attacks with a fungicide but protect soil. Dutch elm disease may affect mature trees, but is not a problem in bonsai trees.

Japanese grey-bark elm (*Zelkova serrata*)	Styling notes	Soil/repot	Feeding	Notes	Pests and diseases
There are five species within the *Zelkova* genus, but only four are propagated: *Z. abelicea*, *Z. carpinifolia*, *Z. sinica* and *Z. serrata*. These have a number of variations, such as dwarf and variegated forms.	Although *Zelkova* are commonly grown in broom styles, they are equally good as formal and informal uprights. I also like them in groups. They are popular subjects for both penjing and bonsai because the foliage develops very quickly as a result of pruning and pinching.	**Soil:** *Zelkova* do well in most soil mixes, but do not like soggy soil conditions. A mix of 50% grit to 50% organic is normal. The same proportions apply if you are using Akadama™ and Kiriyu™ or clay granules. **Repot:** when repotting, use 50% grit to 50% organic or even 40% grit to 60% organic in dryer climes.	Feed high nitrogen in spring; a balanced feed in early summer; and low nitrogen in late summer, before the onset of fall. Maintain an intense feeding regime in the early period of the tree's development, but reduce feeding to once a month when it is mature. Give *Zelkova* pellet feed once they are mature, which will retain their shape rather than develop it.	*Zelkova* require protection from the frost and wind and need partial shade in mid-summer. When pruning, cut back to the first set of new leaves at the top, to the second set at the sides, and to the third set in lower areas to form a 'traditional' tree shape. (You can also create other forms, of course.)	*Zelkova* may be attacked by scale and aphids. Treat scale by removing one at a time. Use a general systemic to clear out most pests. Spray with Malathion for others but read the instructions. Treat fungal attacks with a fungicide but protect soil.

Shelving and placement

When deciding where to place a bonsai in your garden, you may wonder whether it should be in full sun or shade. Remember that the primary requirement to enable any plant to grow healthily is sufficient light. That apart, although no single rule of thumb applies, some basic guidelines follow.

·   Deciduous trees need some sun and some shade. Depending on the climate, morning and afternoon sun should be fine, but hot or midday sun may be too fierce, in which case provide some shade with shade nets. (Summer is usually the only season when the heat of the sun can cause damage; the sun is lower in the sky and generates less heat earlier and later in the year.)

This shelf at Dream Gardens, Texas, is the right height for small to medium-sized bonsai.

A typical bonsai display on three shelves. Allocating one shelf to larger trees makes them easier to work on than if they were placed with smaller trees.

Trees suitable for bonsai

Some coniferous trees, such as pines and larches, prefer more shade and cooler conditions than deciduous trees. Although most conifers are pretty tough, they really don't like high humidity levels and damp conditions. Many conifers prefer cooler conditions, but there are some tropical and semi-topical pines, so seek out those that are suitable for your climate. Do not, however, use mountain junipers or Scots pines in hot climates.

Reiner Goebel often uses single-column poles with rotating shelf attachments.

In northern climes, indoor trees or trees that originate from warm or tropical areas should be protected from the cold and frost. This fig, at Monastery Gardens in Atlanta, Georgia, is kept in a well-ventilated greenhouse and is regularly misted to maintain the necessary humidity level.

Shade netting is better for trees than solid shade, and in cooler climates you may need wind netting to reduce the force of the winds that may blow through your bonsai. In hot climates, I recommend net shade over other types of bonsai, but again be aware that adequate light should reach all parts of your bonsai and make sure that the area does not become too steamy. I do not recommend polythene-tunnel

The late Peter Visagie, of South Africa, created this wonderful false olive buddleja. It has been placed on a section of tree trunk (which has been treated with preservative to prevent moisture from permeating the wood) wide enough to accommodate the pot.

These beautiful tables for bonsai can be seen at the Golden State Bonsai Federation Collection in San Francisco, California.

Different levels of shelves can also be created to house different sizes of trees.

environments because the lack of freely flowing air encourages disease, while slow-moving air similarly assists the development of disease and soil-insect attacks. Following a house move, some of my own bonsai lived in a poly-tunnel for over a year and were so badly damaged by this environment that I realised that I had to remove them. Most of the sick-looking bonsai recovered after three months of intensive care outside, and it was only when the first frosts arrived that I put them under shelter. Despite these countermeasures, I still lost two wonderful bonsai as a result of their previously inadequate care. So even if you live in a cold climate, be careful about using poly-tunnel-type structures throughout the year for mature bonsai, that is, unless they are semi-tropical or tropical trees that need a lot of humidity. The golden rule is to provide ventilation at all times to ensure that the air can circulate freely.

Checklist

Pines and most other conifers prefer some shade during the day. In addition, try to ensure that they are kept in dry conditions. Deciduous trees need shade to protect them from the midday sun. Although I recommend shade netting as the best solution, you could alternatively watch the sun's progress over your garden over the course of a day to determine the best placement for your bonsai.

This chapter of *Bonsai school* gives some guidelines on how to care for your bonsai, and covers potting and repotting, watering, feeding, preventing pests and diseases, and seasonal care.

Soils for bonsai

When I started growing bonsai, I was nervous about repotting them, so much so that I often neglected to repot my ever-growing collection, much to the trees' detriment. I was especially worried about how much of the roots to remove and what type of soil to use.

It seemed that bonsai-growers all used their own soil mix, blend, or recipe, and none of the books that were then available (and these were few and far between) told me which types of soil to use for different trees or where to locate such mysterious materials as long-grain peat, red loam, and sand and clay mixes (I was not even sure what was meant by loam!) I really got into trouble when I read about soil mixes that had Japanese names, such as Tenjingawa-suna and Fuyo-do. And when I eventually discovered that Tenjingawa was river sand, I had no idea what that meant because every river with which I was familiar contained huge stones and big boulders. Leaf mold, a component of organic soil, is leaf mold the world over, but I learned that it harbors insects, their larvae and eggs, fungi, and other things that would be detrimental to the roots of my precious bonsai.

As for clay, this is the bane of all gardeners in Glasgow, where I live in Scotland, and although I read at one time that peat had fallen out of favor because it can dry out and turn to dust, causing compaction of the soil, a few years later it was decreed that you could use peat after all, the reason being that because you should never allow bonsai soil to become bone dry, peat will therefore remain in its constituted state and will act as a vital nutrient-holding medium after a feed. Another area of confusion surrounding peat concerned climatic conditions. Some people complained that in a wet climate peat became so waterlogged that a tree could not develop its roots in it. This, however, depends on what genus or species of tree is grown in peat, inasmuch as although pines (*Pinus*) do not normally like waterlogged soil, swamp cypresses (*Taxodium*) and willows (*Salix*)—apart from alpine willows—love these wet conditions. (I should also point out that, despite pines' general preference for dryer soil mixes, I have collected trees from bog- or swampland in the south of England and the north of Scotland. And while the reason why the trees were worthy of collection was their stunted growth, which was caused by some of their roots having failed to develop normally because of the wet conditions, it illustrates the pines' ability to persevere in such hostile conditions.) All in all, everything to do with bonsai soil seemed very confusing.

My introduction to Japanese soils

A breakthrough came one day during the early 1980s, when I visited Ruth Stafford Jones, an extremely experienced bonsai-grower who had been collecting bonsai since the early 1960s. A wonderful teacher, Ruth generously shared her knowledge of a Japanese product called Akadama™ (a dry, clay-fired, particle soil) with me. Ruth told me that she sieved it in order to grade its particles into similar sizes and to filter out the dust that could have compacted the soil mix. She used it both neat and mixed it with organic materials, such as peat.

After Ruth introduced me to Akadama™, I started to use it myself. Clay fired at a temperature of 1,112°F (600°C) changes into a hard, vitrified material, which should not break down. Although I was originally told that Akadama™ is clay that has been partly fired at a temperature of over 1,292°F (700°C), the Akadama™ that I then had access to did tend to break down, both in the hand and in the pot. In addition, although it lasted for two or three years, which, under normal circumstances, is acceptable for bonsai, I needed a longer-lasting soil for my very old and large bonsai, which needed repotting every four or five years.

When using Akadama™, I also discovered after a while that it slowed the growth of pines (*Pinus*) because the soil stayed damp beneath the surface (it dries quickly on the surface, however, which I'd taken as an indicator that I should water the bonsai). I then started to mix it with peat and grit and began to work out formulae for each tree's specific needs, having found, for example, that that pines needed more grit and less peat, while azaleas needed more peat and less grit. Nevertheless, further questions kept arising: my azaleas were not flourishing as much as I'd expected—could this be due to the soil? I then discovered that there is a special soil for acid-loving plants like azaleas named Kanuma™ (because it comes from the Kanuma region of Japan), consisting of low-fired, soft granules, which you can use neat or as part of a mix. I also learned about a soil that is suitable for pines called Kiriyu™ (which you can mix with Akadama™).

Pre-prepared bonsai soils

Nowadays, the guidelines concerning bonsai soils are thankfully far clearer, and more pre-prepared bonsai soils are sold today, too. There are, for example, different qualities of Akadama™ available, either soft, low-fired Akadama™ or harder, high-fired Akadama™, along with different sizes of grain, either small granules measuring between 1/16 and 3/16in (2 and 5mm) or medium-sized granules measuring between 1/8 and 3/8in (4 and 7mm). Always buy a brand with two red bars on the pack. Remember that if you mix Akadama™ with organic material, you'll need to include grit to enable fast water drainage; all brands of Japanese soil will retain water; that they can be used either neat or mixed with other types of soil; and that all young bonsai planted in them require regular feeding as they are developing.

In North America, other commercially available soils include Hollow Creek™ bonsai soil, which is manufactured in four grades that cover most soil requirements. All four grades contain 70 percent aggregate or grit (Haydite™, fired clay, and sized bedrock) to 30 percent organic pine-bark mulch and micronutrients.

Note that the products that are available in different countries will vary according to the prevalent climate and that it is important to seek local advice both on the soils that are sold in your area and those that suit your climate. (At one time, when bonsai teachers visited another country, they sometimes advised their students to switch to the soil mix that they personally preferred; having done so, however, the students often found that many of their trees died because the soil mix did not suit them.) Japanese soils are a good general solution, however, and I have used them in many countries around the world, although it is important to tailor the proportions of the soil mix's constituents to the prevalent climate. Many bonsai dealers will also make up a mix for you that will suit your local conditions.

Mixing your own bonsai soils

Alternatively, you could make up your own mix using the materials that are available in your country. Pure aggregate consists of the following materials, either entirely or in part: expanded shale or Haydite™, fired clay, such as high-fired Akadama™, and sized grit, such as granite grit or hard, crushed limestone (but remember that this will not be tolerated by such lime-hating species as azaleas, *Stuartia* and *Styrax*), and in Europe, for example, many growers use cat litter as the aggregate, or grit, element of a soil, while Haydite™ is popular in North America. Another option is the type of expanded shale that is used in the building trade, and common expanded-clay and shale products in the United States include Haydite™, Isolite™, Turface™, and L.E.C.A.™ .You can buy many such types of grit from building merchants, gravel- and construction-supply companies, garden centers and, of course, bonsai dealers. If you buy your grit from a building-supply company, always sieve and wash it thoroughly. Note that grit does not absorb water.

When preparing a soil mix, remember to sieve any dry ingredients, such as Akadama™ and grit or aggregate, both to remove the dust and to enable you to grade their particles into similar sizes.

(You can buy three-sieve kits from most bonsai dealers.) Although bonsai-growers also used to divide soil into two or three different thicknesses, I gave that up some time ago for most bonsai, except when I need to use a big, deep pot, when I place coarser particles at the bottom for drainage, medium-sized particles in the central section and slightly finer particles at the top. This instance apart, a soil consisting of medium-sized particles will do for most bonsai. Never include the sieved dust in your soil mix because its powder-like particles will work their way down through the soil to become compacted further down the pot, thus preventing water from draining away freely. (You can, however, save the dust to include in a suiseki arrangement, such as a suiban or dhoban, when a smooth effect is required; see Felix Rivera Page's section on suiseki, pages 245 to 250.)

Sterile, single-material soils can be mixed with organic material, as can clay-based soils, such as Akadama™, which, although water-retentive, also allow excess water to drain away freely. This means that they will dry out quickly, so if this is of concern to you, mix them with organic material. Although composted pine bark is a good organic substitute for peat, most soil-less seed composts will also do.

Soil mixes for different types of tree

The following section details the soil mixes suitable for different types of

A maple tree (*Acer palmatum* 'Seigen').

Deciduous trees

Mix 60 percent organic to 40 percent grit or aggregate (the grit should measure around 3/16in (5mm) in diameter). An alternative soil mix for young deciduous trees and freshly planted collected material is 50 percent organic to 50 percent grit or aggregate.

Azaleas and rhododendrons

Mix 50 percent organic to 50 percent grit or aggregate (the grit should measure around 3/16in (5mm) in diameter). Alternatively, you could use Kanuma™ only. I like to use a mix of 80 percent Kanuma™ to 20 percent aggregate for mature bonsai because it provides extra drainage, but be warned that because the soil will dry out quicker, you will need to adjust your watering régime accordingly.

This fig (*Ficus retusa*) is an example of a bonsai from a tropical or semi-tropical region that can be grown inside in colder climates.

A satsuki azalea.

A Chinese juniper (*Juniperus chinensis*).

Conifers, yews (*Taxus*), junipers (*Juniperus*), and pines (*Pinus*)

Mix 30 to 40 percent organic to 70 or 60 percent grit or aggregate (the grit should measure around 3/16in (5mm) in diameter). For young material, use a mix of 40 percent Akadama™ to 60 percent Kiriyu™. Pines require a soil with a higher grit content, however, making the most suitable mix 30 percent organic to 70 percent grit or aggregate.

Indoor bonsai

For most indoor trees, it's advisable to use a mix of 70 percent organic to 30 percent grit or aggregate. Depending on the size of the tree use the above sizes of grit as a guideline. Many tropical bonsai are supplied growing in soil with a high clay content, but if you live in a cooler region, it's best gradually to remove this and to replace it with a mix of 70 percent organic to 30 percent grit or aggregate.

A soil glossary and checklist

Grit (also known as aggregate or sand)

Grit particles should measure between 1/16in and 1/4in (2 and 6mm) in diameter. Although you can buy both rough and smooth grit, rough is preferable. Remember to wash the grit well to remove the dust.

Organic

Organic soils include rotted pine bark, leaf mold, peat moss, and soil-less compost.

Loam

Loam does not mean garden soil, but a mix of the above and clay or else a proprietary brand.

Akadama™

Akadama™ is general-purpose, proprietary-brand soil comprising clay granules of differing sizes and qualities that is suitable for most deciduous trees. Although it absorbs water, it soon relinquishes it.

Kanuma™

Kanuma™ is a proprietary-brand soil that is suitable for such acid-loving plants as azaleas, satsukis, and heathers (*Erica*).

Kiriyu™

Kiriyu™ is a proprietary-brand soil that is suitable for conifers.

Potting or repotting: a seventeen-point checklist

If you are frightened of potting or repotting a bonsai (as I was when I started growing them), you should find the following checklist both helpful and reassuring.

1 Prepare any dry components by passing them through a sieve to remove the fine particles or dust.

2 Prepare the pot by: a) making plastic-mesh covers for the drainage holes b) making wire retainers for the mesh. Then cut the wire with which to retain the tree in the pot.

3 If you are using a shallow pot, you do not need to create a drainage layer (just fill the pot with the appropriate soil). If you are using a deep pot, however, create a drainage layer consisting of large particles of grit, add a layer of slightly smaller-sized particles and then add your soil mix. Create a mound of soil on the spot where you intend to plant the tree.

4 When removing the tree from its existing pot, use a knife or blunt blade to ease the soil away from the edges.

5 Having removed the tree from its pot, check the soil for insect attack, especially of root aphids. The difference between root aphids and the beneficial mycelium fungus that helps pine (*Pinus*) roots to grow is that while mycelium is creamy-white in color, root aphids are bluish-white and may be spotted as small, oval, seed-like shapes within the webs that they weave (which look similar to mycelium).

6 If the tree is a pine, check the soil for mycelium, too. If you can't see any, consider adding some to the soil. (You could either gather it from just below the soil surface around trees growing in the wild or buy a specialty mycelium-growing kit.)

7 Remove between a third and half of the old soil by gently shaking off any loose particles or carefully teasing off sections of soil with a very blunt chopstick.

8 If the tree has a small root ball, trim only a little off the edges of the roots (this will encourage the roots to divide at the cut points).

9 If the root mass is surrounded by a large "beard," gently tug at it to ascertain whether it can be removed safely. Cutting it off is generally not advisable because this would weaken most trees, although some, such as mountain maples (*Acer palmatum*), can tolerate drastic root removal if they are healthy. Check for damaged or dead roots and remove any that you find. If you have cut any large roots, remember to seal them with a wound-sealer to prevent rot from setting in.

10 Because they can quickly dry out, keep fine roots moist during the potting or repotting process. Use a plant-sprayer to mist them with water every few minutes, taking care not to soak the remaining soil clinging to the roots.

11 Place the tree on the mound of soil that you prepared earlier.

12 Gently press the tree a little way into the soil.

13 Add more soil to the area around the tree and press it down with your fingers.

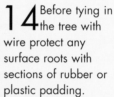

14 Before tying in the tree with wire protect any surface roots with sections of rubber or plastic padding.

15 Using a rubber hammer or your hands, tap around the outside of the pot to ensure that the soil settles around all of the roots.

16 Water the tree using a watering can fitted with a fine rose-head-type spray attachment.

17 Do not feed the tree until the bonsai has settled into its pot and its roots have started growing. This will take about six weeks.

A front view of the bonsai in its new pot.

Caring for bonsai

Most bonsai need more than one component in their soil.

When mixing a soil, use dry components.

Mix the soil components thoroughly.

Remember to cut the retaining cores or wires under a bonsai pot before removing the tree for repotting.

When removing a tree from its pot, check for aphids, mites, and other pests.

You can see moss spores on the surface of the soil in which this fifteen-year-old, broom-style *Zelkova serrata* is growing.

This small yew (*Taxus*) has been planted in a shallow slab, which means that its roots will have to be checked each year. The roots of healthy trees develop very quickly and require sufficient fresh soil to accommodate their growth.

Root-over-rock-style trees can be root-pruned once they are well established. When you are repotting a young tree, you will need to support the roots and rock. This tree is a trident maple (*Acer buergirianum*).

This well-established Scots pine (*Pinus sylvestris*) has been planted a little higher than is typical in order to give its roots the space in which to develop nebari.

A bonsai pot should ideally be no wider than the tree's apex. In the case of this hawthorn (*Crataegus*), a shallower, wider, oval pot would also emphasize the tree's beautiful shape.

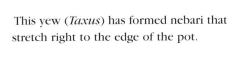

This yew (*Taxus*) has formed nebari that stretch right to the edge of the pot.

Watering bonsai

The most common question that people ask when visiting my bonsai information website is, "Do bonsai need watering?" It may sound crazy, but when someone is given a bonsai, they are apparently often told that they don't have to do anything to it, so they don't. When the bonsai starts to shrivel and its leaves fall off, they start to become worried, and it is at that point, when the bonsai is a past bonsai, that they seek information.

Using a long-necked watering can with an upturned rose head will enable you to pour water gently onto the soil without disturbing the surface.

Attaching a rose head to a hose also makes watering a gentler process. You can use feeder attachments to water your trees and garden, too.

A bonsai therefore needs to be watered, but how often throughout the year? The answer depends on the prevailing climate and the type of tree. Here are some general guidelines.

If you live in a cold or temperate climate, you may need to start watering your bonsai once a week from early to late spring, that is, until the buds start to swell, when you should

Not only can over-watering damage a tree, but when the water sits on top of the soil, it can indicate a serious problem below, such as compacted soil, root rot, a damaged subsystem, or an insect infestation.

increase your watering régime to every three days. As the summer sets in, water every day and then twice a day throughout the summer period until the fall. When the leaves of deciduous trees start to change color in the fall, reduce your watering to three times a week or simply keep the soil damp. In winter, only water if the soil is looking dry, as opposed to being dry. Scrape away a little soil to get into the sub-soil to check if the soil is damp. This means that you will need to inspect the soil at least three times a week over the course of the winter, although this depends on where you live and how you over-winter your bonsai. In the south-west of Scotland, where I live, we have cool summers and mild winters, with regular light frosts and lots of rain, which means that most of the trees that I keep outside never need watering during the winter, although I still have to water the larger bonsai that have heavy canopies because these act like umbrellas. Those that I keep under cover to protect them from the frost, such as deciduous trees or more tender species like olives, elms, and maples, need watering only occasionally because these trees are static during this period and the air is cold and damp. Although I check such trees once a week, I may only have to water them once a month when the soil starts to appear dry.

If the prevailing climate is warm or hot, the changing of the seasons may not be so obvious: you may have cooler periods, a rainy season, a dry summer, and maybe a hot period of dry wind, for example. Most trees display seasonal changes, however, and you will have some that lose their leaves during the cooler part of the year. You may need to place these trees in a position away from winds, cold nights, etc. Make sure that while the tree is leafless you keep the soil slightly damp because if you let it dry out, it may become unable to reconstitute itself when the tree starts to grow again. (The tree may have lost all of its foliage, but the roots are still alive and need damp conditions in order to survive.) During warmer periods, you may have to water your bonsai between three and five times a day.

A Kotohime maple, *Acer palmatum* 'Kotohime,' measuring 18in (45.7cm), which has been trained from a cutting and is now thirty years old. (From the collection of William Valavanis.)

Caring for bonsai

If you have a large and varied collection of bonsai, there are a number of solutions to your watering problem, as follows.

· **Misting**

Having advocated misting at various points throughout *Bonsai school*, I should explain what it involves. Misting allows the leaves to take in moisture through the leaf system. Soft spraying emulates soft rain and this is beneficial to the bonsai. Use warm, not cold, water for misting (the rain that you are trying to recreate is generally warm). If the water supply in your area contains lime, do not use it without taking certain precautions, for two reasons. The first is that many bonsai trees do not like lime, and if you are at all uncertain about a tree's preferences, it's best to play safe and avoid harming the tree by using it. The second is that it will leave a white deposit on the tree's leaves, which will not only look unattractive, but will clog up the leaves, possibly causing die-back. Either use distilled water for misting, or else let tap water stand for twenty-four hours to allow the lime to settle or run it through a lime filter.

Before using an automatic watering system, make sure that you've checked the deliverable rate of water and that the water jets are in working order and are not clogged up.

· **Automatic watering systems**

Automatic watering systems are probably the best option for trees in warm and hot climates. The daily watering routine is controlled by rigging the system to a faucet or a small timer (often grandly called a "computer"), which may control a fan jet or drip-feeding system.

· **Drip-feeding systems**

Drip-feeding systems consist of a series of tiny water-release nipples attached to a thin tube, attached to a thicker tube, attached to a water-pressure reducer, attached to a hose, in turn attached to a "computer" or control system.

Dripper nipples and computer.

Feeding bonsai

Giving your bonsai a suitable feed will ensure their survival. In general, it's advisable to use a general organic garden food once a week and a seaweed-based fertilizer every other week. Seaweed is a popular feed for bonsai, and some companies are developing root-growth stimulants containing it to use immediately after repotting. (I've discovered that using rooting hormone powders when repotting can cause a problem that many growers are unaware of, in that many contain fungicides that can kill the beneficial mycelium fungus that grows on the roots of many trees.)

A full-moon maple, *Acer japonicum*, measuring 29in (73.6cm), which was trained from a cutting and is now twenty-five years old. (From the collection of William Valavanis.)

I also use three types of liquid fertilizer (or rather powders that can be dissolved in water): low or zero nitrogen, high nitrogen, and a balanced feed. To explain further, plant food is composed of three main elements, plus trace elements. The three main elements are nitrogen (N), phosphate (P), and potassium (K), a combination that is abbreviated to NPK. (The trace elements or nutrients that commercially available feeds contain include boron, copper, magnesium oxide, manganese, molybdenum, zinc, calcium, and sulfur.) The three main elements can be further broken down if nitrogen is divided into its three components, nitric nitrogen, ammoniacal nitrogen, and uric nitrogen, while phosphate can be broken down into phosphorus pentoxide and potassium into potassium oxide. Broken down into a basic formula, high-nitrogen, low-nitrogen, and balanced feeds comprise the following proportions:

- a high-nitrogen food consists of 15% nitrogen (N), 10% phosphorus (P), and 20% potassium (K): 15-10-20;

- a low-nitrogen feed contains a very low level of nitrogen, and in bonsai culture it may even be zero, such as 0-10-10;

- a balanced feed consists of an even level of nitrogen, phosphorus, and potassium, in the proportions 10-10-10, for example.

The feeding guidelines are as follows:

- a low-nitrogen feed should be used early in the growing season because it encourages leaves to harden off. It is also better for pines than many other feeds because it does not force the rate of growth too much.

- a high-nitrogen feed should be applied to deciduous trees as the leaves harden off after the first flush of growth.

- a balanced feed should be used from late spring to early summer. It should not be applied during mid-summer because trees enter a state of semi-dormancy during the hottest period of the year. Feeding should be resumed from late summer to fall, when deciduous trees lose their leaves, and in the case of evergreens, feeding should be stopped before the winter or cooler weather sets in.

A penjing *Celtis sinensis* created by Wu Yee-Sun.

If a foliar feed is advocated, use the appropriate low-nitrogen, high-nitrogen, or balanced feed and apply it from late spring, when the leaves are in place, until late fall.

Using different feeds for different types of bonsai

The trees that we use for bonsai fall into two principal categories: lime-hating and lime-tolerant plants. Lime-hating plants, or ericaceous and acid-loving plants, can suffer from chlorosis, a condition caused by iron deficiency, malnutrition, or an alkaline soil that causes the leaves or needles to turn a pale greeny-yellow. A lime-hating tree planted in the wrong soil will end up suffering, if not in its first year, certainly in its second.

Although some soils, like Kiriyu™ and Akadama™, have a vitrified-clay content that remains more or less neutral, I use Kiriyu™ for lime-hating conifers and Kanuma™, a speciality soil, for azaleas and rhododendrons. In other cases, when trees show signs of discoloration, such as yellowing, I use Miracid™ feed, which stimulates healthy growth by gently lowering an alkaline soil's pH level and supplies such essential elements as iron, manganese, copper, and zinc in a fast-acting water-soluble chelated form, which the plant's roots and life structure will absorb almost immediately. Because Miracid™ is sold all over the world, it is one of the few names that I can confidently give you. When buying a feed for rhododendrons or heathers, look for one whose label says that it is suitable for these plants, and as long as the NPK balance is correct, it should be safe to use. (Never use lawn food, however, because it is far too high in nitrogen.)

A general list of lime-hating, or acid-loving, genera includes: stewartia, azalea, rhododendron, Berberis, most conifers, pine (*Pinus*), spruce (*Picea*), cotoneaster, dogwood, fir (*Abies*), larch (*Larix*), tree heather (*Erica*), hawthorn (*Crataegus*), holly (*Ilex*), laurel (*Laurus*), juniper (*Juniperus*), styrax, honeysuckle (*Lonicera*), oak (*Quercus*), magnolia, and mountain ash (*Sorbus*).

Most other tree genera fall into the lime-tolerant group.

Pellet feed

Pellets on the surface of the soil.

As a tree matures, you will need to make some effort to maintain its shape, and over-feeding will probably cause unwelcome branch and foliage growth, as well as overly fast root growth. One way of feeding bonsai without encouraging excessive growth is to use a pellet feed, which enables a small amount of food to leach into the soil. Essentially a food in cake form, the commonest kind, called rapeseed cake, is made from the material that is left after rapeseed oil has been processed. Such a cake will last for about six weeks, after which it should be removed and, if desired, replaced. Small plastic cages are sold to lace over rapeseed cakes (which are about half the size of a boiled egg), partly to prevent birds or animals from dislodging the cake, and partly to discourage flies from laying their eggs on it (alternatively, spray the cake with an insecticide).

A number of excellent bonsai pellet feeds are now available (some bonsai nurseries make their own), and one of the new products that can be used instead of rapeseed cake includes my own favorite, Bio Gold™, which contains some trace elements and takes the form of small, triangular pellets. Protect such pellets from insect attack by spraying them with an insecticide and follow the instructions on the label before using them.

A Kiyohime maple, *Acer palmatum* 'Kiyohime,' measuring 13 x 32in (33 x 81.2cm), trained from a cutting and now twenty-four years old. (From the collection of William Valavanis.)

An American larch, *Larix laricina*, measuring 21in (53.3cm), pictured after having been trained for ten years. (From the collection of William Valavanis.)

Checklist

Note that the brand names of products that are popular in the United Kingdom may differ from those in the United States, Canada, Australia, New Zealand, Greece, Spain or South Africa. Ask your local bonsai nursery for advice, but alternatively remember that it's generally fine to use a houseplant food (but not lawn or grass food because these products contain such high levels of nitrogen that they will damage the tree's roots). A list of some recommended brands follows:

*   general foods: Miracle-Gro™, Baby Bio™, Peters;
*   slow-release soil-surface cakes: Green King™, Bio Gold™ and rapeseed cake;
*   for acid-loving plants: Miracid™ ;
*   low-nitrogen feeds: 0-10-10™, and tomato fertilizers, such as Tomorite™;
*   Chempack™ makes a number of chemical feeds, including low-nitrogen, high-nitrogen, and balanced feeds.

See also pages 204 to 205 for Michael Persiano's advice on following a "superfeeding" regime.

Preventing pests and diseases

Space does not, unfortunately, allow me to discuss all of the pests and diseases that may attack bonsai, but a few common culprits, along with their antidotes, are outlined below. Contact your local bonsai club for advice on the pests and diseases that are prevalent in your country or climate and how they should be dealt with.

Pests and diseases

Pests	Period of attack	Visual indications	Treatment	Species
Aphids Aphids are the most common of the sap-sucking insects. Commonly green, there are also more voracious, black forms.	Aphids tend to attack from spring to fall, but green aphids, especially in early summer and, black aphids, from late spring through summer. All aphid attacks set in quickly, but black aphids are particularly rapid, they can work through an otherwise healthy tree in a few days.	Leaf droop and stickiness are the first signs of aphid attack. On closer inspection, you will see that the tips of new growth are covered with aphids.	First remove as many aphids as you can by running your fingers up the infested stems to clear the aphids from the tree. Spraying them with a suitable insecticide will also rapidly clear the tree. Always wear a protective mask and gloves and remember to spray downwind. Do not inhale the insecticide and wash your hands as soon as you have finished.	Many different types of aphid are prevalent in temperate to cool climates, as well as in warmer climates. Consult your local garden center for information and advice.
Root aphids Root aphids attack the under-soil system by attaching themselves to the root area, usually near the edge of the roots at the pot. They suck the sap from the roots.	Root aphids attack throughout the growing season, from early spring to late fall.	Poor growth and lack of vigor are indications of root aphids. The best way to check is to inspect the root mass. Carefully support the root mass and do not disturb the roots when easing the mass out of the pot. Root aphids look like pale-blue fungus at first sight, but on closer inspection you will see little oval, seed-like shapes.	Use a systemic insecticide poured into the soil and sprayed on the tree's branches. The roots, leaves, and needles will absorb the systemic and the root aphids will die off as they feed. Treating the tree once a month for three months should eradicate the root aphids. Check the root mass two months later and then every month.	There are many different types of root aphid, which, in cooler climates, mainly attack conifer bonsai, probably due to the type of free-draining soil in which these trees should be planted. I usually see root aphids in soil that contains a high proportion of peat or leaf-mold.

Pests	Period of attack	Visual indications	Treatment	Species
Adelgids and woolly aphids These are small sap suckers that are covered in a white waxy fluff. Usually seen on conifers and especially pines.	Adelgids and woolly aphids attack throughout the growing season, from early spring to late fall.	Absorbent cotton-like clusters of insects between pine needles are often attributed to the presence of woolly aphids, but are more likely to be adelgids, similarly sap-suckers.	Although a systemic insecticide will move through the food source, the tree's sap, the waxy fluff is difficult to eradicate. The best way of dissolving this coating is to rub it with a cotton swab or child's toothbrush dipped in denatured alcohol. If you use a hose you will damage the buds and growth. A hand sprayer with the sprayhead adjusted to jet should be ok but be careful.	There are similar species of adelgids and woolly aphids in various parts of the world. The treatment is generally the same.
Scale Many deciduous trees are affected by scale, including elms. They are small, oval, or round, pimple-shaped pests that are brownish in color and can cover the stems and trunk of a tree quickly.	Scale attacks throughout the growing season, but is usually only noticeable in late summer.	Scale presents itself as small, brown, or gray scales, sometimes with fluffy edges.	Although a systemic insecticide will move through the food source the waxy "scales" are difficult to eradicate. The best way of dissolving this coating is to rub it with a cotton swab or child's toothbrush dipped in denatured alcohol.	There are many species of scale, most of which look similar and are bad news when they attack. Some affect a tree's roots, as well as its upper portions.

Pests	Period of attack	Visual indications	Treatment	Species
Lopho Lopho (full name Lophodermium pinastre) is also known as pine-needle cast. This is a fungus and is spread by air and infection.	Lopho may attack at any time.	Yellow, horizontal stripes in a tree's needles are the most common indicator of Lopho infection. Although poor health and die-back is another, these symptoms could also have been caused by poor soil.	Because a Lopho infection is tantamount to a fungal attack, treat it with a fungicide (I would use a copper-based fungicide). You need to protect the soil from any drips, so cover it with plastic sheet and a dishcloth or two. Treat the tree every seven days for five weeks.	Lopho presents itself in much the same manner around the world, and I have seen imported trees from China and Japan that have been affected by this disease.
White fly, thrips, black fly, and other tiny insects These small insects usually affect indoor trees. They are soil pests and jump from pot to pot. They feed on the roots.	Because these insects thrive in greenhouses and inside, they may attack at any time.	If you see little black or white flies flying around you, these are likely to be white fly, thrips, or black fly. You may also see tiny insects in the saucer or container that you may have placed beneath the bonsai's pot.	Spraying with a suitable insecticide should quickly get rid of them. Remember to wear a protective mask and gloves, always to spray downwind, never to inhale the insecticide, and to wash your hands as soon as you have finished. In addition, don't spray near children and keep the area off limits until the spray has dried. Follow the instructions on the label and don't drench the leaves, but mist them lightly. Drench the soil, however, because this will kill the larvae. Treating the tree every week for five weeks usually eradicates the problem.	There are many species of white fly, thrips and black fly, so read the label of the insecticidal product that you are using against them for advice on their different tolerance levels.

Water sitting on the surface of the soil may indicate, among other things, rotten roots.

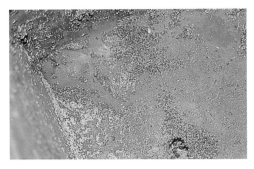

Tiny mites, like the hundreds that you can see in this pot during a repotting exercise, can damage a tree's roots.

Root aphids are oval in shape and form small clusters within a bluish-white web.

A web made by pine-needle caterpillars. A serious infestation of these needle-eating larvae can quickly strip a tree of its foliage.

If you split the web open, you can see the pine-needle caterpillars' pupae. The web itself is composed of chewed-up bark and pine needles.

Vine weevils, which are found the world over, can cause serious damage to a tree because their grubs feed on its roots.

This photograph illustrates the damage that wood-eating larvae can wreak beneath a tree's bark.

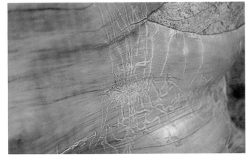

If an infestation of wood-eating larvae is not serious, or if the grubs leave their host for whatever reason, the tree will start to recover and its bark will start growing again around the edge of the damaged area to create natural shari.

Always check under moss for any pests that may be lurking beneath the surface. Fast-moving insects are usually hunting for slower-moving ones. All beetles go through a grub stage, and it is these grubs that can damage a tree's root system.

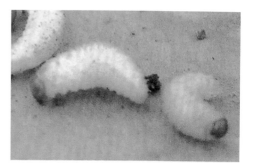

Mycelium is a beneficial fungus whose presence in conifer roots you can recognize by its pale-cream color. In this example, it has grown around the base of a bonsai pot.

In this instance, the mycelium fungus has become so prolific that it has grown up the tree's trunk, and although it is usually beneficial, it has now become a pest. Remove it by hand, using a soft brush, not a fungicide.

Because the grubs of vine weevils feed on a tree's roots voraciously, they can kill it very quickly. Some pots can have one weevil while others can have many hundreds.

The particles of processed wood that small, wood-boring insects may leave on the surface of an infested tree may cause fungal damage, which may in turn either kill an adult tree or else seriously damage its structure.

These examples of insect damage are almost architectural in form.

Seasonal Care

Although I would love to cover every climate in detail, this is primarily a book about bonsai techniques and space doesn't allow it. Whether you live in a warm, temperate, or cold climate, you are therefore advised to seek local information about the best times to institute seasonal care in your area. The following pages will give you a framework into which to slot that information. In warm climates, most jobs can be done throughout the year (except for the middle of summer), but it's best to work seasonal jobs into your calendar. Slow down your feeding régime when the weather is cooler, but do your repotting during the third period of the cool season, for instance, or your wiring at the end of summer, before the cooler weather sets in. In more tropical climates, there may be a rainy season, during which you can perform the chores that you would during a cooler period if you lived elsewhere. Ask your local bonsai teachers for advice, however, because bonsai chores in Florida or Sicily will be quite different to those in Pennsylvania or Moscow, for example, inasmuch as their type and timing will differ.

	Spring	Summer
1 Notes	Spring means many things in many countries. In cooler areas, there is early, middle, and late spring while in warmer areas spring means very little, other than it's warmer after the winter slightly cooler period. Warmer areas can have two or even three growth periods while in many countries, spring really means the start of the growing season. Early spring is the time before bud growth to repot your trees while late spring means the trees have grown their leaves and you can now start feeding, bud plucking, and other techniques to get the trees to develop. Spring can also mean high winds and lots of rain and you will need to protect your bonsai or penjing from the elements.	Although summer can be divided into three main periods—early, middle and late—these divisions are more pronounced in temperate climates than in hotter countries. You won't have to work as hard during the summer as you would in spring or fall (and you can't do much in mid-summer in any case because trees go into a period of dormancy), but late summer is the time to wire conifers and perhaps do some repotting.

Fall	Winter

If you live in a temperate country, where there are four distinct seasons, you will also know that there are three fall periods: early, mid-, and late fall. Although the jobs that you'll need to do during the fall are not too onerous, they nevertheless need doing. Early fall is the last part of the year in which you can rewire conifers, and you can also pot or repot now as long as you protect your bonsai from a cold winter or frost. Mid-fall is the time to check whether any moss is growing on tree trunks. If you find any, remove it, taking care not to damage the bark. (Now is, in any case, a good time to remove moss from the soil surface and to plant moss on sand and peat ready for the coming year.) And in late fall, your trees may start to change color and lose their leaves.

As the weather becomes cooler, and after a tree's leaves have either fallen or turned brown (as in the case of the *Fagus*, or beech), you will need to protect your bonsai from the cold and wind. Although this should be a matter of course in cooler climates, unless you live in a tropical country, you should still be prepared to protect your trees from a sudden bout of inclement weather. (I have seen snow in Florida, while desert areas, such as Utah and Arizona, can have freezing nights, even though it is hot during the day.) If you live in a tropical area, continue providing your bonsai with shade, while in colder areas you will need to protect your trees from the wind with netting, and in very cold areas your bonsai should either be housed inside or in a deep pit.

Your climate will dictate whether you need to insulate your bonsai during the winter. If you do, remember that poly-tunnels or greenhouses are not a good option unless they are fully shaded because they can warm up significantly during sunny spells, causing the trees within them to begin a period of false growth. If you decide to use a greenhouse, however, make sure that the glass has been painted in to provide shade and open any doors and vents on sunny winter days. While they are in their period of winter dormancy, most deciduous trees do not need light. Although many growers transfer all of their trees to a dark place for two or three months after winter's arrival, I like to give my evergreens as much light as there is in my temperate climate. If you live in a very cold area, you may need to create a sunken area in which to over-winter your bonsai. If you do this, ensure that no water can seep into the pit. Alternatively, place your bonsai in a shed that has a double layer of insulation and install a small ambient heater to remove the severe chill from the air. I move my more delicate trees to my garage and leave the rest outside and, as I mentioned previously, the only time that my trees suffered from winter dampness and cold was when they were over-wintered in a large poly-tunnel without an ambient heater.

Frost and wind damage can be a serious problem, and if your climate is subject to winter frosts, note that you should also keep your trees out of the wind, which may pose more of a threat than the cold. If you don't, the frost will freeze the soil so that the roots can't move, while the wind will buffet the foliage of evergreens and the twigs of deciduous trees, sometimes freeze-drying it. The soft tissues of smooth-barked deciduous trees, in particular, may suffer in extremely cold conditions, perhaps even splitting open if there is a particularly severe frost, so make sure that you protect such trees by moving them into or under shelter for this period. It's also important to keep maples out of the wind because it may cause their branch tips to die back.

	Spring	Summer

2

Chores

The main chores that you will need to perform in spring are much the same the world over. The early spring is the time to pot or repot, although precisely when to do this depends on an individual tree's growth pattern. In most non-tropical climates, it's best to pot a tree before its leaf buds have opened, just before they start to swell. (Some species, however, prefer you to wait until their buds have started to swell, so seek the advice of your local club or teacher.) An emergency repot can be performed at any time, as long as you do not cut, or significantly disturb, the roots. Certain genera, such as pines (*Pinus*) require a dryer soil, while bald cypresses (*Taxodium*), and willows (*Salix*) require a wetter soil. (See the section on soil, pages 69 to 77).

If you live in a mild climate, you can root-prune and to do a little branch pruning in spring as well, as long as you seal all of the cuts with a latex tree-wound sealer, such as Kiyonal™ or Lac Balsam™ (don't forget to seal the roots, too, to prevent them from dying back or rotting).

Plant moss on the soil, but if your bonsai is an outdoor tree, cover the moss with netting to stop birds in search of insects from removing it.

Check that no pests, such as scale insects, are over-wintering in your bonsai, apply a little systemic insecticide to the soil and also spray the branches and twigs.

Now is also the time to tie your tree into its pot with 2mm–4 aluminum wire—depending on the size of your tree—to stop it from being rocked by spring winds.

Tag the front of your bonsai to remind you to turn them every week (and to avoid confusion, always turn them in a clockwise direction). If all of the tags are facing the same way, you'll know that you have turned all of your trees, but if one is pointing in a different direction, it's a reminder that you need to turn that bonsai.

Early summer is the time to defoliate some deciduous trees (but only healthy ones), especially maples, elms, and zelkovas, because creating a false fall in this way can encourage new twigs to develop. The defoliation technique involves cutting just below the leaf, leaving a little stalk, which will then die off naturally; you do not need to seal the cut. Although the new leaf that will grow at the base of the stalk may be smaller in size than its predecessor, the main purpose of defoliation is to generate more twigs, that is, to create better ramification. The leaves of other genus's can be nipped out during the early summer to encourage denser growth.

The new inner growth (the new growth at, or near, the main trunk) of some genera, such as *Cryptomeria* and *Juniperus*, should be plucked because leaving it in place could weaken the tree. To tip-pluck, hold the base of the leaf section with one hand and then pluck upward, without twisting (to avoid damaging the growth beneath, causing it to die off), so that you remove only the tip of the new growth. Tip-plucking should be an on-going process during the tree's period of active growth, but not during the fall and winter.

Fall

Continue to turn your pots, and if your climate is temperate or cool, take the appropriate watering and shade-provision measures if you suddenly have an Indian summer or hot spell. As the fall season unfolds, remember that there is a danger of wind damage, too.

Drench bonsai soil and moss trays and spray leaves with a systemic to kill any pests. (Wear a mask when applying systemic, and do not perform this job on a windy day.)

Winter

Your main chore at the start of winter is to protect your trees from frost and wind. In cold climates, wait for the first frost before doing this (except in the case of tender material), however, because most trees need to be jolted into dormancy, which the first frost should do. If you live in a warmer climate where the winter weather is cold, but free of frost, the cooler nights may still damage a tree's soft tissues, so if you keep your bonsai on a shelf, it's best to move them underneath it, which will also protect them from the wind.

If you intend to place your bonsai on the ground, either put down slug pellets first or slightly raise your trees above ground level by standing them on wooden packing pallets. Protect your trees from rodents, dogs, and cats by surrounding them with either fencing or meshed chicken wire.

Repotting should normally be done between late winter and early spring, before the leaf buds of most trees start swelling. Pines and most evergreen conifers can also be potted at the start of the late-winter period.

	Spring	Summer
3 Feeding	You should only commence feeding when a tree's leaves are fully open. To start with, use either a very low-nitrogen or even 0-10-10 feed to enable soft, deciduous leaves to harden off or to reduce the length of pine needles. Later in the spring, switch to a normal feeding régime and make sure that you use the appropriate fertilizer for your trees. Do not add proprietary pellet feeds to the potting mix because these have a tendency suddenly to leach out and damage the roots. If you have repotted a tree, do not feed it for at least six to eight weeks, and before doing so make sure that the tree is growing, otherwise you will harm the newly developing tender roots.	During the early summer, step up your feeding régime to once a week for young bonsai after their leaves have hardened off. Mature bonsai need feeding more carefully, and I recommend that you use a pellet food, such as rapeseed cake or Bio Gold™ (and lightly spray any cake feed with an insecticide to stop flies from laying their eggs in them). If you have repotted it, do not use any feed until you are sure that a tree has settled into its pot. Use a balanced feed if you want to apply a liquid feed to soil and foliage. I stop feeding my bonsai in mid-summer because most trees, even in very hot climates, simply "shut down" during this period of hot weather to conserve energy. When we were walking through his collecting area in the Dolomites region of Italy, Valerio Gianotti told me that the reason why the trees are so stunted here is that they receive no rain for two to three months and just stop growing, which is why you should pay particular attention to watering during this part of the summer.

Fall

| Winter |

Although you should continue to feed all of your trees during the early fall, do this only every two weeks and use a low-nitrogen fertilizer because the tree's woody parts now need strengthening rather than its foliage, while feeding its roots will help it to survive the coming cold spell. Give deciduous trees their last feed in mid-fall, but continue to feed evergreens and evergreen conifers until late fall and pines until early winter.

Check to ensure that pines have swelling leaf buds, but if they do not, do not feed them during this period because it may be a sign that they are struggling, perhaps due to root problems, insect attack, or the wrong soil composition following a spring repot. Carefully remove the tree from its pot to check for any signs of problems. Root rot may be identified if the roots look lifeless or there are no light-brown or fine, cream-colored roots (which are associated with the beneficial mycelium fungus). If you see a bluish-white-colored webbing that looks like mycelium, but you can also see small, oval-shaped life forms on closer inspection, these may be root aphids. Mite attacks can be identified if you see lots of white, fast-moving, miniscule insects or, if the situation is really bad, the fat, cream-colored larvae of the vine weevil.

If your tree has root rot, two courses of action are open to you. First, if only a small area is affected, simply cut off the dead roots and seal any cuts that you've made to living roots. Second, if the situation looks really grim, you may have to treat the whole bonsai like a giant cutting to give it a chance of survival. Although it is generally the wrong time of year to do this, transplant the roots—or what's left of them—into either a mixture of sphagnum moss and a little Akadama™ or a sterile cutting medium. You may also have to reduce the foliage to match the remaining root mass, but this may only mean reducing the height of the foliage pads rather than removing any branches. Once you have transplanted it, cover your tree, but ensure that there is good air circulation, protect it from cold and frost during the winter, and keep an eye open for mold, particularly Botrytis. If your tree is infested with pests, remove as many as you can by hand, especially any large grubs, and then drench the soil with a systemic insecticide.

Unless they are evergreen conifers, do not feed your bonsai until their leaves have opened fully in spring (and remember to remove any solid food pellets from the surface of the soil). If you intend to repot any evergreen conifers in late winter, do not feed them for at least six weeks beforehand. If you are not going to repot them, however, you can give them a little low- or zero-nitrogen fertilizer in late winter.

	Spring	Summer
4 Wiring and pruning	As soon as you see any buds, or indications of leaf buds, do not wire or prune your bonsai. Make sure that no wire has been left on any actively growing areas of the tree, that is, the tips of the branches and the apex, because it will bite into and damage the new growth.	It's best not to undertake any wiring or pruning until a tree has entered its period of mid-summer dormancy. (Some bonsai-growers prefer to wire between late winter and early spring, but in my opinion trees should be free of wire in spring, otherwise it will bite into new growth and inflict unattractive wire marks.) If you leave the wiring until later in the summer, just after the hottest period, you can also defoliate a healthy tree. First, however, you will need to work out when the tree will start growing again to ensure that you don't defoliate it too early. Although I have tried to take a seasonal approach instead of specifying months in *Bonsai school*, perhaps I should be a little more specific in this case. In the colder climates of the northern hemisphere, it's best to defoliate some time between the end of July and the beginning of August; but in the warmer climates of the southern hemisphere, defoliation should not be carried out until at least the end of January or the beginning of February, and usually a few weeks thereafter, and it's also best to wire quite late on during the hotter part of the year (seek the advice of experienced bonsai-growers in your area about the best time to undertake this work). Major pruning is best performed at this time, too, and remember always to seal any cuts.

Fall	Winter
Do not wire or prune your trees after the early fall period has ended.	I do not like to wire my trees during the winter, but if you intend to do so you must do it toward the end of the mid-winter period. Carving can also be done at this time, as long as you seal all cut edges with Cut Paste™ or sealing putty for bonsai. If you live in a cold climate, it's important to give your trees extra protection after wiring or carving because the cold or frost can damage the newly exposed wood, which cannot repair itself until it starts growing again. (This is why it's inadvisable to wire, carve, or prune during the winter.) It's also best not to do even very light wiring or shaping during the late winter before the leaf buds have started to swell because the wire will later bite into the new growth. If you live in a warmer area, and your trees do not go into full dormancy, seek the advice of local experts about the best time to wire and prune.

	Spring	**Summer**
5 Watering	Water your bonsai once or twice a week in early spring to keep the soil damp and increase your watering régime as your trees become more vigorous, so that by early summer you may be watering once a day. If you live in a warm climate and the weather is dry, make sure that the soil is damp and start misting your bonsai once a day.	Depending on the strength of the sun, water your trees every two days in early summer and simply prevent the soil from drying out over the mid- and late-summer periods. If you've installed a watering system, make sure that all of your bonsai are indeed receiving water and that the feeder drips have not been blocked or the pipe disconnected. You should mist the foliage as well, and the best times to do this are in the early mornings and early evenings (but if you live in an extremely hot climate, your bonsai should be positioned in the shade, in which case you can mist at any time during the day) Beware of misting when the air is still, however, because the humidity level may rise and temperate trees may develop Botrytis, a fungal mold. Note, too, that depending on the type of soil in which you have potted your bonsai, there is a danger of over-watering, causing mold to grow on the surface of the soil, and also that because many trees stop growing during the hottest period of the year, you should be careful to water just enough to keep the soil damp, not soggy. Many soils contain a high quantity of free-draining material, such as grit or sand (grit-sized particles measuring no less than 1 or 2mm), but finer sand (of the consistency of beach sand) offers poor drainage because it will clog up the soil. Don't even use it as a top dressing because it can leach down into the subsurface, where it will obstruct the free flow of water, damage the tree's roots, and cause root rot. Remember that after the tree's period of mid-summer dormancy its leaves should start growing and signs of life should be noticeable. If they are not, you may have to remove the tree from its pot to check that the roots are healthy, which means that they should be white, with no signs of rot or root aphids (the tell-tale sign being a bluish color). The cream-colored mycelium fungus, a beneficial fungus that aids a tree's feeding and growth, that you may see in the soil around conifers, particularly pines, is a sign of health, however, so leave it alone.

Fall

Winter

Although trees need less water during the fall, they still need some. If the early fall period is warm, continue watering them once a day, and if it's really warm, twice a day.

By mid-fall, when the trees' growth is slowing, restrict your watering to four times a week. Make sure that the soil is draining well, whatever the tree, and that the soil is damp in the case of deciduous, soft-leaved trees. The soil in which conifers are planted should always drain fast, and the subsoil just beneath the surface should be damp. Using a mixture of Akadama™ and Kiriyu™ will enable you to determine this because Akadama™ turns light brown when it is dry, so if you remove a little soil from the surface and the color of the soil beneath is slightly darker, this tells you that all is well. I recommend doing this every day to check whether the tree is receiving sufficient water.

If your climate is temperate or cool, reduce your watering further during late fall. This is a time when it may rain a lot, and you may therefore feel that you do not need to water your bonsai. However, if any of your trees have large, thick canopies of foliage, these may act as umbrellas and prevent the rain reaching the soil. After it has been raining, it's therefore best to check the soil to see if it needs watering. (My neighbors used to think that I was quite mad because I watered my bonsai when it was raining—now they do it for me when I am away teaching!)

Do not water your bonsai until late winter, when they start growing again. In the meantime, keep the soil damp, but not soaking wet (unless you keep your bonsai outside). Tilting one edge of a bonsai's pot to one side slightly will help any excess water to drain away.

	Spring	**Summer**
6 Checklist	· Pot or repot bonsai early in spring, before the leaf buds start to swell. · Seal any cuts made to roots and branches during the repotting process. · Don't feed a bonsai until its leaves are fully open. · Remove any wire that has been left on a bonsai over the winter. · Water just enough to keep the soil damp.	· In milder climates, defoliate a tree in early summer to encourage a second flush of growth (but if you live in a colder climate, think hard before undertaking this task). · Reduce feeding during the mid-summer period. · Wire and prune in late summer. · Increase your watering and misting regimes in early summer.

Fall	Winter
At the beginning of fall, start using a low-nitrogen feed. Check both soil and foliage for signs of insect attack. In mid-fall, stop wiring and potting. Reduce your watering as the season progresses, but only if the weather is cool.	· Prepare your bonsai's winter-protection areas and move them there when necessary. · Do not expose your bonsai to the wind or frost. · Do not feed deciduous bonsai until their leaves have opened fully. · Do not feed evergreen conifers for six weeks before repotting them. · Reduce your watering to almost nothing, but make sure that the soil does not dry out completely.

The increasing interest in bonsai has also seen a return to the traditional method of growing them from seed. A time-consuming process, it is rarely done well due to the lack of available information, however. By contrast, this class looks at seed propagation in detail. (See also page 134 for Xiaojian Wang's advice on propagating *Pyracantha crenulata*.)

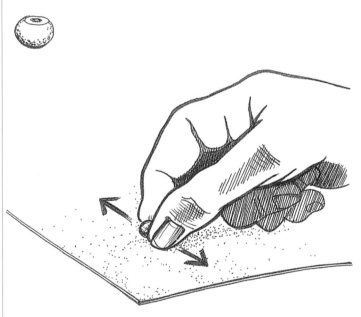

Rub one side of a hard-coated seed with fine sandpaper to wear it down a little, taking care not to damage the embryo inside.

Propagating from seed,
by Gary Field

I asked Gary Field, of Angelgrove Tree Seeds, who are based in North America, to give us the benefit of his extensive experience and research. He gives his advice over the following pages.

Strategy 1: the cold stratification of tree seeds

Pre-treating seeds (cold stratification) is a simple measure that helps to break a seed's natural dormancy, causing it to become more amenable to a quicker, more 'unified' germination process. This section gives an overview of the process, followed by some more detailed tips.

To accomplish cold stratification, you will need to mix the tree seeds with some thoroughly moistened vermiculite (or sterile peat), using ten to fifteen times more vermiculite (or sterile peat) than there are seeds. It is important to dampen the vermiculite (or sterile peat) thoroughly, but only slightly, and to make sure that the seeds are in contact with it during the stratification process. Although too little moisture will not be effective, excess moisture may cause seeds to become moldy. It's therefore best to err on the side of drier, rather than wetter, vermiculite (or sterile peat). Moisten a handful of vermiculite (or sterile peat) thoroughly and uniformly and then squeeze out any excess water before mixing it with the seeds.

Transfer the mixture to a clean, clear-plastic, sealable bag, seal the bag and then place it in the lowest compartment of your refrigerator (not your freezer), where the temperature usually hovers around about 35 to 42°F (2 to 6°C).

Seed growth.

Having spent the recommended period of time in your refrigerator, the seeds can then be removed and sown in a flat tray, nursery bed or pot, which should be placed in a warm place to encourage germination. Try to time the germination process so that it finishes in late spring to early summer.

Preparing and maintaining your stratification medium

- Buy a bag of clean, dry, milled or shredded peat or vermiculite or else a sterile potting mixture.

- Moisten the vermiculite or peat slightly before mixing it with the seeds.

- If you do not squeeze any excess moisture from the vermiculite (or peat), there is a danger that fungus or mold will start growing on the seeds, especially if you haven't applied any horticultural fungicide. If left unchecked, mould or fungus can damage the seeds and interfere with the pre-treatment process.

- It's advisable to check your stratifying seeds regularly, for both fungus and signs of germination. If any seeds begin to germinate during the cold-stratification process, remove them from the bag and sow them.

- If you notice an outbreak of mold or fungus, remove the seeds from the bag and spray them with fungicide mixed with water. You must not reuse the vermiculite (or peat) or bag, so throw them away. Slightly moisten a new handful of vermiculite (or peat), mix it with the seeds, transfer the mixture to a new bag and place it in the refrigerator, as before.

- Always keep the bag sealed to prevent the stratification medium from drying out. If the mixture appears to have become too dry halfway through the storage period, spray it with a gentle misting of water. Remember that seeds need moisture in order to germinate and must therefore be in constant contact with the moist vermiculite (or peat).

Preparing your seeds for cold stratification

Because seeds need to begin imbibing moisture before they will sprout, it helps to soak them in some tepid water immediately before placing them in cold storage. Some seeds have what is known as a "mechanical dormancy", which refers to the seed's hard (or thick), and sometimes stony and impenetrable, coat. When working with such hard seeds, it helps slightly to rupture (or "nick") a portion of the coat with a knife or file, or else to rub it with sandpaper to reduce its thickness before soaking it. Try not to damage the white embryo at the center during this process.

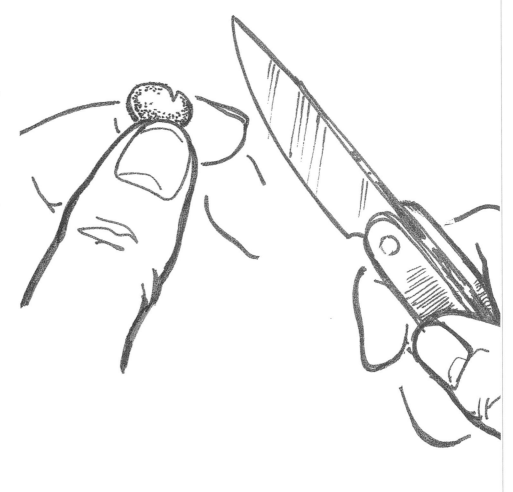

Use a knife or file to nick a hard seed's tough outer coating to help the growing seed to break through the shell.

When preparing tough-coated seeds for cold stratification, another option is to be a little more aggressive during the soaking process. Place the seeds in a shallow container, slowly pour some very hot tap water (the temperature should be approximately 110°F (43°C) over them a few times and then leave them in the cooling water for twenty-four to forty-eight hours before starting the cold-stratification process.

Starter material for bonsai

Timing the cold-stratification process

You should ideally begin the cold-stratification process so that its ending coincides with the beginning of your late spring or early summer season. Doing this will ensure that the seeds are ready to be sown shortly after the weather has become warmer and the earth has warmed up considerably. The chances of a pre-treated seed germinating are greatly enhanced if the seed is sown in a warm and moist (but not wet) situation.

An oak (*Quercus*) seedling starts to break through its tough outer shell.

Within two days, the shoot has tripled in length.

Within five days, the shoot should have broken through the surface of the soil. It is very brittle at this stage.

Sowing and seedlings

Once the seeds have finished their pre-treatment, extract them from the vermiculite (or peat) and either spray or wash them with some fungicide mixed with water. Now prepare your planting medium. Using a sterile potting soil will ward off such problems as stem rot and damping off, both of which are more likely to occur if the soil contains excessive numbers of bacteria and is then exposed to overly moist and cold conditions.

Most tree seeds need to be planted to a depth of up to 5in (6 to 127mm) only. If you are planting your seeds in a nursery bed outside, plant them a little deeper, however, to a depth of about ¾in (127 to 190mm), because heavy rainfall may otherwise disturb the soil and expose the seeds. Make a hole for each seed in the soil and spray that with the fungicide mix as well.

Place each seed in its hole and then lightly tamp down the soil around it. The soil should be in contact with the seed, but should not be too heavily compacted because this would restrict aeration.

Placement and care

Because bacterial problems are more likely to occur if the air circulation is poor, it's best to germinate your seeds, and to grow on your seedlings, outside, where they'll have the advantage of being exposed to the breeze, as well as the benefit of sun-warmed soil. (Dappled, or lightly screened, shade will also protect your seeds from frying in extremely hot sunshine.) That having been said, seeds can also be germinated inside as long as they have sufficient light and good air circulation.

Keep the nursery bed or pot uniformly and lightly damp, but never soaking wet, and never let it dry out completely.

This sequoia cone, which is less than 2in (5cm) long, may have to wait for up to forty years before the conditions are right for it to shed its seed.

Strategy 2: the natural way, sowing seeds in autumn

Planting seeds directly into a nursery bed or pot in late fall, after the hot days of summer have definitely passed, for germination the following spring, or a spring season thereafter, naturally satisfies their requirement for cold stratification, that is, as long as your climate is cold during the winter months.

Depending on the genus and depth or degree of dormancy, some seeds will not sprout until the second or third spring following their planting.

Some of the seeds that require only a short (from four to six weeks) cold-stratification period will often germinate after receiving an overnight soaking in water before they are sown.

How long does it take for seeds to germinate after sowing?

The time that it takes for seeds to germinate after you've sown them differs from seed to seed and from genus to genus, also depending on the prevalent conditions (the temperature and moistness of the soil, for example, and the temperature and length of the days and nights) during their germination phase and how effectively those conditions broke the seeds' dormancy. That having been said, it usually ranges between one to eight weeks, although late stragglers are common, as are seeds that hold out until the following spring, depending on how effective any pre-treatment may have been.

Seasonal care

Pine cones hold seeds, which are scattered when the cones drop. The cones of some trees, such as the sequoia, may distribute their seeds only every forty years. Others, such as the *Pinus coulteri* drop their cones every two or three years.

The *Pinus coulteri* cone splits open to release its seeds.

Key points for seed propagation

Remember the following key points when stratifying and sowing seeds:

- Only use good-quality seeds.

- Think sterile! Use new vermiculite, peat or soil whenever possible.

- It is vital that seeds remain in constant contact with moist vermiculite or peat during the cold-stratification process.

- When stratifying seeds, be patient: let them stratify for the recommended period of time and then add on a few days for good measure.

- Once they have been sown, pre-treated seeds need warm, moist conditions to enable them to germinate, not sopping-wet, cold ones.

- You don't have to cold-stratify your seeds. Alternatively, sow them in a mulched bed, garden nook or pot in the late autumn for natural germination in spring.

- Some batches of seeds will sprout before you expect them to, and some later.

Gary Field.

Cuttings and air layers

Two other methods of propagating trees are taking cuttings and making air layers, and the best time to do both is in late spring.

There are two main types of cutting that you can take: soft-wood and hard-wood cuttings. A soft-wood cutting is still green when it is cut, while a hard-wood cutting's bark is no longer green, but has turned brown (or whatever color the bark of the adult tree is). Having taken a cutting, you then have to encourage roots to develop.

Air layer—standard method

When making an air layer, the cutting is left in situ, on the tree and is fed by the main plant while developing roots in the cut area. You will then need to protect the cut area to allow the roots to develop. As this is an open wound, you now need to make a kind of pot as follows.

The bark is removed around the trunk or twig and soil or moss is placed around the cut area, so that roots form within this "container."

Cuttings—standard propagation method

To take a cutting, first make a clean cut with a sharp pocket or cutting knife – please be careful – then expose a little of the lighter-coloured wood under the bark and dip that part just over the edge of the bark into a rooting gel or hormone powder. Place the stem of the cutting at a slight angle near the edge of a pot filled with cutting compost, cutting sand, vermiculite or even Akadama™. The cutting should be protected from inclement weather and kept in a warm place. Keep the planting medium moist, but not soaking wet, and mist the cutting once or twice a day, more often if you live in a warm climate. Watch out for mildew or fungus and if you see it, lightly spray the cutting with a suitable fungicide. Do not feed the cutting. Transplant the cutting either after three months or when it has taken root.

José demonstrates his Rooter Pot™, with the lid open, on a vertical stem.

The Faura method of taking air-layer cuttings

José Ileo Faura, from Valencia in Spain, has invented a unique tool with which to obtain mature air-layer cuttings from trees. Having worked for many years on his idea, he eventually came up with the hydrocapillary Rooter Pot™, which can take a thick stem cutting, measuring up to 1in (25mm) in diameter, from almost any species of parent tree (and José has successfully taken air-layer cuttings from hundreds of species).

I have spoken to José a number of times, and am fascinated with his invention, which enables you to obtain good-quality material within a very short time. All that you have to do is find a suitable branch, with a nice foliage head, and then apply his Rooter Pot™ and soon the air-layer cutting will not only have been taken, but will have rooted within the same season. José's invention also allows you to make an air-layer cutting at any height on the parent tree's stem.

Due to its hermetic design, the Rooter Pot™ is a self-heating container that promotes rooting by maintaining a constant inner temperature level. Essentially a mini-greenhouse, it also contains self-regulating water reserves that compensate for any evaporation and keep the dampness of the soil at the correct level. You can open the Rooter Pot™ at any time to check on the rooting process and can then close it again without damaging the new roots (which take two to three months to develop). The Rooter Pot's™ technical details are as follows:

* it is vertically articulated so that it opens up around the stem and then locks easily;
* the base holds two water reservoirs that keep the soil permanently damp at the correct level;
* the wall contains six capillary channels that allow water to rise by means of surface tension, causing the roots to grow directly downwards and not around the inside of the Rooter Pot™.

After two months, healthy roots have developed within the Rooter Pot™. To remove your new bonsai material, cut below the root mass, carefully tease it out of the Rooter Pot™ and then plant it.

Using the Rooter Pot™

Follow these steps, and within two to three months you will have a new starter bonsai to work with. I have used the Rooter Pot™ and was delighted with my success.

1 Choose a stem for air layering and, if necessary, keep it vertical by tying it to another branch or other type of support.

2 Make two circular cuts about 3/8in (1cm) wide, on either side of the bark. Remove the bark.

3 Place the Rooter Pot™ over the area of stripped bark and then close it firmly. Use the cable that is supplied with the Rooter Pot™ as well.

4 Fill the Rooter Pot's™ two reservoirs with water.

5 Using your fingers, firmly press some soil into the four base cones to activate the Rooter Pot's™ capillary action.

6 Fill the Rooter Pot™ with soil, pressing it down firmly with your fingers so that it is in contact with the stem.

7 Water the soil well and then press it down firmly with your fingers again (this step is essential).

8 Close the Rooter Pot's™ lid and pass the two pins through the pin sockets.

9 The pin sockets also have two holes to which you can tie cables to support the Rooter Pot™ (which has now become heavier) and keep it stable. These can be tied to either a post or another part of the parent stock.

Seedlings

Seedlings can be obtained from most nurseries. You will need to give them nutrient-rich soil and plenty of food to encourage them to develop strength and bulk, and many growers advocate planting them outside, too. In order to develop a good foundation, you will need to lift them each year to prune and shape their roots.

Nursery material

Much of a bonsai-grower's material is obtained from nurseries. When looking for a suitable tree, remember that lots of branches growing low down on a trunk indicate a good surface-root structure. By contrast, a tree with a long trunk whose first branch starts quite high up suggests a one-sided root structure and a tree that could therefore be very hard to make into an attractive bonsai. (See also the chapter on styling nursery material, pages 140 to 153.)

This chapter explains many of the bonsai techniques that appear in *Bonsai school*'s pages.

Wiring is the most important element of modern bonsai design. Crossing wires, not wiring to each tip, missing branches or twigs, wiring too tightly or too loosely are some common errors, and it's vital that you learn, and then continue to use, the correct wiring techniques.

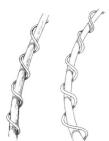    

One mistake is wiring too loosely. You can, however, use a thicker or stronger wire on young or thin shoots to form a cage within which a branch or twig can develop without constriction.

Wires that are too close together will damage the bark as you bend the wood, nor will they hold the wood as well as correctly placed wires. Wires that are too far apart will not hold a bend either.

Wiring too tightly will damage the wood as a tree grows. It is especially important not to wire the tips of branches and the apex of a tree too tightly because these areas grow much faster than other parts of the tree.

The ideal wiring method when approaching a fork is to place the wires evenly in opposite directions; this will hold the bend , support the branch and stop the branch from moving.

Do not wire trees with thick barks, such as pines, in case you damage the texture and platelets of the bark. If you wire from the trunk, try to use the least amount of wire possible and protect the bark first with special tape or raffia.

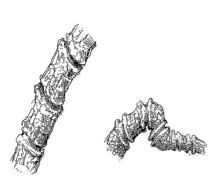

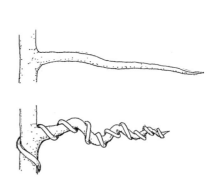

This image shows the irreversible damage that can be inflicted on a pine's bark and branches when wire has been left on for too long. Although you can scar the channels and fill them with Cut Paste™ to encourage bark growth, you will be lucky if the damage is repaired. It matters less if the wire marks are in the body areas of the foliage pads because they will be less visible, but they will still make the tree's twigs and branches vulnerable to wind damage and breakage.

Although thinner-barked trees, such as maples, can repair wire damage to a certain extent over a number of years, a brown, flaky scar will still be visible, especially if the tree has a colored bark.

The length of branches can be reduced in three ways. Firstly, by cutting back to the shortest twig and then redeveloping the branch. Secondly, by wiring and bending the branch upward before taking the foliage section down again (but you will need to do this with other branches, too, so that the image is balanced). And, thirdly, by wiring along the length of the branch and shaping it in a series of bends.

Wire can sometimes become embedded, but removing it would wea the branch. Remove as much wire as you can, the channel with Cut Paste™, cover it with ra and seal the ends of the raffia with Kiyonal™ or latex wound sealant.

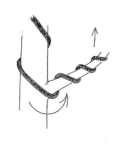

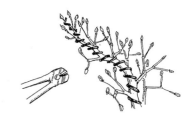

Before bending a branch upwards or downward, you need to understand how the wire will support the branch. If you are wiring downwards, the wire should be taken down over the top of the branch, and if you are wiring upward, the wire should be taken under the branch.

In the old days, bonsai artists wired from the trunk, but nowadays we tend to wire only from the starting point of the section that we want to shape, which limits the stress and damage that wiring can cause a tree. In summary, wire only where you need to wire.

When removing a wire, it's crucial to use short-bladed wire-cutter (see the section tools, page 240–44). Never unwind a wire because, if you do, there's a danger that y will damage the bark or developing buds.

Always wire to the tip of a branch. And when you are wiring conifers, especially pines, elevate the tips to encourage the structure to develop.

I have been promoting the multiple-wiring technique for many years, a technique that was originally developed to assist the styling of new material and that is easy for a beginner to learn. By using the correctly sized wire and spurring off as you reach each twig, the time spent wiring can be significantly reduced. Multiple wiring is best reserved for new material (the careful and slow design process for older, more mature, trees demands single wiring). If you intend to leave the wires in place for some time, do not twist them together because it would be difficult to remove a single wire should you need to.

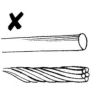

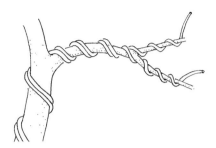 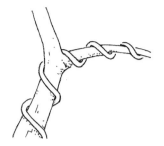 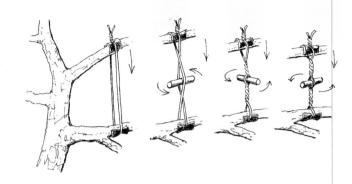

An example of multiple wiring.

Single wiring enables the creation of finer detail when working with mature specimens.

Turnbuckle, or tourniquet, wiring, entails using the strength of one section to change the direction of another, for example, pulling a thinner, usually higher, branch down towards a heavier, lower branch. It is important to protect any areas that the wire will put under pressure by placing small padding of rubber between the wire and tree.

Gary Marchal inserted a screw into the trunk to act as a brace with which to draw down the upper branches. Screwing a steel or brass screw upwards, into the heartwood, will create a secure fixing. This technique is better for rougher-barked trees than smoother-barked ones, on which the resultant mark would be too visible.

A neat example of wiring every section of the tree to its tips by Hotsumi Terrakawa, of the Netherlands.

You can protect pressure points by wiring through a rubber tube, although you may also have to apply additional padding. Having secured the wire, start twisting it as shown here, using a stick or a thicker piece of wire.

Having been secured, the upper branch has now been drawn downward. Had the screw been inserted lower, or a shorter piece of wire been used, the branch would have been pulled even further downward.

Bonsai techniques

When the screws are removed, the small holes that are left will soon be repaired; plug any visible holes with a tiny bit of Cut Paste™. Although this technique works well for rougher-barked trees, I do not use this technique on trees that have smooth barks because no matter how small the holes, they may cause damage.

Wiring techniques

Wiring is used to shape, correct, refine, add detail, anchor a tree into a pot and hold trees within a group-planting scheme together. An overview of some wiring tips and techniques follows.

Branch-wiring

Basic branch-wiring entails wrapping wire around a branch and then bending the branch into the desired shape.

Trunk-wiring

Trunk-wiring is usually undertaken on a young tree to make it grow in the desired direction. It can also be used to wire trees together when creating a group display.

Twig-wiring

You will need to wire every part of a tree if you want to create a certain shape or style. This means wiring even the smallest of twigs.

Multiple wiring

Multiple wiring is a simple and quick technique that is used for the initial training of young bonsai. It is not a better technique than single wiring, just a different one that significantly reduces the time that it takes to wire a tree.

The traditional wiring method is to use a single wire on the area that needs to be shaped. When running my workshops, however, I felt that beginners often became disheartened when asked to perform what I call a 'full wiring', that is, wiring all parts of a tree with a single wire, which can often take two or three hours, frequently either preferring to cut off a branch rather than shape it or simply lacking the confidence to wire it precisely and correctly. I wanted to find a way that would both excite my students and fully involve them in what is, after all, the most important shaping technique for bonsai, as well as a creative process that should not scare anyone. Since I introduced it twenty years ago, it has become one of the most popular wiring techniques among beginners and intermediate bonsai-growers the world over.

Multiple wiring means using a bunch of thin wires instead of one single, thick one. The advantage of using a number of wires is that while it performs exactly the same function as a single, thick wire on the main body of a branch, you can spur off anywhere on the branch to wire the thinner twigs with one of the individual wires without having to wire over an area that has already been wired in order to reach them. Its simply a faster way to get wire onto a tree in the early stages of design.

As you become more experienced in the technique, you can even work out the thickness of wire to use for each individual twig (and I have used over thirteen wires on one branch).

When I started using the multiple-wiring method, many experienced bonsai-growers disapproved, and some probably still do. These days multiple wiring is a popular and easy way to teach beginners how to wire on new material. (note:If you are receiving bonsai lessons from a teacher who does not use this technique, go along with what he or she is teaching you – the outcome will, in any case, nearly always be the same.)

Shaping through wiring

Before wiring a tree, you will need to have decided on the shape that you are aiming for. Always prepare the tree by pinching and pruning it during its formative years in order to develop the density of its foliage pads. If you are wiring a slow-growing tree, leave a little extra wire at the tips with which to wire new growth and thus further develop the tree's shape.

Refining through wiring

After the initial development of a tree's shape has been carried out, some refinements will often be needed: the placement of the branches may be correct, for example, but the foliage may be all over the place or may have grown out of shape, in which case wiring will enable you to reshape or restyle it. When undertaking a refinement, it is best to use the single-wiring technique because this is more suited to finer-detailed work.

Correcting through wiring

Wiring can also be used to correct a displacement of a branch from the overall shape. The tips of maples (*Acer*), for example, tend to grow upwards, and a little wiring at these points, as well as a bit further down the branches, will correct this elevation. If you have wired a tree to correct its shape, remove the wire as soon as you can thereafter, and certainly do not leave it on for longer than six weeks if it is growing rigorously.

Using the correct pressure

Never wire a tree so tightly that the wire bites into the bark because wire marks, which are extremely difficult to remove (if at all), will result as soon as the tree starts growing into the wire. Fast-growing young trees require what I call "cage wiring," in which you use a thicker wire than the branch actually needs, but barely touch the bark, so that a little space is left between the bark and the wire, thereby ensuring that the wire will not bite into the tender bark as the branch grows. Remember that the fastest-growing areas of a tree are the tips of the branches and the apex, or top, of the tree.

Removing wire

Never try to unwind a length of wire because this could damage developing buds, scratch fine bark or otherwise wreak havoc. Instead, always cut off the wire with a short-bladed wire-cutter (see the section on tools, page 240).

Bending thick branches

Although you can use most types of wire to bend smaller branches, in the case of a big branch, you may need to create a framework of wire, as follows.

To bend a thick branch, first wrap it in raffia and then lay two or three relatively thick wires along the length of the branch. Hold these wires in place by tying either thinner wire or electrical tape around them, but do not allow either wire or tape to come into contact with the wood. Wrap more raffia or tape around the wires and then wire a thicker wire around the whole unit. (See also the illustrations that accompany Valerio Gianotti's class on pages 156 to 161.)

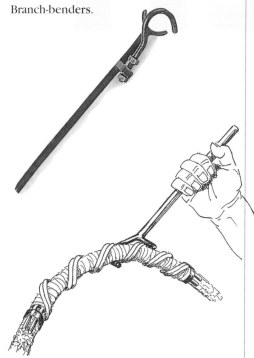

Branch-benders.

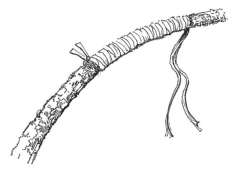

Your hands will probably not be strong enough to lever a thick branch into the required position, so use branch-benders (which are sold in a range of sizes) instead.

Applying lime sulfur jinn seal, which contains sulphur, to wood will turn it yellow, but only for a few hours.

After jinning a tree, treat the cut with lime sulphur jinn seal. If you colour the lime sulphur jinn seal with a little sumi or black watercolour ink, the wood will turn a pale-gray, rather than a bleached-white, color.

Wire can be stored on looms.

Pruning techniques

Most pruning (and wiring) techniques are covered more fully in the styling sections of Bonsai school. The salient points are as follows, however.

Pruning branches

When pruning a branch, it is important to use a cutter whose size matches that of the branch. Do not use a cutter if the branch material is very hard, however, because this would either damage the edge of the cutter or twist its joint. Use a pull saw (which cuts when you pull it back rather than forwards and produces a very smooth cut) to cut thicker branches. Cut at an angle, and preferably start on the underside of the branch.

After you have finished pruning, it is vital to seal every cut you have made. If you don't, the pruned branch or twig will almost certainly die back and that part of the tree will then be lost. An unsealed cut will also seep fluid that may attract aphids or other insects, thereby further damaging your tree.

Pruning twigs

Carefully observe how a branch supports its twigs and then prune the twigs to enhance your design. A flat, untapering cut will cause you trouble as the design develops, so prune at an angle, preferably starting on the underside of the twig.

Pruning the trunk

Although you may sometimes need to remove major portions of a tree's trunk, cutting to a side branch is often all that a design requires. When pruning a trunk, cut at an angle and then channel out a shallow groove around the cut to encourage the bark to roll inwards, into the cut area. Seal

the cut with a suitable sealer or wound putty, such as Cut Paste™. When designing a broom style for a fast-growing tree, you could also cut the trunk into a "V"-shaped wedge at your preferred point.

After you have made a slight groove around the edge of the cut and have sealed the cut, wrap the edges with wet raffia to force the new leaf buds to grow straight upward (otherwise the buds will force the edge of the bark outward, causing it to swell unattractively).

Pruning to shape

When working with a fast-growing genus, such as *Zelkova*, *Ulmus*, *Ligustrum*, *Lonicera*, *Sageretia*, *Ehretia* or *Cotoneaster*, you can often prune the overall shape to improve the tree's appearance. Always prune out any crossing branches (or else rewire them into a better position), prune any upward-growing branches that break the shape of the foliage pad and remove any downward-growing twigs that are not part of your design development before they thicken up.

Pruning for maintenance

Unless you are developing a branch, trim any twigs that are growing out of the existing shape. Also trim or prune any overly large leaves that may be developing on bonsai

whose leaves have reduced in size (a reduction in leaf size occurs naturally in bonsai, but the balance of growth can be upset by overenthusiastic feeding or watering in early spring, thereby forcing larger leaf development).

Pruning for styling

When you are developing material into a specific style, you will need to remove any branches that break the pattern. If you want to create a windswept style, for example, you will need to bend the branches on one side of the tree so that it looks as though they have been buffeted by a severe wind. Although you can develop this windswept shape with wire to a certain extent, you may need to prune off some of the branches on the windswept side.

Pruning for development

We sometimes have to prune a tree to force it to develop new branches. This could result in the tree forming clusters of new growth that will need to be pruned out, leaving selected leaf buds only. It could also mean pruning a specific bud to encourage it to grow in a new direction and then pruning another bud along the new branch to change the direction of the growth yet again.

A Cotoneaster group.

In this example of pruning for development, I have used a small indoor tree, namely a Chinese elm (*Ulmus parviflora*). The question that is most often asked of me is how to undertake a basic pruning, and although this little tree is not as fully developed as many of the bonsai featured in *Bonsai school*, it is a good subject for demonstrating important pruning techniques. In any case, starting with a young tree will result in a wonderful-looking, mature tree after it has grown and developed.

In order to establish a deciduous-tree image, you will need to prune to the first set of leaves at the top, to the second set of leaves at the sides and to the third set of leaves at the bottom of the overall shape.

A four-year-old air-layered Chinese elm (*Ulmus parvifolia*) before pruning.

The first series of cuts is made to the first set of leaf buds on the new wood. Prune about twice during the growing season, and remember to prune all round the tree, not just the front and back, to avoid the tree appearing flat and without depth as it matures.

The second series of cuts is made just beneath the apical area, to the sides of the tree. Prune to the second set of leaf buds and remember to prune evenly all the way round.

Finally, prune to the third set of leaf buds around the skirt, or the bottom of the tree, to balance the overall image, which should initially resemble an upturned teacup.

The finished image.

Modern techniques for displaying bonsai draw on other materials to suggest size and atmosphere. Placing this little tree behind a stone wall (which was built by sticking small, rough stones together with latex), for example, recalls a common country view in the United Kingdom.

The back of the image.

Glossary of Techniques

This is a good point to introduce you to the Japanese names of some of the techniques that are used in bonsai. Although these names are not commonly used in everyday Japanese, they are part of the international language of bonsai, much in the same way that Latin is the international language of plant nomenclature. More detailed examples of these techniques appear later in the pages of *Bonsai school*.

Shari and sharimiki

Shari describes when the bark on one side of a tree is removed, leaving one or more veins of live wood supporting the foliage mass. Sharimiki is similar to a 'fish back', when jinns are left in the wood, an image that bonsai artists find particularly attractive.

Natural shari on a
Manzanita bush.

Shari on a cedar
(*Cedrus*).

Jinn

Jinn (or jin) describes the stub of a dead branch on the side or top of a tree (in the latter instance, the entire apex has died, exposing the wood).

Juniperus osteosperma

Jinn on a Scots
pine (*Pinus
sylvestris*
'Beuvronensis').

Nebari

Nebari describes a surface-root formation, ideally one in which the roots circle the base of the tree, which swells out to form a surface-root pad, as seen on mature trees.

Nebari on an old oak (*Quercus*).

Uro

Uro refers to a hole in a tree's trunk or a large branch.

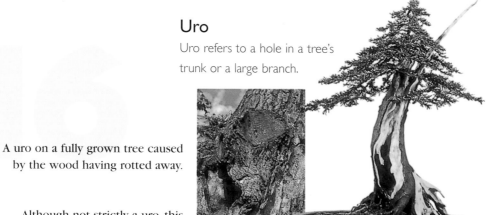

A uro on a fully grown tree caused by the wood having rotted away.

Although not strictly a uro, this example shows the creation of a hollow trunk.

Nebari on an
English elm
(*Ulmus procera*).

Old nebari, as seen on this swamp cypress (*Taxodium distichum*), are best achieved on collected bonsai.

Jinn on an old juniper (*Juniperus*) at the Ginko Nursery in Belgium.

Ageing techniques

Although a bonsai may look very old due to the use of certain ageing techniques, it may actually be only a few months into its training. Some of the most prevalent ageing techniques are discussed below.

Jinning trees

Why jinn a tree? There are a number of reasons: when a tree becomes old, it may lose some branches; as a tree grows taller, the lower branches may die back due to having been shaded; or a tree's apex may become frozen or wind-blasted or something else may have caused it to die back. Jinning is a way of recreating these images.

To make a jinn, first carefully cut around the edge of the branch that you intend to jinn. For example, if the branch is near the trunk, gently press the blades of an angle-cutter through the bark without cutting the branch. Using a pair of pliers, compress the bark and twist it off the branch. Take your time and take special care when working around smaller twigs. Removing the bark will reveal the pale-yellow wood beneath, and I recommend immediately applying lime sulfur to the exposed wood to ward off insect or fungal attack.

If you think it necessary, the next step is to wire the branch into the shape required. Although you could use heat (from a small blow torch, for example) to bend a very thick branch, I prefer to use wire. You must wire the branch as soon as you have applied the lime sulfur because it will then be soft. When the lime sulfur dries, the branch will become brittle, and although heating the dried wood can soften it enough to enable changes to be made, it's better to wire wood that has been freshly cut.

To prevent die-back, always seal the edge of the cut nearest the trunk with Cut Paste™ or tree-wound putty. Latex soft wound-sealers like Kiyonal™ or Lac Balsam™ can leave stains, so if you have to use them as a last resort, protect the edges of the new jinn with masking tape before sealing the edges of the living tissue.

Making shari

Why make shari? The main reason is to recreate bark die-back on an old tree's trunk and branches. In some genera, such as junipers (*Juniperus*), the bark dies back naturally, leaving a living vein on one or two sides of the trunk.

To make a shari, use chalk to draw directly on the bark the area that you want to expose. If you use a marking pen and you change your mind you will be unable to remove the ink. If you go round the tree's circumference, make sure that you do not accidentally ring-bark the tree. Using a sharp knife that can be locked so that it does not fold back and cut you, start by pressing into the bark of the trunk. You should feel the knife cutting through the bark as you follow the outline of the mark you have made. When you have finished, ease the knife under the top of the area that you have cut and gently force the bark down, easing it off the cut section. When working on a large area, make a shallow channel in the debarked section by using a hollow curved chisel or a small grinder, to encourage new bark to grow into the hollow, but not to rise over the edge. Seal the living tissue with Cut Paste™, not a latex sealer such as Lac Balsam™ or Kiyonal™ .

Carving trees

Why carve a tree? Although it is hard to simulate the effect of old shari, in which the wood has cracked, peeled or rotted, you may be able to do so using a carving technique, and the most popular genera with which to create such effects are conifers like pines (*Pinus*), junipers (*Juniperus*) and yews (*Taxus*). The primary problem, however, is that over-carving can make the image look false. It's therefore advisable to photograph a good natural example to act as a guide and perhaps to practise on some dead logs. (See pages 202 to 205 for Michael Persiano's detailed instructions on carving and refining bonsai.)

The tools that are used for carving are either chisels or power tools, such as grinders and cutters, which will remove the wood quickly. Remember that power tools are dangerous and that you must wear protective clothing when using them. I would also urge you to join a woodcarving workshop to learn how to use power tools correctly. (See pages 240 to 244 for more information on tools.)

Before carving a bonsai, however, consider whether it really needs to be worked on in this way. You would be a poor bonsai artist if you carved a tree simply because you enjoy the carving process rather than because the image requires improvement.

When you have debarked an area of your tree, you can now either leave the resultant image alone (not a bad option in most cases) or else enhance it by carving it to give it the semblance of having been affected by splits and cracks, scars or rot.

Both apical jinn and shari can be seen on this wonderful example of a forest group created by my late friend Werner Bub, of South Africa, using false white olive buddleja (far right).

Shari on a white pine (*Pinus parviflora*).

Shari on a California juniper (left).

Jinns on a larch (*Larix kaempferi*).

Jinns on a four-hundred-year-old Mugho pine (left).

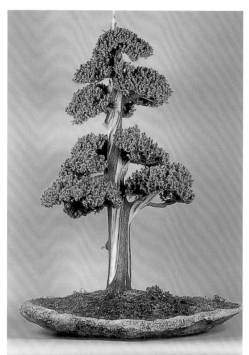

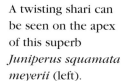

A twisting shari can be seen on the apex of this superb *Juniperus squamata meyerii* (left).

This spruce (*Picea*) also has a jinn on its apex.

Recreating splits and cracks

To recreate splits or cracks, first mark their outlines on the tree with a very fine pencil, such as a 2H. Then, using a hammer and a selection of small, sharp chisels of different sizes (but as narrow as possible), gently hammer your chosen chisel along the length of the lines that you have drawn to give them some depth. You can make thin or wide splits by using progressively thicker chisels, but use a fine chisel at each end to refine the split or crack. Try not to twist the chisel as you are working.

Rub a little charcoal stick into the splits or cracks that you have made and then gently mop the rest of the trunk to leave the splits or cracks a darker color. If you mix some lime sulfur or Jinn Seal with a little black watercolor or sumi ink and apply the mixture to the trunk, it will turn gray when it dries, a more natural color than bleached white. To find your preferred color, experiment on a dead log rather than your bonsai.

Recreating scars

To recreate a scar, take a chisel and cut slightly inward (without a hammer if it is a softwood tree and with a hammer if a hardwood species) at one end of your prospective scar. Then, using a pair of pliers, pull a strip of wood downward from your cut to leave a torn hollow that is rougher than a split. (This is also a good technique to use when creating jinned tips on branches.)

Recreating rot

A popular way of recreating rot is to use a grinder to make a series of progressively downward-moving cuts. If you are trying to create the image of an old oak (*Quercus*), for example, you could even hollow out the entire tree using this method.

Natural shari in a Manzanita's trunk.

A yew (*Taxus*) that has been shaped.

Preparing your material prior to carving it

The time to carve a tree is during its dormant period, either in late winter or mid-summer. Before carving it, however, make sure that the tree is healthy and has been growing in its container for at least two years. Do not carve a newly lifted tree.

Another important tip for inexperienced carvers is to spend at least a month planning the cuts that you are going to make. Although experienced artists often make instant decisions based on years of knowledge, as John Naka once observed, "Even monkeys can fall out of trees." So take your time—after all, this is a crucial point at which you will either create a masterpiece of bonsai or kill your tree. John Naka is one of the most important founding fathers of bonsai in the West today. He is a highly honoured Bonsai Master in North America and is one of the most respected teachers in the world. I studied a number of times with him in the UK and in America, where he lives with his wife and family. Known for his huge knowledge and even greater humor, John is a well-loved Sensei. A number of his bonsai sit in some of the world's leading bonsai collections.

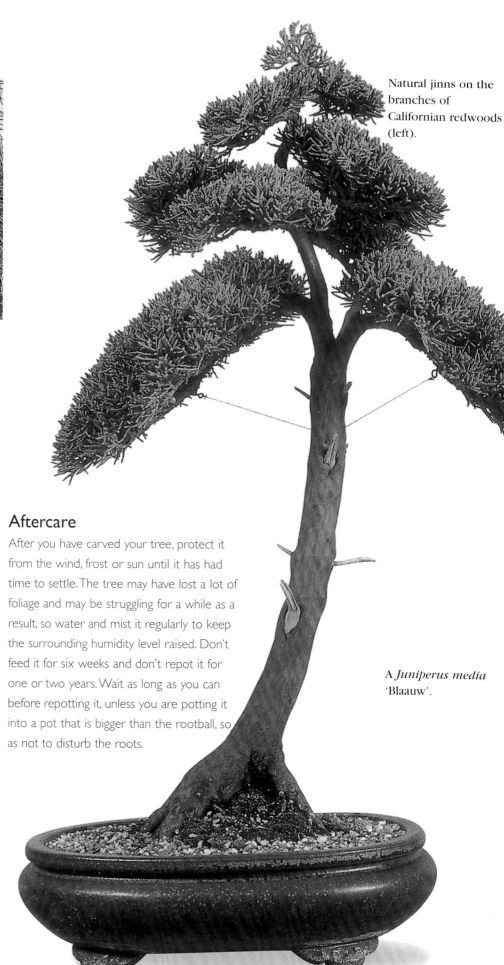

Natural jinns on the branches of Californian redwoods (left).

A *Juniperus media* 'Blaauw'.

Aftercare

After you have carved your tree, protect it from the wind, frost or sun until it has had time to settle. The tree may have lost a lot of foliage and may be struggling for a while as a result, so water and mist it regularly to keep the surrounding humidity level raised. Don't feed it for six weeks and don't repot it for one or two years. Wait as long as you can before repotting it, unless you are potting it into a pot that is bigger than the rootball, so as not to disturb the roots.

Some popular bonsai styles

When creating a bonsai style, the effect that you should be aiming for is that of a natural tree, and in order to be successful, you need to understand the elements of a mature tree's growth pattern, as well as how to recreate these elements in a miniature version. "Can any tree be turned into a bonsai?" you may be asking, and in answer to your question, the subjects of the photographs that illustrate the various bonsai styles.

A Chinese juniper (*Juniperus chinensis*).

Informal upright

In the informal-upright style, the trunk is bent or twisted. An extreme informal-upright style is known as a sangan.

A European larch (*Larix decidua*), measuring 24in (62cm).

Formal upright

In the formal-upright style, the trunk is straight, without any noticeable kinks or bends.

Slanting

In the slanting style the tree is planted at an angle in the pot. The style can be formed by wind pressure early on in the tree's life but as it grows older the shape is retained and the branches grow normally.

A Japanese larch
(*Larix kaempferi*).

A Chinese juniper
(*Juniperus
chinensis*).

Windswept

Most coastal and exposed areas have windswept forms in trees. This is where the tree is not only bent slightly or extremely, but the branches are growing away from the direction of the wind. In some cases the wind is only at certain times of the year so the tree will grow normally but as the season for wind arrives, the foliage is whipped away again into the windswept form.

Clump

Different from a group, the clump style is where the trees emanate from a single or closed root stock, e.g., where a number of trees have grown together at the base. The clump can be any number from three to seven. Larger clumps are also possible but uncommon.

Cascade

There are a number of cascade forms but all have "hanging branches." Forms include growing slightly down to the edge of the pot, below the edge and below the bottom of the pot. Placement is crucial when working out branches as the cascade has to look like a tree cascading down a mountain side.

A hawthorn (whitethorn, haegthorn, quickthorn or May tree - *Crataegus monogyna*) measuring 22in (55.9cm).

A *Zelkova serrata* measuring 24in (61cm).

Broom

When you consider the shape of a tree, you invariably think of a perfect form. This style, the broom, is most folks idea of a miniature tree. The branches in a broom style grow out and up. Out at the base and upwards to the apex. The Broom name comes from the image of a broom or brush for sweeping.

A hornbeam (*Carpinus betulus*).

Group

Group forms, also known by the Japanese name of Yosue (pronounced yo su eh) can be from three trees to as many as you like. In smaller numbers where it is easy to count, you need to use odd numbers. Never plant one tree behind another if that tree will be disguised. Look at the front and at one side to see if any tree is hiding another. Remove or adjust when planting up. This is one of my favorite forms of bonsai or penjing.

Root exposed

Trees growing on the sides of embankments, hills or steep slopes often have the soil washed off their roots. Growing this exposed root style is a derivative of that. However, this style of penjing or bonsai became quite rigid over the years and in many cases the roots are more important than the shape of the upper portions. It is a popular style in China.

A Korean trident maple (*Acer triflorum*).

Literati

Also called bunjin, the literati style means in the style of the traditional painters of Sumi-e, Zen or Chinese painting, in which the ideal is a tree that appears to be struggling for life. Conifers are the main subjects of this style.

Split trunk bark at base and perfectly placed branches make this literati larch bonsai almost windswept.

Part 3
Styling from nature

"What we have to learn to do, we learn by doing."
Aristotle (384–22 b.c.),

This part of *Bonsai school* consists of highly detailed, hands-on demonstrations of bonsai styling techniques, many of which are illustrated with images that were especially commissioned for this book. In this chapter, Gary Marchal, from the United States, Xiaojian Wang, from China, and Kevin Baillie, from Wales, share their expertise in styling bonsai from nature with us.

Flat-top, mature-typical styling, by Gary Marchal (United States)

Gary Marchal is highly respected throughout North America, both as a bonsai master and as probably the leading expert on the bald cypress (*Taxodium distichum*), among many other species, in the United States. A native of Louisiana, he takes an unassuming, but extremely detailed, approach to his art. Although his section focuses on the bald cypress, the techniques that he covers can be applied to most species.

I have visited Gary a number of times (and spent a week with him as I photographed material for his class for *Bonsai school*), and am always impressed by his bonsai, his knowledge and his dedication as a teacher. I have learned a great deal from him.

The bald cypress (*Taxodium distichum*)
The swamps of the southern United States are home to the bald cypress (*Taxodium distichum*), a botanically unique conifer. These large, buttressed trees are attacked by few insects and diseases, shed the current season's growth each fall and are well-known for their "knees," which are nodules that grow up from the roots. These knees are not young trees and their use is thought to allow for better sap and auxin flow to the parent tree in such wet conditions. They are popular trees with foresters, botanists, landscapers and bonsai enthusiasts. Although much can be written about the description and morphology of the species, we will focus on the design of the bald cypress as bonsai.

Before we begin the design of any tree as a bonsai, we should understand how it grows in nature. With this understanding,

Alligators and water moccasins don't worry this native Cajun from Louisiana. He's made of sterner stuff and even eats raw chillies!

an accurate representation of the tree can be obtained while taking into account the horticultural requirements of the species. To simplify how the bald cypress grows in nature, we could use two styles: the immature and the mature style. Both of these styles can be further identified by the typical or the variant growth of the species. A definition of these styles is as follows.

· The immature-typical style has a gradually tapering trunk, with many branches growing upright to horizontal.

· The immature-variant style has a short, stout trunk, with many branches growing upright to horizontal.

· The mature-typical style, also called the "flat-top" style, has the majority of the growth in the flat-top canopy, with the branching making sharp, directional changes.

· The mature-variant style, also a "flat-top" style, has graceful and fluid movement in its branch structure.

1 This bald cypress was photographed growing on the banks of the Tickfaw river in south-eastern Louisiana. Notice how the branching on its crown makes sharp, directional changes. This branch structure exemplifies the true nature of the mature-typical style of bald cypress. Note, too, the trunk's diameter near the root base and the tree's height. You will see that the trunk diameter to height ratio is somewhere around 20:1. This ratio is a very important factor in the design of a mature bald-cypress bonsai, and it needs to be addressed if the bonsai is to look believable.

2 This bald cypress was collected from a swamp outside New Orleans, Louisiana. It was nearly 46ft (over 14m) in height, with all of its branching near the top of the tree. The root base measures nearly 13in (34cm) and displays the typically buttressed base of a mature bald cypress. After it had been collected, the tree was reduced to nearly 35in (90cm) in height. Before it was planted in a nursery container, all of the old soil and swamp muck was washed from the roots. The cypress was then planted in well-draining soil, with the root base at a depth of nearly 6in (15cm) beneath the soil surface. The root base was planted at that depth to ensure that the tops of the hard-root cuts would not dry out between the morning and afternoon watering sessions. (If they were allowed to dry out, no roots would emerge from the top of the cuts, resulting in die-back further up the trunk.)

3 Two years later, the bald cypress is finally ready to be designed as a bonsai. Because its root base was planted deep in the nursery container, the top layers of soil need to be removed in order to identify the best root-base presentation.

4 One of the most important considerations, and the first step in the design of a bonsai, is to identify the best root-base presentation. The front of this bald cypress is pictured not only because it shows a wonderfully buttressed root base, but also because of the balance and symmetry of the roots. Notice how the roots have a welcoming feeling, inviting you to look up at the rest of the tree.

5 The bald cypress shows its fluting, which continues around the whole of the root base.

6 Although the front of the bonsai has been selected and the initial designing is about to begin, the bald cypress needs to be studied without its foliage before a decision can be made on the style of bonsai to be created. The best time of the year to undertake the initial design of a bald cypress is in early spring, before the tree begins to bud. However, the initial styling can also be performed in mid-summer, thereby allowing enough time for the tree to leaf out before autumn and to build up food stores for the following year. The foliage is stripped from the branches by hand.

a: The immature-typical style

The immature-typical style of a bald cypress has a gradually tapering trunk line. This can easily be created by removing all of the top growth, recutting the top to encourage a new bud to emerge at the new cut at the chosen front of the cypress and then growing the new trunk line. However, taking into account the root-base diameter, if an immature-typical style was created, the height of the tree would have to be approximately nearly 6ft (2m) in order to be believable, and this would take the tree out of the realm of bonsai.

b: The immature-variant style

The immature-variant style of bald cypress has a short, stout trunk that tapers steeply. This effect, too, can easily be created. However, because there is no leader at the chosen front of the cypress, the top would have to be regrown as described above for the immature-typical style. This style possibility would require another two years of growth before the initial design could be considered.

c and d: The mature style, both typical and variant

A mature bald cypress typically has a root-base to trunk-height ratio of 20:1 or greater. Using a bald cypress with a nearly 13in (34cm) root base would make the tree too tall to be in the realm of bonsai. The diameter of the root base of a bald cypress that would normally be used to create a believable mature-style bald-cypress bonsai would be around ¾in to 3in (2 to 8cm), which, depending on the trunk size, would make the finished height of the bonsai between around 15¾ to 47in (40 and 120cm), well within the size of normal bonsai and in scale with the typical size ratio of a mature bald cypress.

On reviewing the information presented thus far, one might ask, "Why collect large bald cypresses for bonsai if the only style that is believable is the immature-variant style?" The answer to this question is very simple: believable large-scale bald-cypress bonsai can be created by telling a "story," one that can be related by observing the variations created by nature.

The initial design choice of the subject tree will be the mature-typical style. The impression given will be of a very old bald cypress that was naturally reduced in height due to a lightening strike. The "story" will tell that the top of the cypress died and rotted away over time, leaving a hollow trunk at the top of the tree. In it's efforts to continue growing, the cyprss sent out the new leaders that form the "flat-top" crown of the bonsai. Some lower branching also grew upward, reaching for the rays of the sun from under the cypress' massive crown.

7 With all of the foliage removed, further design decisions can now be made. The front of the bald cypress was selected because of its outstanding root-base presentation. Now a decision must be made as to the style of the bonsai to be created. What "story" would we, as artists, like the bonsai to tell? Let us review the four basic styles of a natural bald cypress and consider what we can do to create that "story," bearing scale and proportion in mind.

8 The work begins with the selection of the branching that will create the basic framework of the tree. Note the multiple branching growing from the trunk, seemingly from one location. This occurs naturally because the collar where a branch joins the trunk has many buds and these buds create multiple branches emanating from the collar. If these multiple branches are allowed to grow from the collar, the collar will swell, resulting in a very unpleasant look. These branches and collars therefore need to be removed to enable new, single branches to grow.

9 When removing branches from a bald cypress, make a deep, concave cut. Fast-growing callous tissue will fill in the concave cut and create a natural look upon closure.

10 Seal all cuts with Cut Paste™, which will help to prevent the live tissue at the edge of a cut from drying out, thereby encouraging the scar to heal faster.

11 Having decided on the basic structure of the mature-typical-style bonsai, it is now time to consider the creation of the jinn and shari that will tell the "story" that explains why such a large bald cypress is not very tall.

12 The hollow section of the trunk will be at the front of the tree. Three branches were selected to form the basic structure of the canopy. The branching of the crown will frame the hollow section of the trunk, with the crown's back branch providing foliage depth. The "typical" part of the mature-typical style will be created by wiring the branching using sharp, directional changes (these can also be made using the clip-and-grow technique).

13 The locations of the jinn and shari are outlined with a black marker pen. This will give the artist direction when using power tools and should prevent too much tissue from being accidentally eliminated. When using power tools, care must also be taken not to damage the upper branching, and the best advice that I can give is to take your time.

14 The removal of the live tissue begins using a die-grinder and carbide burr, a combination of tools that gives the artist great control over them, thereby preventing the tree from being damaged unnecessarily.

15 Once the live tissue has been removed from the area that will become the hollow trunk, a different tool is used to remove the bulk of the wood: a side-grinder with a chainsaw blade.

16 When using any type of power tool, the wearing of protective equipment is strongly advised to safeguard your face and respiratory system. Work very slowly and remove small amounts of wood at a time. Be warned that a side-grinder with a chainsaw blade can grab the wood, causing the artist to lose control and resulting in damage to the tree and perhaps also to the artist.

17 With wood shavings flying everywhere, control is maintained with the help of a side handle on the tool. Take care not to remove too much wood. The final wood-removal and detailed carving will be done using a die-grinder and carbide burr.

18 Detailed carving is also undertaken on the back and side of the top of the jinn. Although the final carving will not take place for more than a year, it is important to outline the approximate location of the dead-tissue line at this stage.

19 Additional detailed carving continues on the inside of the hollow trunk. This leaves ridges, which form naturally due to the density of the old hardwood. A natural, jagged appearance has been given to the top of the jinn. With the hollow section of the trunk now complete, the wood will be treated with lime sulfur and allowed to dry for a year. At the end of the year, the wood will be hard and dry, which will enable greater detail to be included in the carving. Very detailed carving, along with etching of the wood, will replicate the effects of weather and time.

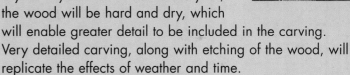

20 The left side of the tree shows live tissue between the side and back branches. This will also be left for a year so that the direction of the branches' vascular connection to the roots can be determined. After a year, a distinctive callous line will have formed, indicating the vascular connection and the line along which to make the final carving.

22 The carving performed on the mature-typical-style bald cypress tells a "story" and justifies the root-base to trunk-height ratio. Another type of carving is undertaken on bald cypresses to create the tapered trunk line that is required for the immature style. In the past, the carving was mostly done using a 45 to 60° cut. The fast-growing leader will quickly develop a reverse taper where it meets the point of the cut. By leaving a tapered ledge for the callous tissue to grow over, it is possible to develop a tapered trunk line that not only looks good from the front, but also from all sides of the tree. The photograph shows an example of this tapered-ledge type of carving. If you can imagine a leader measuring 1 to 2in (4 to 5cm), you will understand how the callous tissue will heal over the carved section and look natural.

21 The right side of the tree shows that some live tissue was removed between the right and back branches. This was done to force the vascular connection of the right side branch to grow directly downwards so that the right side and back branches do not heal together, thereby resulting in a build-up of heavy callous tissue. Again, the final detailed carving on the right side of the tree will be done in a year's time, after the vascular connection has been determined.

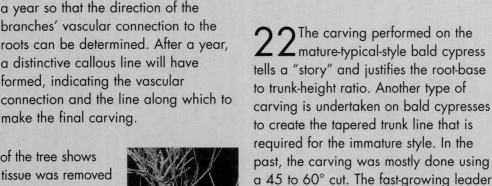

These photographs show the right, left, back and front views of the completed flat-top mature-typical-style bald cypress, which will develop over the next three or four years.

23 The initial design and wiring having been completed, the mature-typical-style bald-cypress bonsai will be planted in an oversized bonsai container to enable the development of the spreading flat-top crown to begin. The shari has been brought down the trunk and all dead wood has been treated with lime sulfur. The heavy, original bark has been removed to deny insects the opportunity to set up home in it. The three large, main branches of the crown have been guide-wired into place rather than using heavy wire that could damage the bark. From this simple basic structure, the crown of the flat top will be created using secondary and tertiary branching.

Gary Marchal.

24 A natural flat-top-style *Taxodium distichum*.

25 Gary Marchal pictured with one of his international-award-winning bald cypresses.

These trees, which I discovered growing in the wild, have flat tops similar to the one that Gary created for his class. As Gary observes, it's important to try to "read" nature if you want to emulate its effect successfully.

These photographs show some of Gary's bonsai, as well as the beautiful landscape of the Louisiana swamps.

Pyracantha crenulata, by Xiaojian Wang (China)

Note from Craig: There are many species and varieties of *Pyracantha* (firethorn). In the West, some have colored berries, such as *Pyracantha coccinea*, which has red fruit. *Pyracantha crenulata*, which originates in the Himalayas, is a subspecies of *P. coccinea*. It has oblanceolate (blunt-tipped) leaves, smaller flowers (and leaves) than *P. coccinea* and berries that are orange-red in color. A large tree, *P. crenulata* grows in western China and was first brought to Europe in 1911. Two of *P. crenulata*'s subspecies are *P. rogersiana* and *P. rogersiana* 'Flava', which have yellow fruit. In the West, we mainly use both orange- and red-berry species for bonsai.

Xiaojian Wang regards *Pyracantha crenulata* as one of the most suitable trees for modern penjing.

The characteristics of *Pyracantha crenulata*

Pyracantha crenulata is a member of the evergreen prickly-rose family, which, never having been domesticated, has retained many of its primal characteristics. Its branches are short, with opposing pairings of leaves. From spring through early summer it bears white, five-petaled flowers. In the winter *P.* crenulata bears large numbers of vividly colored deep-red to orange-red, pear-shaped berries, measuring about ¼in (6mm) in diameter, giving the impression that it is covered with burning torches (which is why it is also known as "torch fruits" or "flaming tree.") The fruits, which ripen in autumn, are used as a raw ingredient in the fermentation of wine.

Although *Pyracantha crenulata* thrives in warm, moist climates, it can also withstand cold weather and may be placed outdoors throughout the winter, other than extremely cold climates. In addition, despite its liking of sunshine, it will grow in semi-shaded areas. It grows best in a deep, fertile soil, yet will also survive in a less nutrient-rich soil and does not need artificial fertilizers or watering if it is planted in the ground. All in all, *P.* crenulata has strong powers of adaptation.

Compared with many other plants, *P.* crenulata is easy to cultivate because it is evergreen, it bears plentiful fruit over a long period and the rate at which the fruits drop is low. And with its attractive appearance, displaying as it does numerous red berries among its foliage, it is therefore not surprising that modern penjing artists favor *P.* crenulata as a subject for styling, and that many attractively designed trees have featured in exhibitions of their work.

A forty-year-old *Pyracantha crenulata*, measuring nearly 43in (110cm), styled by Zuo Hong Fa.

An eighty-year-old *Pyracantha crenulata*, measuring 17 ¾in (45cm), styled by Zuo Hong Fa.

A forty-year-old *Pyracantha* measuring 10in (25.4cm) across the base and 28in (71.1cm) in height. Purchased from a nursery in the United States and then imported into the UK, the carving-out of this bonsai, and the forming of its branches, was undertaken over twenty years.

A *Pyracantha* styled by Reiner Goebel.

Propagating *P. crenulata*

The propagation of *Pyracantha crenulata* may be carried out by growing its seeds or taking cuttings.

To grow specimens from seed, collect *P. crenulata* fruits in early spring, wash off the flesh, dry the seeds, place them in a seeding bed or shallow pot and cover them with about 3/8in (1cm) of soil. Water the soil and then keep it moist. If the seeds are kept in a greenhouse, they should germinate in around forty days. Do not plant seeds in the open until mid-spring and they will germinate by early summer.

The best period in which to take *P. crenulata* cuttings is from early to mid- spring. The cuttings, which should be taken from the year's new growth, should measure around 4¾ to 6in in length (12 to 15cm). Plant them in a seeding bed in a shady area to a depth of around 2 to 2¾in (5 to 7cm). Rooting should take place in about six weeks' time.

Do not allow a seedling or a cutting to follow its natural inclination to grow as a single shoot, but instead try to cultivate it so that it becomes a strong shoot with numerous branches and plenty of leaves, which will make it a better subject for potting. Potting should be carried out in fall, winter or early spring. Some of the old soil should be used for potting as it will contain mycelium, the beneficial fungus that will help the tree to grow.

Pruning *P. crenulata*

Both evergreen and prickly, when *Pyracantha crenulata* is used in landscaping, open management (forestry and woodlands) or landscape conditions, it is often pruned into a spherical shape to serve as lawn decoration or hedging. Potted *P. crenulata*, however, is usually designed to maximise the appreciation of its fruits. (From the start of the growing season to when it starts to bear fruit, fertilisation is necessary to ensure a good crop of berries, and it is advisable to use a cake fertilizer.)

When pruning *P. crenulata*, prune out the middle shoot in a group of young shoots, but retain the side shoots. Repeat this procedure as new shoots emerge to ensure a plentiful display of flowers and hence berries.

The placement of *P. crenulata*

When the plant is flowering, it must be kept indoors on windy and rainy days because the pollination and fertilization processes could otherwise be disrupted and the fruiting process hence negatively affected. The fruits will begin to change color, turning from green to red, in early winter, but will not start to drop until the following spring. In China during the Christmas, New Year, Chinese New Year and spring festivals, potted *Pyracantha crenulata* plants are in great demand, and when different varieties are in short supply, they are hotly sought after on account of their attractive red fruits and bright-green leaves. Some penjing artists even painstakingly develop these potted plants' old roots into penjing, a practice that has significantly upgraded the status of *P. crenulata* as a material for penjing.

The berries and foliage of *Pyracantha augustifolia*.

Repotting *P. crenulata*

Pyracantha crenulata has a tenacious survival tendency and possesses a well-developed root system, which frequently grows at the expense of the rest of the plant. It is therefore necessary to uproot a plant every year in spring in order to cut out any dead roots and thin out the surviving ones. After replanting it in new, fertile soil, place the pot in a shaded area to allow it to recuperate for a few days. Then move it to a sunlit spot to encourage it to grow and bear masses of flowers and fruits over the coming year.

Design elements for an oak (*Quercus*), by Kevin Baillie (Wales)

Kevin Baillie is an authority on the indigenous trees of the United Kingdom. He is also enthusiastic about propagation from seeds and cuttings and has a special interest in suiseki. He regularly collects trees with his equally enthusiastic friend, Alan Dorling, and both are also great friends of mine.

1 Year one—winter, just lifted.

2 Year two—summer, front.

3 Year two—summer back.

4 Year three—summer, front.

5 Detail of bench growth.

6 Detail of branch growth and development.

7 Year four—winter, front—in new pot.

8. Year 4 – summer.

The sumo oak

The following example illustrates how you can identify a natural oak style and then create a bonsai from this image.

A sturdy little oak caught my eye as Al Dorling and I were prospecting a disused quarry in North Wales in November 1997. The rock waste was being landscaped around its edges and the bulldozers were paying no heed to the ancient, dwarfed trees growing there, which had struggled for decades to survive the ravages of sheep, rabbits and the weather. Once the industrial waste had been shaped to the developers' satisfaction, the trees were being replaced with a selection of landscape "whips" or seedling trees, the thickness of pencils, wrapped in bright-orange, rabbit-proof collars.

The oak that I'd spotted had a thick trunk, with well-developed bark platelets and dense, low branching, making it an obvious bonsai candidate. We made some quick decisions about which of the existing branches had to be removed. Although one branch that emerged from the top of the tree had escaped the ravages of the sheep, its first 4ft (1.2m) was naked. It obviously had to go, but we left a stub as a possible future jinn. The rest of the low, mounded growth had two very long branches that hugged the ground and spread too widely from the trunk. We carefully shortened these into secondary branches.

With some difficulty, we then dug the oak from the loose rock rubble, and I was very pleased to find that it had masses of fibrous roots close to the base of its trunk, which had developed in a couple of inches of leaf litter and dead grass. We sawed off the much thicker roots radiating from the trunk, just beyond the drip line of the foliage. Because it just dropped away as we lifted the oak, little of the original growing medium could be saved. It was a wet day, so I wasn't unduly worried about the roots drying out, but I nevertheless carefully wrapped as much sodden moss around the fibrous roots as I could. We then enclosed the root ball in a large plastic bag and sealed it tightly with parcel tape before carrying it home.

On arriving home, I boxed up the oak in a free-draining mix of calcined clay (cat litter) and chipped bark before placing it in an unheated conservatory for the rest of the winter. My regular misting with a hand-operated sprayer, along with my fervent desire to see signs of budding, increased as winter dragged on into spring. With trees of this quality, early spring is always a nail-biting time. Has the tree survived? Are those leaf buds, inspected daily, really starting to swell? Then, at last, an unmistakeably fresh green color rapidly started to show as one, then another, then many, plump buds began to grow.

The apex of Kevin's oak before shaping—year four.

The apex of Kevin's oak after shaping.

After the length of the main branch has been reduced, the secondary branch is extended.

Having been planted by a French settler during the early eighteenth century, all of the trees in the Oak Alley Plantation in New Orleans are now around two-hundred-and-eighty years old.

Styling from nature

Craig liked the look of this tree and had just the pot in mind for it. He was happy to barter his pot for a thick *Escallonia* stump from my garden and kindly threw in another huge pot in which to grow the remaining *Escallonia* stump that I had kept to work on myself.

By spring 2000, the wooden box in which I had housed the oak had deteriorated to the stage at which I knew that it had to be replaced. Al and I worked in cold conditions, fumbling with numb fingers, to remove every last trace of the original "soil." Masses of new roots had by now filled the box, which was quite a bit larger than the new pot. Some root reduction was therefore needed before it was transplanted. After transplanting it, I wasn't too happy with the tree's almost central position within the pot, but it was the best that could be achieved in a first potting without removing too much of the new root mass. The tree was then once again given special treatment by protecting it from extreme conditions as it was still tender until the last frosts had passed.

Some minor refinements, such as removing branch stubs and cleaning or pruning out crossing and long, straight, uninteresting shoots, were undertaken during the year 2000. In the fall, I was pleased to see two varieties of fungi spring up through the soil surface, indicating that healthy mycelia colonies had been generated (mycelium, a mycorrhiza fungus, works in association with the roots and assists in nutrient uptake).

I worked on the tree with Craig in spring 2001. He repositioned a top branch to act as a new leader, removed the rest of the jinn and arranged some of the finer low twigs. By summer, the tree was looking good enough to be displayed at the National UK Bonsai Federation (Fobbs) exhibition in Manchester. Some important design decisions still remained, so I sought the thoughts of others and visitors to our stand made many helpful comments on future refinements.

The tree's fall color having faded, I trimmed all of the foliage in November 2001 and refined the structure with a light trim and extensive wiring. The tree will be protected from hard frosts in a cold greenhouse while the wire remains in place. It is due to be repotted in the spring of 2002 so that a better placement can be achieved, while trimming the dominant shoots will encourage the further ramification of its twiggy growth. A few more years of growth and refinement should complete the image that I want to achieve of an old, isolated, hillside oak.

One of the trees in the Oak Alley Plantation in New Orleans. It is a majestic specimen, with astonishing nebari.

A close-up of the same tree focuses on its small 'knees', as such knob-like root growths above the ground are called.

This Scottish oak shares some of the sumo's elements.

In New Orleans, I photographed an oak that was in the process of air layering itself (a trait of older oaks). This occurs when branches grow so long and heavy that they break off (which typically occurs in cold climates, but in warmer climates they may even reach the ground and take root).

Kevin is fortunate to have such a good basis for creating nebari in his sumo oak.

Styling from nursery material

In this chapter, bonsai artists from the United States, China, Italy, England and New Zealand explain the characteristics of their chosen bonsai subjects, as well as their styling methods, in illuminating detail.

Joe Day, Alabama, USA.

1 Before planting his maples, Joe needs to create a slab. The first step is to mark out the shape of the slab on a piece of slate.

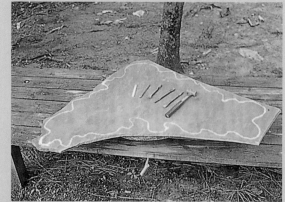

2 Joe shapes the slab using a variety of tools, including chisels, saws and stone-sanders.

3 The slab is ready for its final shaping. Joe now works on the edges and makes the occasional hole to hold wire. Although it is a soft material, slate is very durable.

4 The bonsai material will be young trident maples.

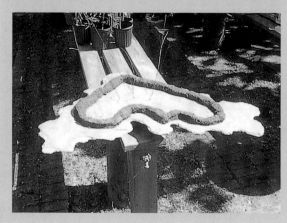

5 Joe constructs a wall of peat and clay within the shaped slab.

6 Having added a soil mix, Joe is now ready to plant the trident maples.

7 Joe positions the first trees to one side, slightly towards the back of the slab.

8 Joe positions taller, thicker-trunked trees in front of the first trees. No trees overlap each other from the side or front.

9 Joe positions smaller trees to one side to give a sense of perspective.

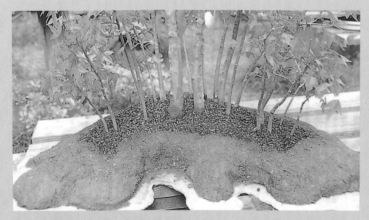

10 Joe completes the group by positioning the remaining trees according to their size.

11 This is a view of the group from behind.

12 Joe removes the trees' leaves to reduce the stress that the transplanting process has put the trees under. This is a view of the group from the side.

13 This is view of the group from the front.

Trident maples (*Acer buergerianum*) and box (*Buxus*),
by Joe Day (United States)

Trident maples (*Acer buergerianum*)

The trident maple (*Acer buergerianum*), a species that originates from the temperate country of China, is a member of the Aceraceae family.

In common with most maples, tridents are apex dominant. They break their dormancy very early in the spring, after which growth is vigorous. They should be fed lightly throughout the growing season, and organic fertilizers will both provide adequate nourishment and reduce leaf burn. Growth will slow when the temperature drops in the fall, but will not stop until the first frost. With the right combination of weather conditions, trident maples will give a beautiful show of fall colors.

Propagating trident maples

Trident maples can be grown from seeds, cuttings and air layers. Seeds collected in late fall should be washed with a mild fungicide, placed in a container (not a glass one) with some moist sphagnum moss and refrigerated for eight to ten weeks (see also the section on propagating from seed, pages 102 to 104). Then plant the seeds in a good-quality seed starter mix.

Cuttings taken from late spring to early summer should root readily, and using a good-quality rooting hormone will increase your success rate. Most trident maples can be air layered, and the procedure is best performed just after the new growth has hardened in late spring. After cutting a ring in the bark, squeeze a large wire very tightly around the trunk to prevent new callous growth. Place moist sphagnum moss over the cut and cover it with poly tightly closed at both ends. Expect roots to appear between six to eight weeks thereafter. (See also the section on cuttings and air layers, pages 106 to 108.)

Placement and growing climates for trident maples

Under bonsai cultivation, providing protection from severe cold, particularly taking steps to prevent the soil mass from freezing, allows trident maples to be grown in extremely cold areas. Although they may survive, they will not thrive in tropical climates. Where I live, in Mobile, Alabama, on the Gulf Coast, where the temperature resembles that of the southern Mediterranean, trident maples go into dormancy in mid-winter and start producing new leaves in early spring. In colder northern-hemisphere areas, they lose their leaves from early fall to late fall and start budding from mid- spring to late spring.

Insect attack

Attacks by chewing and trunk-boring insects are usually the only problems for healthy trident maples.

Suitable soil for trident maples

Trident maples tolerate a wide range of soil conditions, but grow best in soils that drain fast, but remain moist,

A box (*Buxus*) styled by Rob Moak, of Alabama.

not wet. After two long growing seasons, you will need to undertake root maintenance and provide new soil for developing trees. Mature trees should be checked after the third growing season.

Styles for trident maples

Trident maples can be developed into any bonsai style, apart from those that make use of large amounts of dead wood. Large areas of dead wood determine the shape which can be left or carved. In all other styles and when working with young branches, you need to be aware that the wood quickly becomes hard and brittle, you should follow a styling plan before you start.

Wiring and pruning trident maples

Wire new growth early in the growing season, but not too tightly because trident maples grow so quickly. The best styling procedures during the growing season are partial defoliation, wiring new growth and pruning. Large branches should be pruned in the early autumn, a period of less vigorous growth that will allow smooth callous growth. Hard pruning in spring will produce large bulges of scar tissue. Seal all cuts with a good bonsai sealer.

Box (*Buxus*)

Note from Craig: Common boxwood (*Buxus sempervirens* is found in Eurasia, tropical and South Africa, Caribbean, and Central America. It belongs to the family Buxacece, a very small family of only six genera and about thirty species, closely related to the Spurge family—Euphorbiaceae. Joe also uses Chinese boxwood.

Box, or boxwood, is a very hardy plant. It grows in a wide range of soils and tolerates organic and chemical fertilizers. Foliage growth is strong in spring and fall, but slow in the heat of the summer. (We have about two-hundred-and-eighty growing days in Mobile, Alabama.) With its woody and dense roots, its root growth is not as vigorous as its top growth, which means that you can allow up to five growing seasons before undertaking root and soil maintenance.

Placement of box

Box is hardy enough to tolerate cold conditions, but freezing weather can turn its leaves a bronze color.

Insects and diseases

Box suffers almost no insect attack, and any disease problems are usually related to poor root conditions.

Suitable soil for box

The soil mix that I use for box is red lava rock and pine bark, both sifted so that I am left with particles measuring around 1/8 to 1/4in (4 to 7 mm) in diameter and washed to remove any dust. Box trees do not require extra-deep containers.

Styles for box

Boxwood is both rich in oils and very hard, which means that it is one of the few deciduous trees that will hold dead-wood designs. Large, live box branches can be bent a great distance if care is taken to wire them correctly. After a few months of wiring, small branches should hold their position.

This group was created by Joe Day.

A Rocky Mountain juniper (*Juniperus scopulorum*).

Although these trees are probably over a thousand years old, they are no more than 6ft (2m) high.

Most of this tree has died, but it is still clinging to life.

The ground cypress (*Juniperus prostrata*), by

Shangli Bao (China)

Note from Craig: This lesson is on ground-covering junipers, which include the prostrate juniper species *Juniperus communis*, *J. procumbans* and *J. prostrata*, which, in China, is known as ground cypress. Junipers belong to the Cupressaceae family, which is why they are often commonly called cypresses. (Note that it is advisable to use the name commonly given to a tree in its country of origin.) There are around sixty species of ground-covering juniper, such as *Juniperus chinensis*, whose name commemorates the fact that it, and many others, originate from China. It is, however, commonly found all over the world and has found favor among bonsai- and penjing-growers in many non-tropical countries.

Introducing the ground cypress

The ground cypress (*Juniperus communis* variety *prostrata*, is a mutated member of the juniper family. Common all over the northern hemisphere, it was introduced into China from Japan. The plant exhibits a peculiar, yet beautiful, configuration with its lack of straight stem and dense branches that creep outwards in all directions (which is why it is also sometimes called creeping cypress). The tiny leaves are jade green in color. The plant, which stays green throughout the growing season, sometimes turns bronze in colder areas. The variety looks vigorous and is very hardy. It is a popular subject for bonsai because its branches can easily be bent and can therefore be fashioned into many different styles.

The potting and placement of the ground cypress

Ground cypress thrives in almost any type of soil, including neutral, slightly acidic or alkaline soils. When planting it in a small pot, however, it is advisable to use a fertile, moist soil that has been well drained and mixed with humus. Soil for nursery material in China and temperate regions comprises 30% grit-2-4mm, 70% soilless compost or local compost. Wetter regions require more grit while dryer regions require more compost. Potting should be carried out during early spring.

Although the ground cypress prefers a lot of sunlight, it will tolerate shade, making it very adaptable. During hot, sunny weather, the ground cypress should be placed under an awning so that it receives diffused light; it should also be kept reasonably moist. When the weather is dry, the plant should be sprayed with water to increase the humidity of the air surrounding it. During the spring and fall, the ground cypress may be placed in the open, but should be moved inside during the winter.

Watering the ground cypress

The ground cypress prefers a moist environment, but hates a water-saturated soil. It should be constantly watered throughout the summer (especially on very hot days) to ensure that the soil remains constantly moist. Frequent spraying with water is also necessary to enable the plant to stay fresh and green. Watering should be carried out with restraint in winter, however.

Feeding the ground cypress

During its growing period, feed a small ground cypress a diluted organic liquid fertilizer every ten to fifteen days. Do not over-fertilize the plant, or feed it too frequently, because this would prompt the branches to grow too quickly, thereby affecting its overall shape. When the penjing is mature, feed it with slow-release, organic fertilizer cakes (Bio gold™, rapeseed cake etc).

Propagating the ground cypress

The primary propagating materials for the ground cypress are cuttings, (air layers or cuttings) although seedlings, medium- or adult cypress (collected or nursery material) are sometimes also used. If you want to create a bonsai that looks graceful and aged, take a cutting from a prickly foliage cypress such as *Juniperus rigida* (needle juniper), *Squamata Meyerii*, *Arizona*, or any other prickly needle juniper from late spring to early summer. Graft this to the tree and let it grow. When the cutting is well established, usually by early to late fall, cut it from the mother trunk by layering to use as material for an aged-looking bonsai.

Another method is to use a softer, tighter foliage juniper such as *Juniperus Chinensis sargentii* and then attach that to the stem of a mature prickly or rougher variety of species, such as *Juniperus rigida* (needle juniper), *Squamata Meyerii*, *Arizona*, or any other juniper, by grafting. Approach graft or insert graft to the older and more mature parent plant. When the cutting has taken to the mature tree, gradually remove the rougher foliage from the parent tree and develop the softer foliage on its new host.

Juniper communis (which is known as ground cypress in China) grows in the United States, northern Europe, northern China, Korea and Japan.

Wiring and pruning the ground cypress

Juniperus branches are thin, soft and winding by nature, and new branches are constantly being produced. Because they adjust well to wiring and pruning, they are particularly suited to bonsai modelling, and *Juniperus prostrata* is usually modelled in the following styles: the "hanging cliff," the "slanting stem," the "crooked stem," and the "reclining stem." It can also be modeled into an animal or bird form. The branches and foliage should generally be worked into the shape of oval clouds, and the overall arrangement of the foliage should look natural, restrained, yet vital and pleasing to the eye.

Styling from nursery material

Juniper commu-
nis grows in
many forms,
including large,
tree-like bushes,
single specimens
and groups.

The main technique used to determine the shape is wiring (with wire or raffia), supplemented by pruning to refine the shape by ridding the tree of any small, undesirable branches. The tree's growing period starts in mid-summer and extends into early fall, a time when wiring and pruning should not be undertaken because these would cause the plant to "bleed" excessively, thereby retarding its growth. Wiring and pruning should therefore be confined to the period between winter and early spring. It usually takes *Juniper prostrata* about two years to establish its shape. If the wires are detached too early, the branches will spring back to their original position, but if the wiring is left

in place for too long, the branches may be damaged, in turn either damaging the plant itself or leaving unsightly marks.

During the tree's nursery period, branch-pruning should be carried out at the right moment in mid- to late summer during the mid-season dormancy to ensure that the branches are short and dense. During the spring and summer, the middle shoots of the finer new growth should be plucked out to

encourage the growth of side branches.

The ground cypress has a well-developed root system due to its dense foliage. After the plant has been removed from the soil in which it has been growing and the roots have been preliminarily trimmed and shaped, on the surface and just below, add several smooth, different-shaped stones in sizes between 1/4 to 3/8in (6 and 10mm)—depending on the size of the penjing—to the soil to encourage the roots to grow into the interstitial spaces between the stones. Then replant the ground cypress. After repeated watering or erosion by rain, the stones, along with part of the root system, will be exposed and in time the plant will exhibit the characteristics of an aged tree of natural beauty, standing firm, with its robust roots exposed as they grow among the stones.

Pots for the ground cypress

The choice of pot for a ground cypress depends on the shape and posture of the plant. The hanging-cliff type requires a tall pot or large bowl in a purple sandy clay. In this case, the root system should be left long, so that it secures the stem sufficiently firmly to counterbalance the weight of the plant as it hangs outwards. The crooked-stem type would suit a purple sandy-clay or glazed-pottery pot of elliptical shape. For the slanted-stem or reclining-stem types, a shallow, oblong-shaped, purple sandy-clay pot would probably look best. When potting the last two types, the root system should be trimmed short, but the lateral root and tassel (feeder) roots should be retained. Charcoal (carbon powder) should be applied to any cuts to prevent bacterial growth and rotting.

Juniper commu-
nis also grows
along the ground.

Styling a large juniper (*Juniperus chinensis*),
by Patrizia Capellaro (Italy)

Patrizia Capellaro, a student of Salvatore Liporace in Milan, Italy, is a highly respected and accomplished bonsai artist in her own right. She has won prizes in both national and international competitions (and was the runner-up in the International Ben Oki Awards organised by Bonsai Clubs International in 2000) and has been invited to speak at many national and international bonsai conventions. Examples of her superb work feature in this photo-essay by Salvatore and me.

1 Patrizia Capellaro, Salvatore Liporace and my wife Svetlana, pictured in Milan.

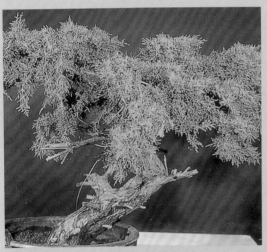

2 The material for Patrizia's bonsai is nursery stock, a *Juniper chinensis* 'Old Gold'.

3 When planning how to style the tree, it was noted that it had a lot of foliage and that much of the lower foliage was removed two years ago.

4 The first tasks are working on the trunk, establishing the front aspect and stripping the tree of any branches that will be redundant to the planned style.

5 The initial shaping of the foliage involves taping and wiring the heavier branches to form the rough outline.

6 The next step in creating the desired shape is to pull down the apex.

7 Some of the bark is removed to create a shari.

8 With the styling completed, the bonsai is planted in a training pot.

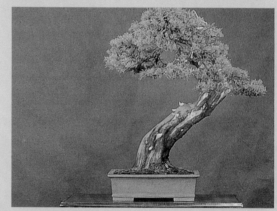

9 The bonsai a year later. Patrizia has repotted it and its foliage has filled out.

10 Two years later, this masterpiece of bonsai is now well established.

11 The completed bonsai next to Patrizia.

12 Another of Patrizia's creations: a large Juniperus that is still being developed.

13 This Scots pine (*Pinus sylvestris*) forms part of Patrizia 's excellent bonsai collection. It was collected in the Italian Alps.

Blue cedar (*Cedrus atlantica* 'Glauca'),
by John Hanby (England)

My blue cedar (*Cedrus atlantica* 'Glauca') originated from a nursery in be the Netherlands, where it had been grown for use as a traditional garden tree. It was one of a batch of garden trees and other types of raw material that I acquired in early 1997. All of the trees were root-balled, and on my return home they were heeled into a holding bed and priced up ready for sale.

Having remained unsold, in the spring of 1998 the tree was removed from the ground and planted in a large mica training pot (fig. 1).

FIG. 1

FIG. 2

   Although the tree had a substantial base, it was generally too tall from a bonsai point of view, with little taper and only a few, somewhat sparse, lower branches. I therefore decided to cut off the top section of the trunk to allow a greater amount of light to penetrate further down the tree to encourage these more desirable, lower branches to grow (fig.2).
   Weeks after its removal, this cut-off section was sprouting almost as vigorously as the rest of the tree. Let this be a warning! Don't assume that a collected or transplanted tree has survived the operation on the strength of a few brightly colored, burgeoning new buds. Give it time,

patient (fig. 3). What you need to remember is that trees retain a lot of moisture and vigor even after being cut down. You will therefore need to wait for a longer period to determine if the roots are developing on large cuttings or collected trees.
   I had been asked by a local

FIG. 3

bonsai club to give a talk on the subject "Dead wood in bonsai: do we really need it?" in November 1999 and decided to use the blue cedar as part of my demonstration. Much of the initial work was done at this demonstration. The height of the blue cedar needed to be reduced, and by creating a dead, jinned apex and taper, a more mature, tree-like appearance could be achieved. The remaining lower branches would be wired and shaped to form the foliage pads.
   For me, the blue cedar can be compared to a potter's lump of clay or an artist's blank canvas. Any artist needs inspiration in order to create something, and what I create are bonsai, illusions, plants in pots that look like old, fully grown trees, but in miniature. I tend to draw inspiration from main sources: one is the trees that I have seen in nature, and the other is images of bonsai from Japan. This blue cedar did not have the necessary taper and branch structure for it to resemble a cedar in the wild, but its powerful root base and needle color reminded me of the classical Japanese white pine (*Pinus parviflora*).
   The bark was removed from the top section of the trunk and the wood peeled back to create a jinn of more natural appearance. The original tall tree had now become somewhat squat, and the thin, extending branches therefore needed to be pulled in closely around the trunk. The transformation made by the first styling was very dramatic and I was pleased with the result (fig. 4)

FIG. 4

FIG. 6

positioned to improve the tapering image and to make the trunk line flow more naturally into the branch that had been used to create the crown (figs. 10 & 11).

FIG. 7

FIG.8

The few branches that were available for styling had been severely coiled and bent around the trunk in order to create the density required for a pine-like image. Longitudinal wires and raffia protection had been used on the heavier branches.

Unfortunately, I had pushed one of the branches a little too far, and by May 2000 it was obvious that the branch was dead, so it was removed (figs. 5, 6, 7)

Over the rest of the year the tree was both watered well and heavily fertilized with Japanese rapeseed pellets. It responded accordingly and was allowed to grow unchecked. (fig. 8). In the autumn, the wire that was biting into some of the heavier branches was removed.

During the tree's growing season in 2001, it was fed and watered abundantly. The remaining aluminium wire was removed in August, after which the tree again looked somewhat unkempt (fig. 9)

Carving was carried out to improve the jinned apex, and a shari was introduced to extend the dead wood down to the base of the tree. This was carefully shaped and

FIG. 5

FIG.9

FIG.10

The strong, squat, pine-like image was not immediately obvious in the original bland, sparse blue cedar. In furthering our education, our technique and our sources of inspiration, we bonsai artists are rewarded not only with breathtaking transformations, but also with the increased ability to use raw material that we had previously labelled unsuitable.

I intend to repot the tree in a smaller, traditional, Japanese ceramic pot. Fertiliser pellets will again be applied in abundance in forthcoming years to improve the tree's ramification and branch structure.

John Hanby.

The tree was then totally rewired, this time with copper rather than aluminium wire because this wiring was for refinement. Copper wire is less conspicuous than aluminium, has better holding powers and the smaller gauges make it possible to wire the smaller shoots.

I was pleased with the progress that the tree had made in the two years or so since the original styling was undertaken. The styling is simply a start, and it is on-going refinement and development that is important if the original, inspirational image is to be achieved within a reasonable period of time.

FIG.11

Japanese red pine (*Pinus densiflora*), by Robert Langholm (New Zealand)

In a quiet suburban street in Auckland, New Zealand, lies a private garden containing a large collection of bonsai. The owners of this garden have a love of nature and an even greater love of bonsai. Robert Langholm and Simon Misdale enjoy sharing their knowledge and open their garden to visitors from all over the world. The garden is so popular that they also host workshops twice a month.

Robert Langholm is one of the most senior bonsai masters in this part of the world and has been growing bonsai for over thirty years. I visited this beautiful country recently and cannot wait to return to savour the landscapes, the bonsai and the many friends whom I made there. Robert and Simon have also visited me in Scotland and Simon, an international-award-winning jewellery designer, created one of my bonsai pins.

When he teaches bonsai, Robert often tells his students a story of how a bonsai is created with loving care. This is the story of one of his trees, a Japanese red pine (*Pinus densiflora*).

1 The pine before being shaped and repotted. The old needles need to be removed.

2 All of the twigs and branches are wired to their tips.

3 The tips are elevated to encourage bud development and back-budding.

4 During the repotting process, a maximum of one third should be pruned from a pine's roots. Because the pine will be returned to its pot, fresh, dry soil is placed in the space that has been made, after which the pine is repotted and tied into the pot. After repotting, do not feed a pine for six weeks, but continue to mist and water it. If, as often happens in New Zealand, and areas with clean air, fast-growing lichens appear, remove them by hand.

5 The foliage is tidied up. The back stub will be shaped and jinned later.

6 Robert Langholm, pictured in the summer of 2002. The pot measures around 25 x 19in (63 x 48cm), while the tree's height is nearly 52in (133cm) and its width, measured from the rim of the pot, is just over 45in (115cm).

The story of my Japanese red pine (*Pinus densiflora*)

When I first came across this Japanese red pine (*Pinus densiflora*) while working for the Auckland City Council Parks Department in 1963, it was an ugly, overgrown pine in a plastic bag. No one was interested in it and it stayed in the nursery, where it was shunted from corner to corner year after year.

After returning home from an intensive course on bonsai with Ben Suzuki in Los Angeles in 1976, I started to take an interest in this tree because I could now see its potential as a bonsai, although it would certainly need a lot of work! Having received permission to take the unwanted tree home with me, I started planning that work. I am sure that I am not the only one who forgets to take "before" and "after" pictures when they start working on a tree, and sadly this is what I neglected to do in 1978.

It has undergone many changes, since then, as well as much wiring and rewiring over the years. Initially, however, I was a little over-awed by the pine. With no one to advise me what to do with it, it remained a potted tree for a long time, whose candles I would pinch during its growing season and on which I lavished loving care.

It was a visiting bonsai-grower from Germany who suggested a change of shape. We started by removing a few large branches to let more light filter through and then rewired the entire tree. (After about six months, the wire had to be removed because it was starting to bite into the branches.) I hung big rocks from the branches to give the tree more shape and, using a fine saw, undertook some undercutting on a few of the large branches to assist the shaping of the branches. (I have practiced this method for many years now and it has given good results on a number of my trees.)

The process of this design: front or back;

The tree needed to be rewired, shaped and pruned to enable more light to filter through the branches. As I needed to repot it, I decided that this would give me a good opportunity to turn the tree in order to give it a new front. What I had previously considered the front of the tree was now, in my eyes as a Bonsai designer, the back.

What I use as a potting mix:

Good loam and well-rotted leaf mold is difficult to come by, so use a tree-and-shrub mix that is made up of peat, fine bark chips that have been well broken down and medium-grade pumice sand. It has a breakdown of 70% organic and 30% horticultural grit 2mm nominal. When mixing, add a slow-release fertilizer. This gives you the base mix. To this you can now add more grit as suits the plant. With pines I prefer to add more grit and I now make a pine mix with 75% grit and 25% of the base mix. This gives me a well-draining mix.

Feeding:

For additional feeding, I like to use a little blood and bone, while for foliar feeding I use Phostrogen™ according to the manufacturers instructions on the packet or on the special feeder bottle that is supplied at most garden centres. For general feeding I use a watering can. I mix the Phostrogen™ at the rate of 2 tablespoons per 10 liter (. I use this about once a month.

Wiring:

Because the New Zealand climate on North Island is very mild, just above temperate but not as hot as tropical, I wire and rewire throughout the year and do most of my pruning in the spring. The next job will be to remove or shape the stub at the side of the pine.

Robert Langholm.

In this chapter, bonsai artists from the United Kingdom, Italy and the United States demonstrate some of the styles, using a variety of trees, that can be created using collected material.

Styling a yew (*Taxus*) as a formal upright,
by Craig Coussins (Scotland)

In this class I shall give a collected yew (*Taxus*) its first styling. When it was discovered by Alan Dorling, the tree measured over 9ft (2.7m) in width and had a huge number of branches. Having been grazed on by sheep or deer, its height was very low, however. Despite its small stature, the yew was approaching nearly a hundred years in age.

Over the next three years, Alan Dorling, the person who found the tree and an experienced collector of yamadori (hill or mountain trees), pruned it into rough shape and kept the branches short to force secondary branching. He also kept it in a deeper pot than would otherwise be usual to help the root structure to develop.

1 The proposed front of the tree before the work is carried out. The tree, which is around 100 years old, displays good nebari and an interesting split trunk.

2 The left side of the yew.

3 The right side of the yew.

4 The back of the yew.

5 Because it will be an initial styling, I shall use the multiple-wiring technique.

6 When wiring a yew, do not twist the leaves, but instead make sure that their undersides continue to face downwards.

7 Between one third and one half of the leaves will be removed.

8 One side of the tree is rough in shape.

9 When styling a yew (and also a pine), you must reach into the centre of the tree and wire every part of it. Remove all juvenile growth, too, such as any leaf buds growing on the trunk.

10 The front of the newly designed tree. The styling took less than four hours, during which every part of the tree was wired. A stubby branch needs to be developed over the next three years, but I have left it for now because it is vital to the bonsai's strength.

11 The left side of yew.

12 The right side of the yew.

13 Because it was early spring and the tree had not been repotted for two years, I decided to check the state of the roots. They turned out to be very healthy, as shown in this photograph. I therefore thought that it would be possible to transfer the yew to a pot that was slightly wider, but also shallower, than the one in which it had been growing.

14 The tree is pictured inside, but only for photographic purposes because outdoor trees like yews will not thrive indoors.

Styling a mountain juniper (*Juniperus sabina*) as an informal upright,

by Valerio Gianotti (Italy) Photos and text by Craig Coussins

Valerio Gianotti is one of Europe's leading bonsai artists. Based in Turin, Italy, he teaches at eight local clubs and has given demonstrations at many Italian bonsai conventions. His personal collection of yamadori is world famous, and some of his trees have received national and international awards (one was even featured on an Italian postage stamp—a great mark of honor).

1 Valerio pictured among the yamadori in his garden.

2 Part of Valerio's collecting area in the Dolomites.

3 Valerio discovered the tree embedded in rocks in 1995. Fortunately, the root system did not extend too deeply into the rocks and the tree was eventually removed.

4 Valerio points at the trunk, indicating how awkwardly the tree is growing.

5 Valerio took the tree home and planted it in pure pumice granules measuring around ¾ to 1in (2 to 3cm) in diameter. The root mass was healthy, but Valerio felt that it needed to be left alone to settle for two years. This picture was taken in 1997.

6 By 1998, Valerio had shaped the foliage mass to produce an amazing image.

7 The tree was deemed an outstanding image for a postage stamp in 1999.

8 I took this photograph in early 2001, and you can see that the foliage has improved still further.

9 A close-up of this beautiful tree five years after it was lifted from the rocks.

I first met Valerio during the early 1990s, and have spent time with him on many occasions since then, either at bonsai conventions or in Turin. I recently spent a week with him, during which I photographed the following demonstration, as well as some of his trees.

The first styling of a mountain juniper (*Juniperus sabina*)

The mountain juniper (*Juniperus sabina*) is a common and variable species of low-growing juniper that can either grow in a shrub shape or more usually, and like many procumbent juniper species, such as *J. communis*, along the ground, where the wood may become so wet that it die backs, pushing the growing area up across the width of the trunk to form exceptional shari and excellent life lines or veins. *J. sabina* is widely distributed throughout the mountains of southern and central Europe, as well as the Caucasus. It has been cultivated for two thousand years or more and has been grown in Britain as a garden shrub since 1548.

This specimen, which is about one to two hundred years old, was collected by Valerio in the Italian Alps and was then kept in a box for three years before the first styling. The following series of photographs documents its styling into a masterpiece bonsai over the course of a busy, educational week.

1 The tree, which has been in its pot for three years, is demonstrating good root and foliage growth.

2 Most of the foliage seems to be sprouting from thin shoots. A view from above reveals the depth of the foliage mass.

3 Having determined the front, or best, aspect, the first task is to remove the redundant foliage.

4 The next task is to reduce the amount of excess wood.

5 Jinned areas are created next.

6 Shari are developed on the inner curve of the trunk. The loose bark is removed and the area cleaned up.

7 Using a large blade, Valerio removes more bark to develop the jinned sections.

8 The next step is to use a flap sanding disc or ball on a grinder on the tree.

9 Always wear goggles or glasses, and a face mask, to protect your eyes and lungs. Stroke the flapper against the tree just firmly enough to remove the outer bark and expose the white wood. beneath.

10 Work to remove the bark on the jinns continues. The jinns will form part of the overall design.

11 A larger sanding disc having been attached, the trunk is shaped next, along with those larger branches that would have been too thick for the design, and now have to be to reduced.

12 The result is wood that looks as though it has been grooved naturally. Perhaps the bark has fallen off as a result of the damage wrought by beetle larvae and channels have then formed.

13 The remaining thicker wood is reduced.

14 Valerio's beautiful work is apparent on this shari, on which no parallel lines can be seen.

15 Valerio now considers how to incorporate this branch into his design. Not only is it in the wrong place, but it needs to be taken up to the tree's apex, where there is hardly any growth.

16 In order to make the branch more flexible, Valerio has to split the branch where he intends to bend it. He is using a pair of branch-splitters (also known as root-cutters).

17 Here you can see the split being made.

18 Valerio wraps the entire branch in a stretchy, narrow tape. Samurai™ branch-protection tape is a new low-tack (low-stickiness) tape that adheres to itself, but not to wood, and is now widely used.

19 Having taped the branch, Valerio now positions two or three thick, copper wires along its length. He uses copper wire rather than aluminum because it's stronger.

20 The wires having been applied, Valerio then retapes the entire structure to increase the pressure on the branch.

21 The small holding wires are clearly visible in this picture. They should either be removed or trimmed before taping is undertaken for the second time.

22 The next stage is for Valerio to wire the tree as one would normally, not only to secure the entire structure, but also to enable him to create extreme bends.

23 This is Valerio's branch-bender, an adjustable tool that he designed to bend branches up to 3in (7.6cm) thick. Its bars can be unscrewed and repositioned to suit different branch thicknesses.

24 Valerio has prepared the branch-bender to undertake this particular job.

25 Valerio works out exactly where this branch needs to be taken.

26 Enrico Stracca, Valerio's assistant, helps him to lift the lower branch, whose length this photograph shows clearly.

27 Using his branch-bender, Valerio starts to "fold" the branch, having protected it by splitting its structure, covering it with plastic tape, attaching wire splints and taping it again.

28 The strain tells on Valerio's face as he maneuvers the branch into the space between the top branch and the curve of the trunk.

29 The branch has now been "folded," or turned upside down, and taken through the target area so that it forms the tree's apex.

30 Now it's the turn of the foliage, a process that must be undertaken extremely carefully and very slowly as you work the soft, breakable foliage and twigs through the spaces.

31 With the foliage in place, Valerio can now push the branch a little further into the space.

32 The preliminary work having been done, the juniper is now ready for shaping.

33 Every branch, twig and bit of foliage is wired individually, a task that took Valerio and Enrico two days.

34 Five different sizes of wire were used.

160

35 Before styling the top, Valerio ensures that the foliage is in place. The density of the apex is now almost double what it was before the lower branch was positioned here.

36 Although jinn seal (lime sulfur) has already been applied to the stripped area, Valerio now decides to create some more jinn using the sanding flapper.

37 The newly jinned areas are carved and then sealed with jinn seal (lime sulfur).

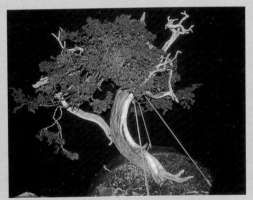

38 The final shaping and placement of the apical jinn is undertaken.

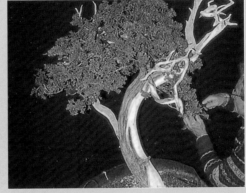

39 A stray branch is rewired and positioned within the foliage mass.

40 By the end of the styling, which took four days, a superb, classical bonsai has been created.

41 The bonsai one year later, in a new pot.

Forest planting styles

This section focuses on the elements of forest planting styles, using drawings for clarification.

A forest planting's basic design

The drawings that accompany this section illustrate the traditional forest-planting approach, in which the dominant tree is at the front and the rest of the trees are arranged as though they are retreating into the background, thereby creating a feeling of depth. Forest groups can comprise five, seven or any other uneven number of trees. The largest tree should be higher than the others and the whole design consequently falls into a triangular pattern. This is clear in the outline drawing, and you should also note that the foliage pads themselves should ideally be triangular, too. All types of group are best planted in a shallow pot or on a slab.

Drawing 1 shows a deciduous forest that has been divided into two. The smaller forest is a five-tree planting and the larger group comprises ten trees. Or does it? If you look carefully at the smaller group, you'll see that the two smaller, central trees are shared and that each group, in fact, borrows from the other. This group design is full of interest and draws the viewer deep into forest without the inclusion of a lot of trees.

Planning a forest planting

In a basic forest planting, the largest tree is set to one side, as are the smaller trees, which are positioned towards the back of the group. The trees at the side mirror the smaller trees that develop through natural growth in a forest, while the ones at the back give the impression of distance.

Depth is the most important consideration when planning a forest planting. Because inner growth can die back if it does not receive enough light, your foliar plan must be spaced in such a way as to give the illusion of depth, but without any foliage pads crossing each other. This is shown in the outline plan.

The design of this group is clear from the outline.

Drawing 2 shows a typical forest of conifers planted in the perspective style. The larger tree at the front dominates the image, while the trees on the other side give the impression of being in the distance, a long way away from the main tree. Interestingly, the central trees belong to neither side: the single tree in the centre has no connection with the distant group, but stands on its own, while the tree directly next to it appears very far away, a perspective that the central tree helps to create.

The outline clearly demonstrates the role of the central tree.

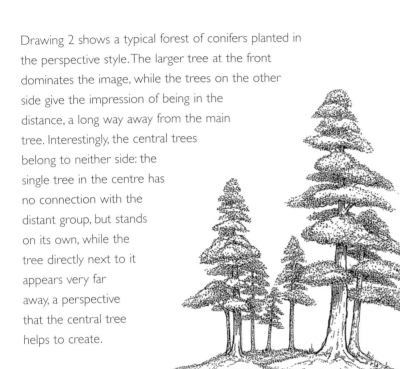

In drawing 3, the large group, whether it consists of deciduous or coniferous trees, is simply a development of the other two groups. When creating a group, remember that no tree should cross another from a frontal view or a side view because this would break the illusion of depth and size.

Here you can see the placement of the foliage pads in relation to the whole unit. If the pot were extended by one-third on the right-hand side, the image would become smaller, and if I did this, I would use either a pot of the same depth with a rounded edge or else a slab.

A cedar elm (*Ulmus crassifolia*) forest planting, by Howard and Sylvia Smith (United States)

I first met Howard and Sylvia Smith, who run the Renaissance Bonsai Nursery in Dallas, Texas, when they invited me to speak at the Texas Bonsai Convention a few years ago. I have since visited them a number of times to work with members of the local bonsai club in Dallas. Here Howard and Sylvia describe how they created a cedar elm forest planting.

Escaping into the forest

At the beginning of our bonsai endeavors, we would obtain a tree and style out a "one, two, three" pattern of branch pads around the trunk, all the way up to the apex. Although the tree often appeared rather barren after we'd removed all of the "wrong" branches, according to our understanding of the rules of bonsai, it looked as it should. We knew that in time it would be a 'better' tree, yet it lacked an ineffable quality. We then began to look for, and acquire, trees with "'personality," but applying the generic techniques of our bonsai training was not enough: the branch structure and foliage did not harmonise with the tree's individual characteristics. With time and experience, we began to "listen" to trees. Each tree is unique, possessing its own strengths and weaknesses, and we have come to realise that it is the bonsai enthusiast's duty to recognize each tree's individuality, to hear its story and to ensure that that story is expressed to all who see it.

Bonsai has not only endowed our lives with beauty, but has provided us with a wonderful escape from the stresses of day-to-day life, especially during the creation of a forest planting. When working with a single tree in a container, we are expressing our artistic and creative freedom by bringing out the best that we can in that tree, limited only by the material, our technique, our horticultural knowledge and our artistic skills. In the making of a forest, we are creating our own little part of the world, one which we inhabit while we reflect and work on it.

The cedar elm (*Ulmus crassifolia*)

Referred to by some as the "king of Texas bonsai," the cedar elm (*Ulmus crassifolia*), also known as the Texas elm, is a strong, resilient tree that responds well to bonsai techniques. Prevalent in limestone soils and native to the eastern half of Texas, it can grow up to 90ft (27.4m) in height. Hardy in the cold and resistant to most pests, the cedar elm's period of active growth is when the Texan climate is hot, and although it is susceptible to fungal infection during unseasonably wet summer weather, this will not damage the tree greatly and can easily be treated with fungicide.

Ulmus is a marvellous genus to work with. Its hardiness allows the artist to commit horticultural and technical errors that would cause the demise of most other genera, yet the elm will show only minimal signs of distress. An elm makes a great tree for beginners, too. It responds well to harsh root treatment, enabling forest plantings to be created using material whose root system is not very shallow. It readily sends out new growth from old wood, allowing branches to be placed in almost any position. It heals promptly and its coarse bark will show little evidence of scarring after medium-sized, and even large, cuts have healed over. Its rapid growth causes ramification to develop within a relatively short period of time (by bonsai standards, at least), and its flexible branches will accept and maintain dramatic movement within a single wiring session (but note that the "Hokkaido" and "Seiju" varieties are more brittle and need to be wired before the branches gain too much girth).

The forest planting

FIG. 1

FIG. 2

FIG. 3

The trees featured in the forest planting (see Figure 1) were chosen for their harmony of character, their varying trunk sizes and their similar rates of taper (that is, they all demonstrated appropriate trunk girth to height ratios). The grouping is in the distant forest style, representing our imaginary land in its entirety. The seven trees shown in Figure 1 were arranged in order of height and trunk girths and were identified as tree 1, tree 2, and so on, to make the building of the arrangement easier.

The slab was crafted by Vito Megna, of Leander, Texas, and is composed of cement and cement fondue, which is a product obtainable from modeling shops. It is a heated fluffy cement mix which is then applied as a light skin over a harder base. It can be colored before mixing or painted after applying. It is useful as natural rock texture

can be worked easily into the mix. The soil mix was composed of peat moss, sphagnum moss, Perlite™ and Haydite™. This mix possesses a spongy consistency that provides good aeration and drainage, yet is cohesive enough to assist in holding freshly root-pruned trees in place without the need for a perimeter border within which to contain the soil.

The roots were washed and the tap roots cut (Figure 2). As was observed above, cedar elms accept aggressive root removal, that is, as long as they are healthy and the removal is done at the correct time (in early spring, just before the leaf buds open). Care was taken to wrap the freshly cut root balls in a wet towel to keep them moist while the arrangement was being composed.

FIG. 4

FIG. 5

FIG. 6

The first tree was positioned towards the front and somewhat off-center (Figure 3), with its most aesthetically pleasing side facing the viewer. Trees 2 and 3 were positioned close to the main tree as we started to develop the triangular silhouette, as well as the triangular aerial view. The root balls were firmly pressed into one another to assist the stability of the planting and initiate the interweaving of the root systems. Final adjustments of the angles of the trees were made prior to adding the remainder of the soil and covering the surface with moss (Figures 4 and 5). With the help of a few lamps, some rough wiring of the branches was completed (Figure 6). Any branches that reached towards the inner portion of the forest were removed and their apices were adjusted so that they were in proportion with one another.

One year later (Figure 7), the large cuts are healing over nicely and some branch development has occurred. In the future, any large, or thick branches in the upper section will be removed, the crown of the forest will become more rounded, some of the unnatural-looking, exposed roots will be removed and the width of the forest will increase as the branches develop. Many more internal branches will also be removed as the external branches and apices develop ramification.

Nearly five years later (Figure 8), the forest has a more refined look. But as the forest has developed, so have its designers, and on reflection some flaws and imperfections are apparent: the opposing initial movements of trees 1 and 2, the straight character of tree 3 and some lack of depth in the overall composition, as well as the lack of randomness of the tree placements. It has occurred to us to pull the forest apart and rebuild it

FIG. 7

FIG. 8

anew, but then too many forests are already being torn down, and we would miss this one.

Howard and Sylvia Smith

FIG. 9

Styling an English hawthorn (*Crataegus monogyna*) in the raft style,
by Tony Tickle (England)

Tony Tickle runs one of the UK's leading design and marketing companies but has a passion for excellence in bonsai. I invited Tony to the second Scottish Bonsai Convention in 1994 where he illustrated a lecture using innovative computer aided bonsai design. Tony has been collecting yamadori (natural material suitable for bonsai) since 1992. He lives in the north of England, where they neither have extremes of weather nor high mountains. What they do have, are areas that are grazed by sheep and deer, and Tony does his collecting in these areas. The qualities that he looks for in yamadori are old-looking bark, good movement and a compact image. Most of his collected material is between forty and three-hundred-and-fifty years old. Working with such choice material is, for Tony, very satisfying, and ultimately very rewarding. Tony discusses the creation of raft-style bonsai, which have two sources in Nature. A raft is where a tree has fallen down and the remaining roots that grow feed the branches on the side facing upwards. In some cases, the fallen tree can sprout a small forest of trees from the calamity that caused the tree to fall in the first place. The second is where a tree has self-layered a branch along the ground. The branch has developed roots from underneath and the branch then develops upward and outward branches creating a new structure.

Craig Coussins

This English hawthorn (*Crataegus monogyna*) was collected in 1993. It was a cold November morning when two of my bonsai buddies and I headed for the hills. I had visited the site during the summer and had approached the farmer who owned the land about collecting a specimen or two, and although he was surprised, he had no objections. I am a lover of English hawthorn, and a good specimen can display all that is desirable in bonsai: bark of great character, a trunk with taper and movement, very small leaves and, if you are lucky, delicate red, pink or white fragrant flowers followed by bright-red berries.

When we collected it, the hawthorn's appearance was very different to what it is today. The tree was a solid mass of twisted branches and large knuckles, points where the tree trunks or branches took a different direction, causing a sharp angle in the growth, or had small suckers growing from that point creating what could even be termed as a burr. There was very little root mass. We took a great deal of care to ensure the survival of this very old specimen which we considered to be be over two hundred years old. I planted the tree in a wooden box containing a soil mix of 30 per cent Akadama™, 40 per cent alpine grit and 30 per cent Biosorb™ (a fired clay that resembles grit, but holds water). Immediately after we had boxed it up, those trunks and branches that I felt were too straight were removed and the whole tree was thinned out to balance the root system.

Although the tree put out very little growth during its first year with me, the following year it began to thrive. During the two years of its establishment in the wooden box, the tree's scars and calluses were dressed with Cut Paste™, the redundant branches removed and the edges and center of the hole carved to make them look natural. This tree displays no jinns, and the only dead wood is inside the holes that I created to disguise the removal of both large and small branches. The tree remained in the box until the early spring of 1996, when it was planted in a bespoke misty-grey, oval pot created by the British potter Derek Aspinall.

I am always trying to improve the bonsai that I have in my collection (and may spend many days deciding how to change a tree). This raft-style bonsai has been modified many times since it was first shown in 1997. The original back is now the front, three trunks have been removed and branches have been restructured. Derek Aspinall, unhappy with his original pot, also created a beautiful rectangular pot, whose colour as you can see, perfectly complements the hawthorn's misty gray bark.

Tony Tickle

In 1993, it was hard to believe that this scruffy bush would eventually become a beautiful bonsai. This is the tree in the wild: a tight, triangular crown of thorns and twisted branches.

The tree pictured shortly after it had been boxed up. The box measured 40in (102cm) in length, 18in (46cm) in depth and 7in (18cm) in height. It held one bag of Akadama™, one bag of grit and half a bag of Biosorb™ Pumice—roughly one third each in the mix – and needed two people to carry it.

Having decided which aspect of the tree would be the front, a large surface root had to be removed accordingly.

The removal of the large root was undertaken at the same time as the tree was repotted. The tree's substantial amount of root enabled major surgery.

With its new front facing the camera, the tree is pictured in its winter garb and new pot.

The tree as it appeared at the JAL–Japan Airlines Bonsai Competition in Tokyo held in July 1999. I have made some changes to the tree since then. I was never happy with the center of the tree, where the rhythm of the trunks was upset by the back branch. The back branch has now been removed and the small trunk next to the main one has been shortened. The tree's lines appear cleaner and easier on the eye as a result.

The tree as it appeared in Munich, Germany, in 2001 at the World Bonsai Convention. The hawthorn has received many national and international awards since its first styling.

Rock and landscape plantings

This chapter focuses on rock and landscape planting. Earlier in *Bonsai school,* I discussed how the Chinese created wonderful gardens from rocks in order to capture the essence of mountains and cliffs, while the Japanese Zen Buddhists monks created gardens with rocks and sand but no plant life. Bonsai and penjing artists have always had a fascination with creating landscapes and in this series of lessons, we have artists from the United States, China, Vietnam and South Africa teaching us how they create this kind of image.

Saikei, by Tony and Frank Mihalic (United States)

Tony Mihalic is a patriarch of bonsai in the United States, having taught it since 1946. He specialises in the rock and forest styles that are respectively known as saikei and yose ue. Frank Mihalic, Tony's son, has been integrating traditional bonsai concepts with innovative teaching techniques utilizing cyber technology for the past twenty-five years. Frank specialises in single-tree bonsai styles and routinely studies with various renowned Bonsai Masters and growers in the Far East to perfect his skills. The Mihalics own and run Wildwood Gardens, in Chardon, Ohio, and I have had the pleasure of leading workshops at this dedicated bonsai family's nursery. This section is introduced by Frank Mihalic.

Father and son are both Bonsai Masters.

The Mihalic philosophy of bonsai

According to the Mihalic philosophy, it is important to understand the basic principles and techniques of bonsai before trying to create a bonsai. The best way is to study, understand and master the elements of bonsai, such as:

- your number 1, number 2 and number 3 branches;
- your one-third trunk and two-thirds foliage;
- balance, taper and exposed root base.

Then, and only then, can you experiment with new techniques and ideas.

Creating the saikei

Because my father has been known for his rock, as well as his forest, plantings for the last fifty-five years, we decided to create a rock planting, or saikei, for our *Bonsai school* class.

First let's look at the materials that we will be using.

- The pot that we have chosen is an oval Tokoname bonsai pot from Japan that measures 24in (61cm) in length, 16in (41cm) in width and 2in (5cm) in depth.
- If they are to complement each other, it is important to use the same kind of stones, and we will use between five and seven rocks in our planting. These rocks are called tuffa rock, fossil shell soft limestone, Karst rocks, or inland coral and are taken from glaciers. They are very easy to carve or drill, making them a great choice for bonsai. The largest rock measures 18in (46cm) in height.
- The plants that we will be using are *Cryptomeria japonica* or Japanese cedars. Originally cuttings, they are now about three years old.
- We will also be using some, *Acorus gramineus* 'Pusillus', a Japanese dwarf acorus rush grass, and *Erodium*, a small mountain geranium, as underplanting. We will also consider whether or not to add a *Onychium japonicum aurea* (Japanese miniature golden claw fern).
- The first step, and one of the most important, is to prepare the bonsai pot. In this case, it means wiring and securing a piece of screening (a plastic mesh used for covering the holes in a bonsai pot when repotting) over the drainage holes to prevent the water from washing the soil out of the pot. In addition, by preparing the pot, soil and of all your materials now, you will not waste time having to do this after you have started to work on the bonsai.

How to make a base for your stones

The next step is to prepare the stones that you are going to use. When you are working with stones, you have two choices, as follows.

1 To cut off the bottom of the stones with a saw or hammer so that they sit in the required position.
2 To make a base for them to sit on. In this case, we will make a base by using a cement water plug used for plugging holes in fish ponds and available from aquatic and garden centres.

Take some clay and form it into a circle on a piece of plastic sheeting. The circle of clay should be larger than the base of the stone. Place the stone inside the circle, propping it up into the required position for your bonsai pot with string or sticks. Then mix up your cement water plug material according to the instructions on the container and pour it into the clay circle. Although it will have hardened within fifteen minutes, it is best to leave it for twenty-four hours before removing the clay circle, after which your stone should be standing in the required position without needing to be propped up. Now submerge the base in potassium magnate, also available from most garden centers to turn the cement's pH level neutral.

A large forest group created by Tony Mihalic.

The step-by-step styling

As a bonsai artist, you should have an image in your mind of what you are going to create. For example, if you were going to create a cascade bonsai, you would keep an image of the style in your mind as you select the branches that you intend to retain. In this case, our design will be a rock planting that conjures up the image of two mountains separated by a river or stream. Keeping the image of this natural rock formation in our minds, we move and rotate our rocks inside the bonsai pot until we like what we see.

Rock and landscape plantings

Tony Mihalic surveys his Koi carp lake at Wildwood Gardens.

We also need to decide where to position the trees in our rock planting. Having added a thin layer of soil around the rocks on the right-hand side, and having made sure that the rocks are sitting firmly on the bottom of the pot, with no soil beneath them, we start to place the trees in front of, and between, the front and back rock on the right. A crevice was created where the two rocks touch each other in which we can put soil and plant trees. In order to prevent the trees and soil from being washed out of the crevice, we will use short moss to hold them together.

Short, or dense form moss, the preferred type of surface-planting moss, is usually found on stone or other hard surfaces, while longer-grain, coarser moss, such as sphagnum, grows on wood. Short moss can be collected from woods or forested areas. When collecting it, one tip is to work a long knife under the moss and then to scrape it carefully away. Using a long knife will also help you to collect a little soil along with the moss, increasing its chances of survival.

(Please note: because carrying a long, sharp, pointed knife may get you into trouble with the police in some countries, it's best to cut off the tip to make it flat and make sure that the blade edge is blunt.)

We will use hairpins or a small piece of wire (but not copper wire, which could leach into the soil and adversely affect mycelium growth because copper has a fungicidal effect) bent into a 'U' shape to secure the moss to the soil. This will do three things, as follows.

1 It will prevent the moss from falling off the planting.

2 It will enable the roots to remain in contact with the soil.

3 It will prevent the soil from being washed off the planting.

Now we shall repeat the process described above for the left-hand side of our planting, starting with the placement of the trees and finishing with the planting of moss on the soil surface.

The total number of trees that we shall use will remain unclear until we have finished both sides of the planting. Only then will we be in a position to decide whether we need to add more trees or else remove some. Whenever possible, however, we prefer to use an odd number of trees because an essential basic bonsai rule for smaller groups is that even numbers of trees are distracting. (In groups of twenty trees and more this is not important, however.) Having finished the planting on the left-hand side, we then decided to place an additional tree in the right crevice, indicated by the chopstick, to give the planting more balance and harmony, as well as an odd number of trees.

When you've finished planting your trees, it's advisable to take a break and to step back from your planting to get a different perspective on your creation. You could now add some under planting to give more perspective and create a balanced, natural, look. We used a dwarf *Acorus* (Japanese grass) to recreate the effect of plants growing close to the river or stream, as well as a dwarf *Erodium* (geranium) to add some pink flowers to the arrangement.

The image that we held in our minds was of two mountains with a river or stream flowing between them. Having positioned all of the trees and under planting, we then made sure that all of the soil surface was covered with moss, apart from the area between the two mountains, which would be the river. Here we placed some small, white stones (you could also add a few small rocks), which, as well as giving the illusion of a river, added three-dimensional depth to the creation

One of the great things about a rock planting is that when you have finished, it looks finished, in contrast to single-style bonsai, when you have to imagine how the tree will look in two to five years, when it will have filled in, the image will look mature and the branches will have developed more ramification.

The Mihalics' nursery, Wildwood Gardens.

1 The pot has been prepared to receive the planting.

2 A rock pictured without a supportive base.

3 The same rock positioned on its base.

4 The rocks in their final positions.

5 The next step is to add the soil.

6 The trees destined for the right-hand side of the planting are positioned first.

7 A chopstick indicates where the next tree will be planted.

8 All of the trees are now in place.

9 Moss is added to prevent the soil from being washed away.

10 A view of the right-hand side of the planting.

11 A view of the left-hand side.

12 A view of the planting from above.

13 Close-up views of the completed rock planting.

When making a rock planting in the traditional way, you will require some knowledge of natural landscapes. You could also use photographs for inspiration, such as this image of Mirror Lake in the Yosemite area of California.

One of my favorite images, of a crevice in Bryce Canyon, Utah, was photographed by my wife.

Images of far-off waterfalls and nearby branches or trees are characteristics of Chinese landscape painting, and I recreated the style of these images in the Yosemite Valley. I look for inspirational images through the lens of my camera to build on after I've returned home.

This twin canyon with a semi-frozen river flowing through it, in the US state of Colorado, would make an interesting image for a saikei.

This image of a small, heavy-trunked, thousand-year-old juniper (Juniperus) growing on a rock face in Vail, Colorado beneath an astoundingly blue sky certainly inspired me.

The Yosemite National Park is one of my favorite places on earth. I am still planning how to recreate this image as a saikei, which should be an achievable task if I exclude the rainbow!

The creation of a rock-embracing Tree of a Thousand Stars, also known in China as the Sixth Moon Snow Plant (*Serissa foetida* or *S. serissoides*),

by Linsheng Zhang (China)

Many people are fascinated by plants grown on rocks and want to know how this can be achieved. This section introduces you to plants that can be grown on rocks and also explains how to do so. The rock-embracing style attempts to imitate the natural posture of trees in the wild whose partly exposed roots appear to embrace the rocks on which they are growing. The purpose is to complement the heroic and unrestrained character of the tree with the aged character of the rock.

2 A root-over-rock bonsai in the Chinese style photographed at Wildwood Gardens, Ohio.

3 Firethorns (*Pyracantha*) can also be grown in this style, as this specimen at Wildwood Gardens, Ohio, demonstrates.

1 The root-over-rock style is also known as the rock-embracing style.

4 Another example of the root-over-rock style at Wildwood Gardens, Ohio.

The choice of materials and pre-styling

The first choice that you will have to make is the rock that the plant will embrace. The best is one that has been well shaped by nature and that is criss-crossed with cracks and fold lines, known in China as a "dragon-bone rock," a "tortoise-lined rock," or a "ying-tak rock".

Your second choice is the plant itself, and the best is a *Serissa foetida* (Tree of a Thousand Stars or Sixth-moon Snow Plant), also known as *S. serissoides*, seedling aged between five and six years, with two strong, opposing branches growing from the lower part of the stem. You will need to plant the seedling in a deep nursery pot in the early spring and then cultivate it for a year or two prior to the styling to make sure that it develops a long root system.

Your third choice is a pot to hold your rock-embracing arrangement, and the ideal would be a shallow one made of purple, beige colored clay. (You won't need this for a few years, however, while the plant is growing in its nursery pot.)

During the year or so when the root system is being encouraged to grow longer, the plant should be shaped by wiring and pruning. Before doing so, you'll need to plan your design, paying particular attention to the ratio of the height of the plant to that of the rock: the height of the plant (the part of the plant above the neck of the root) should be half the height of the rock. The plant's height must not exceed that of the rock (a condition referred to as "the hanging of a long, silk cucumber") because this would lead to a thinning of both the branches and the leaves of the plant, thereby yielding an awful form. Having decided on your design, cut the plant to the desired height and then wire the right-hand branch to form an arch shape and the left-hand branch to form three arches. Now wire the top of the main stem and the small branch on the left into an arch form to represent the tree's crown. You have now established the overall form of the plant (Figure 1).

After pruning and wiring it, fertilising, watering and generally caring for the plant should encourage the branches to grow. When they are between about ¾ to 1in (2 and 3cm) long, prune them to a length of about around 3/8in (1cm). Because *Serrisa foetida* grows rapidly, it will be necessary to prune the branches between five and six times a year, and after about two years the leaves should have grown into clusters resembling cloud formations (Figure 2).

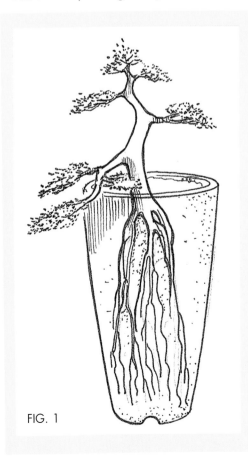

FIG. 1

FIG. 2

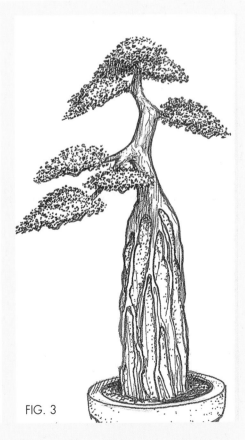

FIG. 3

The step-by-step styling

When the form of the plant has been well established, it is ready for transplanting and attaching to the rock. Do this in the spring or fall.

Take the plant out of its nursery pot, wash off any soil that may be clinging to its roots and then trim off any weak or dead roots. The root system is now ready to be attached to the rock. The arrangement of the roots should look both natural and as though the roots are firmly attached to the rock, so align the roots with the veins and cracks in the rock and along the crevices. Having done this, cover the areas where there is soil with a layer of moss held firmly in place with metallic or plastic wire. (Applying soft plastic mesh held in place with clips will also keep the birds off your moss until it takes hold.)

Position the rock-embracing plant on the right-hand side of the pot (Figure 3). If the rock appears unstable, anchor it into the pot with cement. Remove the soil until you can see the base of the rock. Otherwise, remove the rock and re-set into the pot with cement as before. The base of the rock will be covered by the soil and after the cement hardens (around fifteen minutes to one hour), water must be applied to moisten the moss and the soil thoroughly.

A *Juniperus procumbans* styled by Frank Mihalic.

Place the newly planted arrangement in a semi-shaded area and make sure that the soil and moss are kept constantly moist. If planted in the spring, around fall, cut off the moss covering in stages, taking care not cut off too much each time because if too much of the new root is exposed, the plant's growth and chances of survival will be compromised. There is no set time but essentially you will have to determine the strength of the roots. As a guideline, it will be about two to three years before the roots attach to the rocks. In time, the root system and the rock eventually form a single unit (Figure 3).

You could also add other features to your rock-embracing planting: placing a clay figure of a cowherd or firewood-gatherer beside the rock, for instance, would make the scene appear even more vivid and interesting.

Linsheng Zhang.

Landscape Hon Non Bo,
by Lit van Phan (United States)
Photos by Dinh Nguyet-Mai

The miniature landscapes of Hon Non Bo have a stunning ability to capture the essence of the larger landscapes of Viet Nam, a country that has spectacular scenery, including a long shoreline and many rivers, jungles and mountains.

Many of the mountains are of the Karst, or hard and soft limestone type, soft limestone that has eroded over hundreds of thousands of years to leave the harder parts still standing. (Some of China's spectacular mountains are the same type of limestone.) The mountains have been eroded not only by mildly acidic rain, but also by the sea. Indeed, many mountains have been undercut by the action of the waves, and nowhere is this more evident than in the mountainous islands of Ha Long Bay. Although the Ha Long Bay islands are a fertile source of inspiration, mountains throughout Viet Nam, down to its southern tip, also provide models for miniatures.

The jagged limestone peaks of Viet Nam are my inspiration for Hon Non Bo.

The stones that feature in Hon Non Bo are always mountain shaped ("non" means a mountainous area), while the stones used in penjing may be more abstract in form. Bonkei used representations of mountains, but because the focus is on larger landscapes, mountains generally do not dominate the composition. Another difference is that while Bonkei and penjing were usually designed to have a front—the best-looking side—Hon Non Bo are designed to look good from all sides, as well as from the top down, so that people can walk around them to admire their every aspect.

Chinese penjing are often displayed in beautiful marble trays; Bonkei are mostly found in lacquer trays; and Hon Non Bo are traditionally created in shallow concrete trays. Although Viet Nam does have ceramic ware, the size of Hon Non Bo trays preclude the use of clay because it sags and shrinks too much to make large trays. Indeed, it requires four people to move some concrete trays, even before 200 to 300lb (91 to 136kg) of stone is added to represent mountains.

The way in which the rocky cliffs touch the sea give me guidance when creating this image in miniature.

Hon Non Bo and penjing evolved contemporaneously, graduating from large, outdoor works to smaller, indoor or garden trays. Bonkei, a type of Japanese tray landscape that was Saikei's predecessor, appears to have evolved somewhat later. Comparing the three types of tray landscape, the differences between them are striking. Hon Non Bo in trays always use real water; penjing may, or may not, use real water, while Bonkei used only representations of water.

A Hon Non Bo created by Lit Van Phan and photographed by his wife, Dinh NGguyet-Mai.

Rock and landscape plantings

Making concrete trays for Hon Non Bo is an art in itself, as is assembling the mountain-shaped stones, which requires both artistic vision and technical skill. Because a stone is

An arrangement of rocks over a pool suggests a floating island.

rarely found in the form of a perfect mountain, stones are instead carved or assembled with mortar and epoxy resin to take on the desired shape. Hon Non Bo artists are therefore not only growers and designers, but also sculptors.

Rocks may either be carved to fit a tray or else a tray may be designed around a particularly attractive rock. Mountains and vegetation may extend to within 1 in (2.5cm) of the edge of the tray, but never in a way that would direct the viewer's eye to a point outside it. One mountain must be taller and larger than the others to express the grandeur of mountains or, if you like, to act as the "host" for the rest of the composition. The close fit, the strong, vertical relief, the subordination of secondary mountains and vegetation to the main mountain—all these elements are designed to hold the viewer's interest inside the composition. Techniques to exaggerate perspective, such as placing smaller mountains behind the main mountain, are part of the artistic tradition of Hon Non Bo.

Although it is very big, this Vietnamese Hon Non Bo is a great example of the art.

Hon Non Bo may be designed with one, two, three, five or multiple mountains. Like the Japanese, the Vietnamese avoid using groups of four items in their compositions, however. The Japanese say that the number four is unlucky and signifies death, and the Vietnamese also view four as being unlucky because they believe that this number represents the major stages in a person's life: firstly, being born; secondly, becoming independent; thirdly, becoming old and sick; and, fourthly dying. In practical terms, four elements are difficult to incorporate within a design because one ends up with something resembling either a straight line or a diamond shape. In the same way that many traditional bonsai masters remind novices to use the triangular shape by telling them that the top of the tree represents the heavens, the midpoint, humanity, and the lower point, earth, they may also encourage their students to avoid a difficult compositional problem by telling them that the number four is unlucky. The triangular relationship is also used in Hon Non Bo: everything above the Hon Non Bo represents the heavens; the soil, rocks and plants

signify earth, while humanity becomes part of this trinity, either through its representation as a figure placed on the Hon Non Bo or through viewing the landscape itself.

This example of Hon Non Bo contains few plants, the emphasis being on the jagged peaks that resemble mountains.

Although Bonkei made substantial use of human figures, miniature buildings and other signs of habitation, very few man-made items are included in Saikei, Bonkei's successor. The Vietnamese and Chinese still use figures, however, and in a way that few Westerners understand. Westerners are likely to regard the use of human figures or structures in Hon Non Bo or penjing as contrived, but in Hon Non Bo figures of woodcutters, scholars or fishermen, for instance, should not be taken literally, but rather as representations of the larger world. To give one example, the egret has special symbolism in Hon Non Bo because it represents the faithful Vietnamese wife.

The trees used for Hon Non Bo are not the finely articulated trees found in the bonsai world: they go far beyond the naturalistic style of bonsai and penjing and have a really wild, falling-down look about them. This is because after seeds have developed in small pockets of soil on the mountains of Viet Nam, as they grow

they become too heavy for their roots to hold
 upright and consequently begin to lean towards
the ground, an effect captured in Hon Non
Bo.

There is a related Vietnamese
art, Tieu Canh, which
emphasises trees
 rather than
mountains, but which
requires just as much
skill. Tieu Canh may
be smaller than Hon
Non Bo and are
displayed more like
 bonsai. Indeed, the
demand for
smaller Hon
Non Bo
that do not
require four
men to move them has led to the use of smaller trays and smaller
landscape elements (and a large Japanese suiban—water tray—makes
an excellent tray for a smaller Hon Non Bo).

Other changes from the traditional forms include the use of
aquarium pumps for waterfalls and mist-makers to create fog.
Finally, as Hon Non Bo are adapted to different countries, different
stones and varying types of vegetation are
increasingly being used.

Lit Van Phan

I created these images in my home.

Indigenous landscape planting,
by Koos Le Roux
(South Africa)

Koos Le Roux is one of South Africa's leading exponents of landscape planting. He uses rock found in the Transvaal's higher central regions, which is similar to the Italian material used for suiseki (viewing stones). Koos uses two different kinds of material to great effect to recreate the mountains and canyons of his native landscapes.

South Africa is blessed with great bonsai artists and wonderful material. I have been there a number of times and, having found the growers very friendly and hospitable, recommend it as a place that bonsai enthusiasts should visit.

Inspiration and techniques for saikei

Anyone who has a deep fondness for nature, and who enjoys the beauty of mountains, rivers and trees, will derive great joy from saikei (rock planting). Those who wish to capture and display such beauty on a table in their living room, or those who are deprived of the proximity of nature for whatever reason, will find saikei rewarding. The construction of a saikei should be approached playfully, meditatively, artfully and creatively.

Imagination is the main force behind saikei! If, for example, you are looking at a striking rock, which may resemble or suggest a mountain, close your eyes slightly, and if you can imagine a nesting eagle on a ledge near the summit, you already possess the most important element required to proceed with the construction of a saikei.

In South Africa we are fortunate to have rocks that exhibit strange and exciting shapes, colours and textures.

Indeed, the imagination is most often triggered into action by an interesting-looking rock. The mind picture that ensues determines the scale that you will have to apply to the rest of the material that you decide to use: the bigger the 'mountain', the smaller the other material needs to be.

Rock shapes may suggest mountains.

When you pick up a rock, look at it carefully. Consider every detail and weigh up all of its possibilities in terms of its shape, direction of movement, size and texture, particularly of its surface. A well-textured surface that is full of holes, crevices or fissures is what you should be looking for. Although the rock should also ideally have a sturdy, flat base to give it stability, if it doesn't, you could glue some smaller pieces of rock to the base to rectify its unevenness.

Flat rock faces may resemble faces...

... temples, huts, human figures ...

. . or animals.

FIG. 1

I once picked up a rock with a huge cleft that I thought would be superb to use in a saikei. I decided to make the cleft the focal point. In figs. 1 and 2, you can see the trees, which are leaning away from the rock, on either side. I planted only one on the left and three on the right of the rock. I then placed a small rock of the same color and texture at the front right-hand side to counterbalance the big rock. Because the deep end of the cleft is obviously the center of interest, I created a path to lead the eye to this point. I also used mosses of various colors to cover the mounds of soil that I'd settled on different levels. Doing this adds variety and interest to the saikei.

Another very important principle of saikei is the correct use of positive and negative areas. The positive areas are the ones that are planted and the negative areas are the spaces that are left open to establish a balanced arrangement. In a successful saikei, there must be enough negative, or open, space to emphasise the main elements. The more the main elements stand out, the more the most important guideline, that of simplicity, comes into operation. The open spaces can be covered, perhaps with gravel on the pathway and on other open areas. The gravel pieces should be bigger in size at the front and

smaller towards the back. This is another way to establish perspective and a feeling of depth in a well-planned saikei.

On another occasion, I picked up a rock that reminded me of a temple built in the Eastern style. When I realised the possibility of creating a saikei temple similar to a Chinese temple, I selected smaller rocks of the same color and configuration, but of different sizes, to use as the roofs of smaller temples in the distance. Then something very fortunate happened: I found a small rock that resembled a little Chinese woman wearing a traditional, triangular hat. For this saikei, I selected a big, flat tray large enough to contain the whole lay-out.

FIG. 2

When compiling this saikei, my first decision concerned the placement of the temples. After trying out several possibilities, I chose the position shown in figs. 3 and 4. My decision was based on the balance and aesthetic charm of the arrangement, as well as on other artistic principles, such as repetition, perspective, variation, dominance, harmony and unity.

I placed the main, dominant temple on the left-hand side, somewhat between the left-hand border and the centre of the tray. Then, to balance the weight of the main temple, I placed the Chinese woman on the opposite side, in the front right-hand corner, positioning her so that she appeared to be looking towards the main temple. I placed the second temple on the far right-hand side in a further attempt to balance the main temple. The other temples were placed at different heights so that they became smaller, lost their detail and faded into the far distance.

FIG. 3

FIG. 4

Rock and landscape plantings

The trees that I chose were honeysuckles (*Lonicera nitida*), which I selected to harmonise with the atmosphere created by the temples. Note the movement that is created by the curves of the tree trunks. The bigger trees were placed at the front and the smaller ones at the back to create a feeling of depth. (A word of warning: be wary of placing a tree near a temple or a building in case it diminishes the apparent size of the structure. In addition, it is not a good policy to place a tree near a mountain because it may dwarf the mountain to such an extent that it appears to be little more than a large rock.)

I often use *Lonicera nitida* on account of its beautiful trunk movement, lovely texture and small leaves (fig. 5). Unfortunately, it needs frequent clipping and does not like wiring. It does, however, have a tendency to surprise you by transforming itself from an ugly duckling into a swan after a few years. False cypress (*Chamaecyparis*) is another excellent species to work with.

FIG. 5

Figs (*Ficus natalensis*) make excellent saikei material, especially for root-over-rock plantings, but care must be taken to keep the leaves small.

Of the junipers, blaauw is my favourite because it has a beautifully dense and full crown. Its trunk movement is a little uninspiring, however.

I also like to work with olives (*Olea*), although large leaf size can be a problem in some trees.

Having planted your trees, you should water them thoroughly, especially if they are *Lonicera nitida*, and keep them covered for a week or two with small, clear-plastic bags to prevent excessive evaporation during this stressful period for the trees, particularly if the weather is hot. Keep your newly planted saikei in a cool, shady place until the trees have started to show new growth.

Note that saikei need more regular watering than bonsai and that they tend to grow thin and weedy otherwise, over time. When this happens, patch up any moss, redo and replace any gravel and remove any weeds. And if you decide to redo your saikei, remember there is more than one way to construct a splendid creation! What's more, a few days after you have finished your first attempt, give it a good, hard look and ask yourself whether shifting its components around would improve the composition—after all, we are not in the best mood for creation every hour of every day.

Koos Le Roux.

These examples of saikei were made with a few trees on a rock. Note the roots covering parts of the rock.

These saikei are similar to the Japanese Ishitzuki and Sekijoju styles.

As far as soil is concerned, I recommend using a mix consisting of equal parts of sand, compost and loam. Any gravel used for the negative, or open, areas of a saikei must be sieved and sorted into at least three sizes. Moss is a very important element of a saikei, and you should ideally use mosses that vary in size, texture and color. These should be pressed down unevenly in order to achieve both a good texture and a colorful effect.

Creating a Chinese landscape, by Craig Coussins (Scotland)

These limestone cliffs in the Gweilin (Guilin) region of China typify a Chinese scene.

This canyon in the US state of Montana could also act as a source of inspiration. Note how small the trees on the rocks look in perspective.

This charming arrangement exhibited by the Yorkshire Bonsai Association at a show hosted by the Federation of British Bonsai Societies gave me an idea.

George also gave me some small box plants, *Buxus microphylla* 'Richard', a variety of Japanese origin that was developed in the United States. Their diminutive size would be vital in creating the correct proportions for my landscape scene. A simple planting like this is all about balance, an understanding of space and, most of all, of perspective.

Equally, there are many interesting Western images that you could emulate. This photograph was taken high in the mountains of Colorado, in the United States. Note the split rock, the size of the junipers (Juniperus) at the top and the dry waterfall shape at the front. All of these images could be included in a landscape scene.

While I was working with bonsai-grower George Straw in Dallas, Texas, George cut me two pieces of Featherstone, a lightweight substance that resembles expanded volcanic rock and is porous and very sharp to work with when you are first shaping it. I wanted to use them to create an image similar to the limestone mountains of Gweilin (Guilin).

I marked out the positions of some deep hollows in the Featherstone, which George carved out for me. I then filled these hollows with pure Akadama™ mixed with the soil clinging to the roots of the box plants. Although we'd wired all four trees, I needed to decide which tree would be placed where before determining their final shapes. Having positioned the first tree in its hollow, I then styled it into a cascade shape.

The roots were compacted within the plastic pots in which the box plants had been planted, so we teased them out carefully and removed the "beards" (the excess lengths of root that wind around the inside of the pot).

The remaining three trees were placed on the taller rock. One was styled as a cascade, but the other two were left as uprights because I'd noticed that if they've developed a strong root base, many trees that grow on rocks in the wild grow upwards.

The landscape was placed in a suiban, a water-tray-style earthenware pot made in the old bronze dhoban style. I added moss both to protect the soil and to give the effect of grass. Placing small boats (these are generally available as miniature models and are used in penjing and bonsai) between the rocks enhanced the apparent size of these "mountains."

The landscape viewed from the front.

A view of the landscape from the back.

Bonsai come in a number of sizes. John Naka, the famous American Bonsai Master explained the sizes as follows.

Sizes are measured from soil level to the apex of the bonsai

Height	Name	English or Other Name	
1"	Keishi	Tsubo	Thimble size
1-3"	Shito	Mini size	Very small
3-6"	Mame	Mini size	
6-8"	Shohin	Katade	Small Size
8-16"	Kifu Sho	Small to Medium size	
16-24"	Chu	Medium size	
24-40"	Dai	Large size	

Trees larger than this are referred to as garden bonsai (yard bonsai)

The creation of small bonsai and penjing is one of the most demanding areas of this hobby. The problem is to create perfect form and perspective in a small size. Indeed small-size trees are more difficult to create than larger trees because there is less to work with. Cultivation problems arise because the soil area is so minimal that more care has to be taken to prevent such a small soil area from drying out. Despite all this, small size Bonsai and especially mame and shohin have literally thousand of followers including myself, Craig Coussins.

Although this Natal fig (*Ficus natalensis*) has been grown in the slanted style, it looks balanced when viewed from any angle.

Shohin figs, by Jessie Edwards (South Africa)

I had the pleasure of meeting Theunis Roos, on whose research this section is based, Jessie Edwards, who wrote the text, and Duncan Wiles, who took the photographs, for the first time when I visited South Africa some years ago on a teaching tour. Theunis is one of South Africa's most senior and respected bonsai artists, Jessie is highly regarded as a teacher and authority on South African suiseki and Duncan Wiles is an expert grower of figs (*Ficus*) and other subtropical bonsai. Ian Baillie's illustrations for this section are based on Theunis' original drawings.

Theunis Roos.

How to grow shohin figs from cuttings

A Natal fig (*Ficus natalensis*) grown in the semi-cascade style, measuring 13³⁄₄in (35cm) in height.

A selection of Natal figs (*Ficus natalensis*), all measuring under 4in (10cm) in height.

The Natal fig mother tree from which Theunis has taken all of his *F. natalensis* cuttings. Originally collected in Natal's Oribi Gorge, it measures 17³⁄₄in (45cm) in height.

A young Natal fig (*Ficus natalensis*) in training to become a root-over-rock bonsai.

Figs (*Ficus*) are easy subjects for bonsai, and can prove a welcome addition to your home, whether they live inside or outside.

Among the simplest of trees to grow, figs are usually readily obtainable in all parts of the world. Birds tend to deposit their seeds in gutters, on roofs, in drains or in the cracks of stone walls, and the seedlings that sprout from them are both easy to collect and grow very rapidly. If you require larger specimens, however, you should consider growing cuttings. (As well as this tried-and-tested method of growing figs, another very successful way of propagating them is to grow them from collected aerial roots, which sometimes grow from the tree's branches.)

Theunis Roos, one of South Africa's senior bonsai-growers, once gave a talk on growing this fascinating genus from cuttings and, based on his talk, I shall now set out his method, which I have used repeatedly and very successfully.

To grow a shohin fig that will be ready to style in three years, start with a cutting that has a terminal leaf, is about as thick as your little finger and measures approximately 4in (10cm) in length. Dip the cutting in Seradex™ No 3, or any good-quality rooting powder, and then plant it in sharp river sand in a pot that measures 4in (10cm) in height.

After a month, carefully tip your cutting out of the pot. You should then see that roots have started to grow. Cut off all the leaves, except for the growing tip at the top of the cutting, and leaving half of the petiole to avoid damaging any future buds and encourage branching.

Replant your cutting in the same pot, using the same sharp river sand, and keep it in the shade for two weeks. After two weeks start a vigorous fortnightly feeding programme. Start by feeding Nitrosol™ or a liquid seaweed fertiliser (an organic fertiliser), then, two weeks later, feed Chemicult™ or

Theunis Roos pictured with some of his shohin and mame.

A bonsai measuring 22cm (8 3/4in) that has been trained in the root-over-rock style.

any fertilizer suitable for hydroponics culture. Continue feeding the cutting for three months with the hydroponic fertilizer.

After three months, tip the fig out of the sand again, and you should then see many fibrous roots. Any root thicker than a toothpick should be removed to encourage the development of the fibrous roots that a bonsai in a small pot needs to sustain it. At the same time, work a small piece of clay into a round shape (alternatively, use a small, flat stone) and place it under the roots, arranging them over the clay or stone so that they radiate around the stem. Replant your cutting, but this time at an angle to change the direction in which the stem is growing.

Continue with this programme

feeding and dealing with the roots every three months until the roots have developed into a thick mat and new branches have started growing from the points where you cut off the original leaves. After a year, dating from when you first planted the cutting, cut off the stem at the first branch, replant the cutting and continue with the programme as before, heavy feeding and repotting every three months.

Do not throw away the severed top part of your original cutting, however, but instead grow it as a new cutting. If the stem is too thin, push a toothpick into the bottom to break it all the way round a little, which, as the broken areas heal, will thicken the stem and give your new cutting some taper.

At this stage, to increase the diameter of the stem of the original cutting, allow a few bottom branches to grow as "sacrifice" branches, which, when your trunk has reached the desired thickness, you can cut off. The sacrifice branches will thicken up the trunk. As soon as they have done their job remove them.

One of Theunis Roos' Shohin forests displayed on a walnut table made by Hank Millar.

This semi-cascade-style Natal fig (Ficus natalensis) is 35cm (13 3/4in) tall.

Some tricks of the trade

One of the tricks of growing figs is to be careful not to cut off any superfluous branches too close to the trunk. Always leave a piece of the branch that you are cutting off to die back naturally. There are several reasons for this practice, one of which is that if you were to cut off the branch flush with the trunk, the tree would heal the cut by producing an ugly knob (Figure 1). Leaving a small portion of the branch to die back naturally instead means that you can rub it off without the risk of an unsightly knob developing. Another reason is that there is a healing collar around each branch that enables it to heal itself much more quickly if the branch is left to die back.

Another way to give your trunk shape is by cutting it back to a node that faces the same way in which you want the trunk to grow. Let the trunk grow in that direction until it grows some length, and then cut it back to the next node facing in another direction to alter its growing angle (Figure 2).

You can stop a fig bleeding white latex sap after pruning by spraying it with water. Do not use strong chemicals on a fig, however, because this could make it drop its leaves. Dursban™, a chlorpyrifos pesticide, if obtainable, (also very poisonous and not to be used near children or animals as it is very toxic) has been used on figs with no ill effects, but Malathion™, a chemical insecticide generally available worldwide, can kill your tree.

The key to reducing the size of fig leaves is as follows. If you cut off three of the largest leaves every day (a method that most growers advocate), you will soon be left with a tree that has minute new leaves, which, if left to

grow, would eventually become large and would need to be cut off in their turn. If, however, you observe the growth habit of your fig, you will see that the nodal distance, from the trunk to the first node or first leaf is very short and that the leaf that grows from this first node is also very small. As the branch grows, the nodal distance grows bigger and bigger and the leaf size increases at the same time. The trick is therefore to let your branch grow two nodes from the smallest leaf and then to cut it back to a point halfway between the first and second node (Figure 3). If you continue to do this, in no time at all you will have a tree with the smallest leaves imaginable. Note that you can never stop this treatment when working with figs because if you did, their branches would just grow longer and longer, while the leaves would become bigger and bigger, with correspondingly longer nodal distances.

Some fig trees only produce figs terminally, which means that constantly

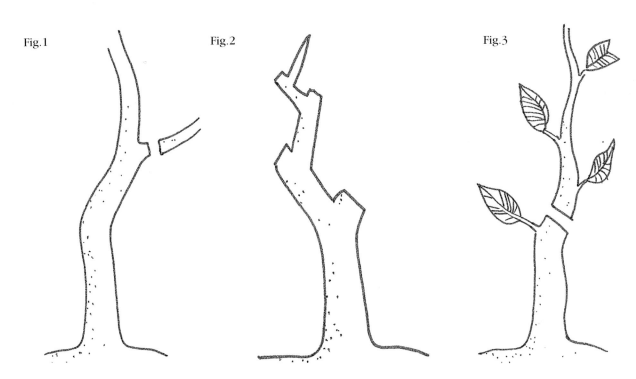

Fig. 1   Fig. 2   Fig. 3

Mini bonsai

pruning the growing tips will stop the fig from bearing fruit, but this is a small price to pay for minute leaves. Several species bear figs along the whole length of their branches, however, among them *Ficus burt-davyii* (the veld fig). Fig trees can bear fruit at any time of year, and a fig fruit, which is covered with minute flowers on the inside, is pollinated when a wasp enters it to lay its eggs, at the same time fertilizing the flowers with pollen from other figs.

If you want to grow larger trees, use nursery stock or collected trees as your material. And if you want to encourage the development of branches that have leaves growing along their entire length, use this method of cutting back to above the first node, starting from the trunk, and gradually developing your branches in this manner.

Styling and caring for figs

Figs can be grown in most of the basic bonsai styles, and are particularly suited to the root-over-rock style. They also lend themselves to being grafted, and if you can't find a tree with a sufficiently thick trunk, you could graft several trunks together to give you the shape and branches that you require. In South Africa, you would not see a fig forest because most of our figs grow into huge specimens that need lots of space, but that having been said, I have seen *Ficus nerifolia* (narrow-leaf fig) planted quite successfully in the forest style.

Figs are, unfortunately, sensitive to frost, and care must be taken in winter to ensure that they are kept warm. Any sudden change in temperature can be enough to make them drop their leaves (which they

can do at any time of year—even when kept indoors and there is a draught, or you move the fig from one room to another). Figs can also be grown very successfully indoors as long as they receive sufficient light (I grow all of my shohin figs on my kitchen windowsill, where they receive the morning sun).

Jessie Edwards.

The biggest trees in the world can also be shrunk to bonsai and penjing size

I asked Bob Shimon from Mendocino Coast Bonsai, California, whose business specialises in collecting and growing sequoias for bonsai cultivation, to share his experience, as a grower, with us.

Sequoia, which include some of the largest trees in the world, are divided into three species (but only one genus): the coastal redwood, *Sequoia sempervirens*; the giant redwood or Wellingtonia, *Sequoiadendron giganteum*; and the dawn redwood, *Metasequoia glyptostroboides* from China, where it can be grown as penjing. Although you can grow bonsai from these species, some of their cultivars are especially suitable for bonsai use, notably *Sequoia sempervirens* 'Prostrata' and *Sequoiadendron giganteum* 'Pygmaeum'.

Sequoia are good subjects for bonsai because a young plant will develop the image of a fully grown tree within a reasonably short time. It has a thick bark and the growth can be plucked as you would that of a juniper (*Juniperus*) to encourage density of growth.

Because of its reputation as a tall tree, the giant redwood should be grown in a formal-upright style. In the wild, mature trees have a flat, and sometimes a dead and jinned, apex, partially hollowed trunks caused by fire and short branches, while younger trees have a more traditional, fir-tree-like appearance. Between these two parameters lie plenty of stylistic options, but remember that the trees grow very quickly and need

A giant redwood (*Sequoiadendron giganteum*) in the Golden State Bonsai Federation Collection, San Francisco, California.

A young sequoia under cultivation at the Price Nursery in northern California.

A close-up of some amazing nebari (surface roots), whose formation resembles those of trees growing in the wild.

regular maintenance be it to develop the image or simply keep it in shape.

In their natural environment, sequoia can reach a height of up to 374ft (114m), and their trunks, which are very large in old trees, are in proportion to their height, making them slim-looking trees. It's important for a bonsai-grower to remember this when creating a sequoia bonsai.

A grove of coastal redwoods (*Sequoia sempervirens*) outside San Francisco, California.

Coastal redwoods (*Sequoia sempervirens*)

The coniferous coastal redwoods (*Sequoia sempervirens*) are native to the West Coast of the United States, ranging from southern Oregon to northern California. The world's tallest trees—some reach a height of over 300ft (91m)—their high-altitude foliage traps the coastal fog, and the moisture then drops to the ground, where it is absorbed by the roots. Thriving in acidic soil, these fast-growing trees can gain 3 to 5ft (90cm to 1.5m) a year.

Styles for coastal redwoods

Coastal redwoods (*Sequoia sempervirens*) make good material for bonsai for a number of reasons: they will sprout vigorously on old wood; branches can be developed within a relatively short time; and they will re-root themselves quite easily after having been collected. Although we tend think of sequoia as being the most suitable material for the formal-upright style, they also lend themselves to twin-trunk, clump, forest, raft and informal-upright styles. Trees that were damaged during logging operations and whose wounds have subsequently healed over, also make interesting material.

Collecting coastal redwoods

Coastal redwoods can be collected all year around, as long as the soil is soft enough to enable you to remove them. When collected coastal redwoods are brought home, there are usually no branches on them because, being higher up the tree, they are lost when the trees are reduced

A sequoia in the formal-upright style.

A sequoia in the abstract style, with a hollow trunk.

in size. Some of the trees that we collect may have been 12.2m (40ft) in height before being reduced to 1.2m (4ft). Some have diameters of 30.5 to 35.5cm (12 to 14in), when measured across the soil level, and trunks of 7.6 to 10.2cm (3 to 4in). All of the large roots should be cut off, leaving a few small, feeder roots. When working with larger specimens, the bottom can be cut flat with a chainsaw to enable the tree to fit into a shallow container.

An informal-upright-style sequoia.

Planting coastal redwoods

Plant coastal redwoods in a sandy mix that will encourage good feeder roots to develop. At Mendocino Coast Bonsai, my son Zack and I use a mix of 25 percent river sand, 35 percent lava rock, 30 percent fir bark and 10 percent compost. This mix drains well, yet holds the moisture that the tree needs.

Coastal redwoods respond well to feeding, and we sprinkle a 6-4-2 dry mix (see pages 81 to 83 for more information on feeding ratios) on the soil once a month during the tree's growing period. We also foliar-feed with Miracle-Gro™ or Mira-Acid™ every two weeks during the same period. During the winter months, we apply a 0-10-10, or very low nitrogen, feed monthly, which encourages a lot of new leaf buds to develop in spring.

After about a year, the tree's container should be full of healthy roots, and lots of new sprouts should be growing from the trunk. Branches will develop from these sprouts, and you can start selecting and wiring the branches in the spring after the tree has re-established itself and has grown for a year.

Pinching-out coastal for shape

When you start wiring your selected branches in spring, this is also the time to eliminate any growth that you do not intend to develop into branches. Look for the sprouts that are just starting to become woody and either eliminate them or wire them to shape. If you wait too long, the branch won't develop an attractive, natural bend at the trunk. You can start the ramification process by pinching out lateral growth on the branches. The tree responds well to pinching out when it is actively growing and well fed.

A sequoia in the informal-upright style.

An abstract-style sequoia.

Pruning coastal redwoods

New branches start to harden off and mature in about three years. The pinching-out process should be continued several times a year, even after the branches have developed. New leaf buds will form and grow on the branches, but will become too long within three to four months, when the tree is most active. As you prune the longer growth, new buds will replace it. I normally remove the growth that becomes too long in late spring, mid-summer and fall. (The tree rests during the winter.)

A group planting of sequoia.

A sequoia grown as an informal upright.

This young sequoia is ready for training.

This giant redwood, or Wellingtonia (*Sequoiadendron giganteum*), has been cultivated for twenty years in the United Kingdom by Dan Barton.

The placement of coastal redwoods

Coastal redwoods tolerate hot weather, but should nevertheless be shaded. (They grow more slowly in warmer areas.) As bonsai, coastal redwoods can cope with temperatures as low as around 20°F (6 or 7°C) for short periods, but it is best to protect them if they are likely to be exposed to more than the occasional frost. I visited the Mariposa Grove of giant redwoods (*Sequoiadendron giganteum*) in the Yosemite National Park, California, with my wife, Svetlana, in the early spring of 2000. Although the grove is open all year, the steep access road closes with the first significant snowfall and reopens in late spring, depending on the weather conditions. Most people visit it during the summer (when a free shuttle bus that leaves from the Wawona Store will take you to there).

Photographing the wonders of Yosemite at this time was a breathtaking experience because the rivers were flowing swiftly and the waterfalls were in full cascade; snow still sprinkled the landscape and we were assured of good weather. Both my wife and I are enthusiastic landscape photographers, but as bonsai and tree enthusiasts there was one thing that we both especially wanted to see: the world's biggest trees, the giant redwoods (*Sequoiadendron giganteum*). (The world's tallest trees, coastal redwoods (*Sequoia sempervirens*) are ranged along the Californian coast, but the giant redwoods are the biggest in girth.)

Arriving in Wawona by car, I was dismayed to find the road blocked by a barrier. I had wanted to drive up to the grove, but we now had to walk instead. After walking uphill for about ½mile (1km) along an apparently never-ending, zigzag road, we took a rest. As we did so, someone walking down said in passing, "Don't worry, it's just around the next corner." Heartened by this, we battled on around the next corner, and then the next, and then many more "nexts" until we finally reached the grove. And when we arrived at the grove, the path leading to the giant redwoods still stretched ahead. It was easy to follow, thankfully, and because it had started to snow lightly, no one else was around: it seemed as though we were exploring virgin territory,

The tiny figure that you can see among these giant redwood (*Sequoiadendron giganteum*) roots is not a gnome, but my wife, Svetlana.

A grove of giant redwoods (*Sequoiadendron giganteum*).

despite the signs and occasional explanatory billboards telling us about the giant redwoods.

We finally reached a flat, open space and saw something looming ahead, huge and tall, with its head in the clouds. Then something magical happened: the clouds cleared, the sun came out for a while, and there it was, the Grizzly Giant, the biggest living thing we'd ever seen. The circumference of its lower branch was as large as many of the trees around us. Its base was so huge that when Svetlana walked to the tree so that I could take a photograph of her standing in front of the tree's full height, she was but a speck in my viewfinder. We were in the presence of a tree that was at least three thousand years old. This was one of the biggest trees in the world and astonishingly gigantic. In the silence, specks of snow swirled softly in the air. It was a simultaneously spectacular and emotional experience for both of us. And then the clouds drew in to cover the apex of this ancient tree, and it seemed as though the Grizzly Giant had gone back to sleep again.

A dawn redwood (*Metasequoia glyptostroboides*) pictured at Hoyt Arboretum, in Oregon, USA, in winter.

A dawn redwood (*Metasequoia glyptostroboides*) displaying its spring foliage at Hoyt Arboretum.

The dawn redwood (*Metasequoia glyptostroboides*)

The dawn redwood (*Metasequoia glyptostroboides*), which is native to Szechwan, China, was discovered by Shigeru Miki in 1941 and introduced to the international community in 1948.

A deciduous conifer, its height ranges from between 69 and 98ft (21 and 30m). It has a pyramid shape when juvenile, and a flat top when mature. When it is young, its bark is reddish-brown, but this darkens, develops deep fissures and is exfoliated in strips when it matures. The needles grow opposite each other, can be straight or slightly curved, reach a length of around ½in (15mm) and are bright green on the upper side and pale green on the underside. The tree bears a solitary female cone measuring around 1in (2.5cm) in diameter (instead of cone clusters).

The dawn redwood will thrive in temperate and northern climates that are free of serious frost and enjoys a sunny position. Easy to transplant, it grows best in a moist, well-drained, slightly acidic soil.

My wife, Svetlana, standing at the base of the Grizzly Giant.

The summer foliage of one of Hoyt Arboretum's dawn redwoods (*Metasequoia glyptostroboides*).

A young dawn redwood (*Metasequoia glyptostroboides*) at Hoyt Arboretum.

One of Hoyt Arboretum's dawn redwoods (*Metasequoia glyptostroboides*).

The trunk of the dawn redwood (*Metasequoia glyptostroboides*) is quite different from those of the coastal redwood (Sequoia sempervirens) and giant redwood (*Sequoiadendron giganteum*).

The needles and cones of a dawn redwood (*Metasequoia glyptostroboides*).

One of the differences between the Swamp Cypress (*Taxodium distichum*) and the dawn redwood (*Metasequoia glyptostroboides*) is that the latter has thinner needles.

A young Dawn redwood (*Metasequoia glyptostroboides*) bonsai that is being developed into a formal-upright style.

Checklist

Soil for redwoods: coastal, giant and dawn redwoods grow best in a moist, well-drained, slightly acidic soil. Use a mix of 40 percent Akadama™, 20 percent organic and 40 percent aggregate or grit, or a mix of 20 percent Akadama™, 20 percent Kanuma™, 20 percent organic and 40 percent aggregate or grit. See also page 196, in the section on coastal redwoods, for another mix suitable for coastal (and giant) redwoods.

Watering: mist redwoods in the morning and evening in order to keep the humidity up as they live in moist areas, Water as you would any other bonsai. Keep soil damp..

Feeding: redwoods respond well to feeding. See page 196, in the section for coastal redwoods, for more detailed instructions.

Summer care: provide redwoods with some protection from strong sunlight.

Winter care: protect redwoods from frost in winter. It's not that they cannot withstand frost, but when they are in a pot that contains only a small amount of soil, frost can cause a tree's roots to become too moist. In addition, frost can seriously damage the soft tips of young leaves.

Design class

The third part of the book starts with an explanation of techniques and styles and then shows systematic photo essays on many techniques of how a bonsai is created. While some of the demonstrations are by me, I have opened up to the reader other artist's methods of making bonsai by showing the work of Bonsai Masters from around the world

Design class focuses on the practical aspects of how to make a bonsai. The material is of the highest quality and these Bonsai Masters demonstrate their art in a clear and easy-to-understand way. This unique section shows a wider aspect of bonsai creation from different teachers and artists living in other parts of the world.

Carving and refining a Juniperus chinensis 'San José', by Michael Persiano (United States)

Michael Persiano, a classically trained bonsai artist, is fast becoming a leading international Bonsai Master. He spends a lot of time researching his subjects and his teaching is clear and easy to follow – the sign of a good teacher. His own bonsai collection is well known and comprises some of the United States' finest. I asked him to create a tree for *Bonsai school* that would cover a number of techniques.

The ascent of the White Dragon

Specimen: a forty-year-old, field-grown *Juniperus chinensis* 'San José'.
Measurements: trunk diameter: 6in (15.25cm); height: 36in (91.4cm); width: 30in (76.2cm).
Notable features: shari, jinn, hollow, brushed bark.
Tools used: a Foredom™ power tool; an AutoMach™, a selection of Masakuni™ hand tools.
Wire selected: aluminum (1-5mm).

Selecting the material

From the beginning of the 1990's, this *Juniperus chinensis* 'San José' stirred my passion for bonsai design. From beneath a wild canopy of foliage, slightly burned by the harsh winds of a retreating winter, what would soon be known as the 'White Dragon' called to be awakened from decades of sleep to embark on a new beginning.

My goal as an artist was to create a bonsai that would reflect my leanings towards classical Japanese design principles while also accommodating what I refer to as 'contemporary' design elements, that is, design features that are not strictly aligned with commonly accepted design concepts. I would also approach this tree as a long-term project, so speed would not enter into the design solution.

The initial design process

After studying the un-styled specimen for several days and envisaging its ultimate design, I selected the front and initiated what would become a multi-year styling and carving endeavor. Unlike some trees that lend themselves to a seemingly mature appearance after the initial design, I knew that this 'San José' would require the elimination of imi-eda (non-essential branches) to survive what would become an extensive exercise in tissue reduction.

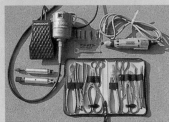

3 The initially wired tree was set up for a period of long-term growth. This would not be an overnight project.

4 The tools used included, from top left to bottom right, a Foredom™ power tool, an AutoMach™ and a set of stainless-steel Masakuni™ tools (the stainless steel tools were a gift from Masakuni San's son).

1 The *Juniperus chinensis* 'San José' before its initial styling.

2 After carving the tree, the wood was allowed to dry out for a period of one week. I subsequently applied a mixture of lime sulfur and white watercolor paint to create contrasts between the dead wood, bark and verdant foliage.

The first phase of the carving work took approximately eight hours to execute, using the Foredom™ power tool. This rotational carving device's effectiveness lies somewhere between that of a Makita™ die-grinder in its wood-chewing power and a Dremel™ tool for precision carving. Numerous hand pieces accommodated the use of various high-speed carving tips, wire-brush attachments and sanding cones.

In the summer of the next year, I introduced the use of an AutoMach™. The AutoMach™, which is produced in Tokyo, Japan, is a pressure-sensitive chisel that allows the artist to create interesting details in carved areas using an assortment of chisel attachments. (Photograph 2 presents the initially carved trunk. Photograph 3 reveals the initially styled canopy of the tree after a season of superfeeding. Photograph 4 shows an assortment of the tools that were selected for the project.)

It is important to mention that the preservation of carved wood is critical to the health of the tree. Trees are all too often carved and then left in the hands of nature. Although this can create an interesting natural touch, the decay that inevitably follows is unnecessary and can easily be avoided.

After-treatment and styling

After carving the White Dragon, I decided to experiment with a product called MinWax™ wood-hardener. After applying the lime-sulfur solution and allowing it to dry thoroughly, I applied MinWax™ wood-hardener to eliminate the chance of decay caused by exposure to the elements developing. Today, after nearly thirteen years, the tree's carved areas remain intact and quite solid. The annual application of this product has worked not only for me, but also for many other US bonsai artists who have adopted this product over the past decade. If you cannot obtain MinWax™ wood-hardener, however, use either a wood-preservation or a wood-hardening product that is absorbed by wood and experiment with it on inconsequential material before applying it to your precious trees. Be careful to avoid applying the product to live tissue.

It is gratifying for me to see that the 'San José' as shown in photograph 2 has evolved into what I view today as being a hybrid of contemporary and classical bonsai design. Rather than attempting to categorize this tree during the design process, I allowed my mind to wander independently of most design conventions. I imagined swelling sap lines, chiseled textures in the carved wood, a hollow running through the tree and reddish-brown bark rising into a majestic canopy of verdant growth. Soon after photograph 2 was taken, I wired the entire tree and then splayed some branches into more horizontal placements to encourage the development of pagoda-like shelves of foliage.

One of the significant structural challenges of working with this 'San José' was the development of a branch on the lower right-hand side to support the integration of the earth, humanity and heaven motif, a classical and recurrent element in bonsai that would lend itself nicely to my anticipated design. To achieve this critical positioning, it was necessary to saw, and then split, one of the forward-pointing branches and then bend it into position using 5mm aluminum wire. My decision to use aluminum was based both on the initial brittleness of the tree's branches and my intention to leave the wire on the tree for a longer period of time than is usual. In effect, some of the branches were "air-wired" (loosely wired) to avoid damaging the bark while accommodating a long period of placement on the tree.

Superfeeding the White Dragon
To advance the rapid growth of the canopy after the removal of the non-essential branches, I used what I refer to as "superfeeding." Superfeeding is a methodical approach that I use to accelerate growth in immature specimens that have yet to achieve their design potential. In brief, the White Dragon was potted in a fast-draining soil and then given a 20-20-20 chemical fertilizer every seven to ten days, organic cakes during the spring and summer and foliar feeds every two weeks during the spring and summer. As a result of the accelerated growth in the root pad and canopy, the tree was repotted every two years. Photograph 5 shows the tree well into its development cycle, approximately nine years after the initial styling.

5 By the summer of 1999, the White Dragon is well on its way to becoming a beautiful bonsai, but major design decisions remain to be made if the tree is to achieve a more sublime level of expression.

Design advancement and detailing
Trees with outstanding potential constantly challenge the artist to explore new ways of releasing their hidden beauty in order to elevate the bonsai creation to a more sublime level of artistic expression. The White Dragon constantly challenged me to support its bonsai ascent.

Having allowed the White Dragon to grow with only minimal maintenance during the mid- to late 1990's, I decided to revisit the tree and advance its design.

During the summer of 2001, I decided to:
· eliminate the lowest branch on the left-hand side;
· eliminate the lowest branch on the right-hand side;
· reduce the density of the foliage pads;
· reduce the density of the crown;
· reduce the width of the canopy;
· refine the carving and re-treat the

wood with lime sulfur;
· remove the old loose juvenile bark to reveal the reddish-brown color of the fresh bark;
· wire the tree as required to achieve a new appearance of harmony;
· place the restyled tree in a more shallow pot that better frames the creation.

The outcome of the 2001 redesign effort is presented as the final image in this chapter (photograph 11). The movement of the tree has been intensified by the elimination of the two lowest branches. The thinning of the foliage, the reduction in the width of the tree canopy, the brushing of the bark and the repositioning of key branches has opened up the tree and allowed the viewer to enjoy the beauty of the wood that climbs sinuously through the canopy of the tree. The newly selected pot emphasises the beauty of the tree's bark and the reworking of the carved elements in the design provides the viewer with a stark contrast between the living and the dead in this creation.

6 The White Dragon before its refinement.

7 Although I also used trimming shears to restyle the canopy, I pinched out leaf buds when possible to minimize the browning that frequently appears on junipers after pruning.

8 I removed several years of accumulated bark to emphasise the beautiful, reddish-brown colour of the tree's younger bark.

9 Carving the essence of the White Dragon.

11 The White Dragon pictured in October 2001.

10 A close-up of the White Dragon's head. Note the strong, well-formed sap lines that feed the canopy of the tree.

The White Dragon's future

The White Dragon is an integral part of me and represents both my earlier days and my most recent efforts in the art of bonsai. After having been nurtured by the earth and then released by the wandering hands of the artist, the White Dragon has begun its poetic ascent through time.

The future of the tree points towards a further reduction of the canopy's width and an emphasis on its movement to the right. As the tree's branch structure continues to develop, additional branches will be removed to expose the workings of its essential branch elements. All of this will take place over a long time.

As an artist, I have found this 'San José' to be one of the most demanding subjects that I have had the opportunity to work on during my thirteen years of practising the art of bonsai. As an exercise in creation, this specimen has taught me well. It is my hope that the White Dragon will continue to advance my skills throughout the years as I continue to release its beauty and, in the process, document what may very well come to be known as the "legendary ascent of the White Dragon."

Michael Persiano.

Styling a *Juniperus chinensis* 'San José',
by William Valavanis (United States)

William Valavanis is the founder of the International Bonsai Arboretum in Rochester, New York, as well as the publisher and editor of *International Bonsai Magazine*. He studied bonsai in Japan with leading Bonsai Masters Toshio Kawamoto, Kakutaro Komuo and Kyuzo Murata, and is today an internationally known bonsai artist and teacher. The author of many articles, he has designed this particular class for *Bonsai school* to cover those techniques that he wishes to share with you. Many specimens from his own collection of superb bonsai are featured in *Bonsai school*.

The initial shaping and potting
The *Juniperus chinensis* 'San José' that I selected for this demonstration was grown from a cutting by Lee Hopkins, of Flowerwood Farms, Pennsylvania, approximately ten years ago in 1991. The tree was grown in a field for nine years and was then planted in a large container in May 2000. I undertook the juniper's initial shaping and potting on 5 July 2001.

FIG. 1

FIG. 2

I liked this 'San José' juniper because of its continuous trunk line, which showed a good, strong taper with diagonal movement, a type of movement that, according to my concept of classical bonsai design, I find pleasing. I selected the front because the trunk was leaning forwards and because it displayed the diagonal movement more clearly (Figures 1, 2).

The back of the tree had a heavy, curved branch growing upward. Although the branch was interesting, it was quite thick and interfered with my planned design. The trunk movement leaned towards the back when viewed from this side.

The first step in the creation of a classical bonsai is to find the surface roots and determine the base of the tree. The surface

FIG. 3

roots were approximately 2in (5cm) below the original soil surface. The tree had been potted a little deeper than normal to provide stability and to allow the development of heavy surface roots (Figure 3).

After finding the base of the trunk and the surface roots, the tree was placed in a shallow container for shaping. The trunk angle was raised to make the upper trunk curves more visible. Although extreme slanting trunks are considered exotic and unusual, I prefer designs that are more dynamic and the original slanting style was too horizontal for my taste.

There were five lower branches that were not necessary for the design of the 'San José' bonsai. I decided to transform these into dead wood rather than remove them

FIG. 4

FIG. 5

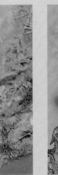

FIG. 7

FIG. 11

completely at this stage. They may provide interest in the future and can be removed at any time. Although they were shortened, they were still allowed to remain extra long. Their bark was crushed with a pair of pliers to make its removal easier. The tip of each dead branch was then split with concave-pruners to shorten it and create taper (Figures 4, 5).

These dead-wood branches, which will probably be removed in the future, are positioned quite low on the rear of the bonsai. They will be treated with lime sulfur to whiten their color and prevent decay. It is important to realise that these branches—and the entire tree for that matter—are young, being only about ten years old. Young wood generally has wide annual growth rings, which tend to decay. By contrast, old, collected trees, junipers in particular, generally have close annual rings, which are excellent for creating dead wood that will not decay.

The interesting heavy branch on top was removed next. It was first shortened, then

FIG. 8

FIG. 12

FIG. 9

FIG. 13

split and part of the wood peeled away to create taper, texture and a smaller size. Although this heavy branch is not visible from the front, it, too, was transformed into a dead-wood element (Figures 6–13).

The heavy lower branch on the left-hand side was removed next. I did not hesitate to remove this branch, partly because it was heavy and a bit low, but, more importantly, because it was growing in a different direction to the

FIG. 6

FIG. 10

main movement of the trunk line. It additionally appeared to be growing on the inside of the main trunk bend, thus spoiling the movement. This branch was transformed into dead wood using the same techniques of shortening, peeling and, in addition, carving to reduce its final size. The final shaping was done using both hand chisels and an automatic power carver.

FIG. 14

FIG. 15

FIG. 16

FIG. 17

The first step in the creation of this bonsai had now been completed. My total concentration on the overall design, combined with undertaking the techniques needed create the dead wood, had absorbed three uninterrupted hours. The time spent on

FIG. 18

creating the dead wood may seem excessive, but when inspecting the carved areas closely, their fine detail suggests that the branches were removed and weathered by nature, not by a bonsai artist. Having carved all of the dead-wood areas, the wiring and shaping of the large branches began. When looking at the bonsai from the front, there were several branches on the left and only a few on the

FIG. 19

right. A dynamic design could have been created using the negative space on the right, but I decide to create a more classical, asymmetrical design. I therefore needed

FIG. 20

FIG. 21

FIG. 22

FIG. 24

FIG. 26

more pronounced curve. I immediately stopped bending it and applied a cut paste

juvenile needles, while the 'Shimpaku' juniper, for example, has dominant mature needles.

Before wiring each branch, a wire brush was used to remove the old, flaky bark and reveal the younger, colorful bark beneath it. This practice also allows the younger bark to receive better light and air circulation, thereby promoting a thicker trunk (Figure 22).

The shaped 'San José' after wiring, trimming and shaping, but before potting. Final adjustments will be made after the tree has been potted, and those will in turn be refined after the tree has recovered from the shaping and potting processes (Figure. 23).

another large branch on the right. Fortunately, there were two branches on the left that I could use. The one on top was wired using heavy copper wire and brought from the back to the right side of the bonsai. This created the basic design that I was trying to achieve. After completely wiring the branch and

FIG. 25

FIG. 23

repositioning it on the right, it was tied to one of the dead-wood stumps with light wire to anchor it in place.(Figure 14–17).

Numbers 6 and 8 heavy copper wire were used to shape the large branches and the top section of the trunk (Figure. 18–19).

The top trunk section cracked slightly when I was bending it to create a

wound sealant to prevent the wound from drying out. To make sure that it would live, I decided to leave the upper trunk relatively straight for now and to reshape it later. After wiring the larger branches, the ends were trimmed to size and then the smaller branches were wired. As each small branch was wired, it was trimmed to promote a tighter foliage mass. (Figure. 20–21).

Many cultivars of *Juniperus*, including 'San José', have both juvenile and mature needles. After drastic pruning, they generally produce a flush of juvenile-needle growth, indicating a vigorous recovery from the shaping process. Continual pinching out will encourage the dominant type of needle to grow, and 'San José' generally has dominant

FIG. 27

FIG. 28

FIG. 29

FIG. 30

FIG. 31

FIG. 32

FIG. 33

This juniper was field grown for approximately nine years and was pot grown for only one season. However, it was grown by an experienced bonsai-grower, who skilfully pruned the root system in the field and before the juniper was first potted in May 2000. Note the lack of heavy, thick roots and the profusion of fine feeder roots (Figure 24).

It now remained to decide which of the three containers that I'd assembled would suit the juniper best.

The first container was of high quality and was made by the Yamaaki Kiln in the Japanese city of Tokoname. This oval container was a good choice, but slightly large. Although I rather liked its "belt" design, I felt that the entire design was slightly too heavy (Figure 25).

The second container was a rectangular, high-quality import from China. The extremely smooth finish of the light-gray clay was attractive. However, I felt that the rectangular shape, even with its softened corners, was too rigid for a trunk with a strong bend. The container also looked small when compared with the existing foliage mass, which would grow larger with the correct care (Figure 26).

The third container that I considered was a modified-oval-shaped, high-quality Chinese import, light brown in color and with a very smooth finish (Figure 27). I thought that

its prominent feet helped to make this heavy-looking container appear lighter. I prefer deeper containers to shallow ones. (And bonsai grown in the world's colder areas tend to overwinter better in deeper containers.) When using deeper containers, I often use a slightly smaller size to compensate for the heavy appearance of the surface area.

Having made sure that the root ball would fit into it, I decided to pot the juniper into the irregular-oval-shaped Chinese container. After preparing the container by using screen to cover the drainage holes, I selected a number 12 copper wire with which to anchor the tree into the pot. I removed further soil from the root ball to make sure that a fine network of fibrous roots would come into contact with the new, bone-dry bonsai soil. (If this doesn't happen, an "interface" problem may occur and the new roots may not penetrate the new soil.)

Having placed a layer of coarse bonsai soil on the bottom of the container, I added finer-grade soil. Because the trunk movement leads from left to right, I carefully positioned the bottom of the trunk slightly left of centre to create an asymmetrical design. I then tied the tree into position to prevent it from moving and added more soil to fill the container. Using a pair of bamboo chopsticks, I gently firmed down the dry soil around the roots. Finally, I added a combination of different species of fine-textured moss to act as ground cover to prevent soil erosion, maintain the soil's moisture level and lend a natural appearance to the planting (Figure 28–32).

The completed juniper bonsai pictured at the end of an eight-hour day (Figure 33). Some final adjustments were made to the branches and foliage masses after the bonsai was potted, but before it was watered and soaked with Superthrive™, a transplanting aid. After its soaking, the newly potted bonsai was positioned out of direct sunlight and wind for one week. Then it was placed under a shade cloth which is usually made of net and reduces the intensity of the sun. Obtainable from most garden centers, this provided the tree with 55 percent shade for six weeks.

The bonsai recovered quite quickly because of the timing of its styling and correct aftercare. Although bonsai artists tend to shape most species in early spring, before growth begins, I have had excellent results after drastically pruning, shaping and transplanting junipers (and many other species as well) during an active growing season.

During the juniper's recovery period, the foliage was misted daily, and sometimes twice on hot summer days. Light fertilizer applications were provided two weeks after the transplanting. Only three small twigs died during the recovery period as a result of the shaping process. The cracked upper-trunk section never showed any signs of stress and quickly produced new growth.

When the juniper was placed outdoors and exposed to full sun in mid-September, the design was refined. The heavy wire in the cracked upper-trunk section was removed and reapplied very carefully. The top was then shaped according to my original design concept. It did not crack this time. Having cared for the bonsai on a daily basis, and having studied photographs of it, I then shortened the branches on the left-hand side. These had lent a symmetrical appearance to the design, but I wanted to create an asymmetrical balance. In addition, I continued lightly to pinch out new growth during the growing season.

After looking at the bonsai through the camera's viewfinder at the time of this final studio shot, slight adjustments were made. Looking at photographs of a bonsai (black and white photographs are best), or through a camera lens, often reveals details that are not immediately apparent when you look at the bonsai itself (Figure 34).

With continued pinching-out and correct care in the years to come, this 'San José' will further its development as a fine-quality, classical bonsai.

William Valavanis.

FIG. 34

Slanting a *Juniperus prostrata* to create the correct angle,

by Salvatore Liporace (Italy)

Salvatore Liporace is a bonsai master with an impressive reputation for producing masterpieces of bonsai. A student of Masahiko Kimura, one of the worlds leading Japanese Bonsai Masters, Salvatore runs a successful international bonsai school in Milan, Italy, at which many bonsai artists from around the world have learned their craft, including Patrizia Capellaro). I have spent a lot of time with Salvatore in Milan, and we often meet when we teach at international events. Indeed, I organised the workshop at which the following demonstration took place.

The material used was a *Juniperus prostrata* that had been collected from a planting area in a shopping center that was being demolished. Having been planted when it was about ten years old, it had then spent approximately thirty years in the planting bed. After it was removed from the shopping centre, it was nurtured for three years prior to this styling to restore its health and vigor. The tree is owned by Robert Atkinson, a bonsai teacher from the north-east of England, and he and I took these photographs of Salvatore styling the tree.

1 The tree before the styling was carried out. It had been in its pot for two years having spent one year in the ground prior to potting up.

2 Viewing the tree from the side gave Salvatore an idea.

3 On turning the tree a little more, Salvatore determined that the side branch could possibly serve as the apex.

4 Salvatore studied the existing apex and checked the health of the tree. Robert, looking on, was not entirely convinced that Salvatore's plan would work.

5 A final look at the tree . . .

6 . . . and then off with its head! It is now abundantly clear what no one, apart from Salvatore, had noticed before —the tree needed to be reduced and angled severely to create the shape that had been hidden. That is the difference between masters and students.

7 The other side of the tree presents a better front because this branch, which has been stripped of its foliage, appears to be advancing towards the viewer, making a better image than if it were retreating.

8 Salvatore instructs Robert to strip off the bark to make a large jinn.

9 Robert's next task is to soak some raffia in ice-cold water to make it both easier to apply and to encourage it to tighten as it warms up and dries out. (Although rubber tape could have been used as an alternative to raffia, none was available at the time.)

10 Every part of the remaining branch is enclosed in a thick layer of raffia to protect the wood while it is being bent.

11 The foliage must be wired before the styling is carried out, and the pot must be well supported during this operation.

12 After every main branch has been enclosed in raffia and wired, Salvatore studies the tree to determine the best placement of the foliage.

13 Work now starts in earnest on the bottom part of the tree.

14 Robert continues to remove the areas of bark that Salvatore has marked.

15 The next layer of foliage is styled.

213

16 Excess growth is trimmed off.

17 The top is now wired into place.

18 The foliage pads are separated to enable them to develop correctly. Robert has applied jinn seal (lime sulfur) to prevent any mould or bacteria from taking hold.

19 The newly styled juniper four hours later. Salvatore has wrought an amazing change.

20 A year later, when the jinn had dried out, Robert first soaked, steamed and heated them and then produced a more delicate shape by bending them downwards, into the body of the image, to reflect the foliage mass. (Salvatore had suggested either doing this or cutting off some of the jinn at a later date.) The bonsai pot is Korean and mid-grey in color. The foliage is starting to develop well and, in response to Robert's steady hand, the bonsai should become a masterpiece within the next four years.

Refining a yew (*Taxus*),
by Craig Coussins (Scotland)

This yew (*Taxus*) was collected by my friend, Alan Dorling, in Wales, and the first time I saw it, I was immediately struck by its beautiful trunk and nebari (surface-root structure). I was judging the local club exhibit at the annual event that Alan and Kevin Bailey organise in North Wales, and Alan had brought this tree along. Although I devoured the image immediately and desperately wanted to work on it, it would be four years before Alan gave in to my constant nagging and the tree came into my possession.

The tree was very low and extremely broad when it was growing in the ground, and we estimated its age to be over two hundred years. Centuries of having been grazed on by sheep and rabbits had kept the yew short, but it had expanded in width. It was growing in a pot within two years of having been collected, and was in its sixth year of development at the time that this series of photographs was taken by Yerbury Studios.

I had previously styled the tree to define its structure, but now needed to refine its shape. The pot that Alan had planted it in was a training pot (photograph 1). We used a temporary pot during its styling, but the tree may need to be planted in a darker, more bronzed container as it develops a denser foliage structure.

The essence of my thought processes when designing a bonsai is that I am trying to create an image that looks like a miniature tree. If it doesn't look like a tree, it isn't a bonsai (in my humble opinion, of course). That is my philosophy. If you want anything more complicated than that, as far as I'm concerned, life's too short!

1 The tree pictured shortly after it was collected.

2 Four years later, and the tree is ready to take its first steps along the road to becoming a bonsai. (The basic techniques for styling a yew are outlined in the styling I did that appears on pages 154 to 155). This is the front of the tree.

3 This is the back of the tree.

4 This is the left-hand side of the tree.

5 This is the right-hand side of the tree.

6 Having examined the base of the tree to ascertain what I could remove, I started wiring all of the branches.

7 Although I continued to wire everything, there is a heavy branch on the left-hand side of the tree whose thickness will need to be reduced once the foliage has developed sufficiently.

8 This photograph illustrates how I wired to the tip of every branch and twig.

9 I have now shaped this side of the tree to create a soft foliage pad.

10 I wired all of the foliage using the single wiring technique. I also removed all of the sucker growth on the trunk. This is the most important area: the apex.

11 Working from the base of the apex, I start to arrange all of the material in flat planes, being careful not to force the image until I can see exactly what I have (or haven't) got to work with.

12 Using the image of an upturned saucer as my design template, the next step is to shape the foliage pads carefully.

13 A view of the front of the yew.

14 The left-hand side of the yew.

15 The yew's right-hand side.

16 A view of the back of the yew.

17 The yew's image from the front.

One of my large maples (*Acer*), which started life as a bonsai as a bare trunk following the reduction of a mature tree. It now has a huge base (I call it Elephant's Foot'), measures 5ft (1.5m) in height and resides in the "Japanese Gardens" in Devon. The tiny tree is a miniature form of *Serissa foetides*.

Refining an American larch (*Larix laricina*),
by Reiner Goebel (Canada)

Reiner Goebel has created one of the finest collections of native trees in North America. A very serious and confident Bonsai Master, I am delighted that he has joined the *Bonsai school* faculty to share some of his considerable knowledge with you.

The American larch: understanding the species in nature and recreating it in miniature

The American larch is a member of the pine family. It grows in most parts of Canada and the north-eastern United States. In Canada, it ranges from the Mackenzie river area in the Northwest Territories through northern British Columbia, Alberta and Saskatchewan, Manitoba and Ontario (except for its southern-most areas), Quebec and the Maritime provinces. In the United States, its range includes north-eastern Minnesota, almost all of Wisconsin, a northern strip of Indiana, all of Michigan, the north-eastern part of Ohio, and the New England states north of a line drawn from about Erie, Pennsylvania, to New York City.

Once they have become established in bonsai pots, American larches form beautiful root systems (indeed, their surface roots may have to be thinned out periodically). The bark of mature trees is very thick and corky and is similar to that of the Japanese black pine (*Pinus Thunbergii*). Larches are usually well branched and, because they grow quickly, their branch structure develops good ramification within a few years. Before the new needles emerge, the impression of ramification is intensified because the fat little leaf buds can look like branch stubs. Flowering on larches is particularly conspicuous in those years in which they produce an abundance of purple flowers, and the cones are in keeping with the tree's somewhat dainty appearance. Larches are attractive to view in all seasons, being well ramified when bare, having graceful spring foliage held in tiny rosettes of grayish-green needles that develop into mature pads of foliage by summer, and turning a golden-yellow by late falll.

The following series of photographs gives a pictorial history of one of those larches, which was originally collected in the spring of 1987 from a fairly open, mixed forest of spruce, jack pine, eastern white cedar and larch in northern Ontario.

1 The tree pictured a few days after it was collected in April 1987. Because the soil in which these trees grow is very shallow, even freshly collected trees can usually be planted into growing pots right away, although not always with the tree's front positioned correctly. Here, the front is on the narrow side of the pot because the tree's root system could not be accommodated in any other way.

2 The tree pictured in June 1988. The amount of new growth bodes well for its survival.

3 The tree in October 1988.

4 Because it had done so well during the previous growing season, I felt confident enough to repot the tree in 1989. Although the tree had a well-developed root system, it was very one-sided, and I therefore had to prop up the trunk with a piece of wood.

5 I was able to remove the prop in the spring of 1990.

6 The tree was repotted again in the spring of 1992, this time into a more shallow container.

7 Shortly after the tree was repotted, it was stolen by burglars while I was away, along with about twenty-five others. The burglars failed to get it over a fence, however, and the damage that can be seen in this photograph, which was taken in August 1992, was caused when they dropped it. When a friend found it, the top was still loosely attached to the tree, but despite his remedial measures, the broken part withered and died. I was heart-broken because I had really liked the elegant sweep of the trunk and felt that the tree was now worthless. My friend convinced me that it was worth making the best of what was left, however.

8 and 9 In the spring of 1993 I wired up a branch in what was now the top foliage pad to create a new apex.

10 The tree was again repotted in the spring of 1996.

11 All of the foliage is in the process of filling in nicely by July 1996.

12 The tree was again repotted in 1999, in the same pot, and the foliage pads were wired and positioned a little lower.

13 The tree pictured in the autumn of 2000.

14 The tree as it appeared in the summer of 2001.

Developing a fire tree (Euonymus),
by Reiner Goebel (Canada)

The fire tree (Euonymus) is one of the most colorful types of plant material that can be transformed into bonsai. Reiner Goebel designed the lovely bonsai that features in this series of photographs, and the story of how he developed it is an instructive lesson.

The advantages of Euonymus for bonsai
The Euonymus, whose common names include fire tree, burning bush and spindle tree, offers a number of benefits to the bonsai-grower, as follows.

· Hardiness in climates that average a minimum temperature ranging from -29.2 to 33.8°F (-34 to -1°C).

· The development of beautiful bark in young specimens.

· Ease of growth in bonsai pots.

· Old wood that buds back well.

· Naturally small leaves that can be further reduced when grown as bonsai.

· Bright-orange berries in autumn and winter.

· Scarlet leaves in fall.

There are some points, however, that you should be aware of, as follows.

· It needs full sun in order to develop good fall foliage.

· It requires lots of moisture in spring and summer and will therefore need a deeper pot than some other trees.

· Branch die-back can occur.

· Elongation of only one shoot's growth occurs during one season.

· The branch development is slower than in other trees.

l The branches need to be wired very carefully to avoid damaging the leaf buds, which are more delicate than those of other trees.

1 Photographed in 1999, this dwarf winged spindle tree (*Euonymus alata compacta*) had been grown in the ground since 1992 and had been regularly pruned to a predetermined shape. The main problem that I had with this tree was die-back when new growth was beginning to develop in spring, although this did not affect the whole branch, just the new growth.

2 The young tree, pictured in 1994, is developing its ramification.

5 The colorful crop of berries that adorned the tree in December 1996.

6 As the tree starts to display its autumn color in September 2000, the image has become a well-developed one.

4 The tree pictured in the fall of 1996. This photograph shows the magnificent color that has inspired one of the common names of the *Euonymus*, burning bush.

3 The tree as it appeared in July 1995.

7 The tree pictured in October 2001.

8 Another of my *Euonymus* bonsai.

Part 4

Pots Pots Pots

Bonsai and penjing are not simply just a matter of growing plants, bonsai also require an understanding of a number of other associated areas, all of which come together to create the bonsai whole.

In this final part of *Bonsai school*, you will learn how bonsai pots are chosen, made, and understood; gain a more detailed insight into bonsai tools; and, finally, be introduced to the viewing stones that can be displayed alongside bonsai or penjing as indications of the tree's native landscape.

This chapter focuses on three areas of interest associated with bonsai: pots, tools, and viewing stones. The sections on bonsai pots and potters provide an in-depth look at shapes and glazes and why it is important to find the right pot to match the style, species, and size of a bonsai. A detailed overview of bonsai tools follows, after which the art of displaying bonsai in stone landscapes, along with the artistry inherent in these viewing stones, is described.

Stories in glaze: the art of the bonsai-pot-maker

Apart from the trees themselves, pot-making is probably the most important element of bonsai. In this section, I examine the work of Gordon Duffett, dating from when he started making pots until his semi-retirement. Alan Harriman, who continues to work as a well-respected bonsai potter, then gives us his thoughts on pot design. Also included in this section are images taken from my own collection of antique Chinese pots.

Although there are, of course, potters working throughout China, Korea, and Japan, I shall concentrate on non-Oriental potters in *Bonsai school*. Gordon Duffett and Allan Harriman are just two of the leading British exponents of this art form, and some other excellent potters working outside the Far East include: Dan Barton (England), Ian Baillie (Scotland), the potters of the Walsall Studios (England), Derek Aspinall (England), William Vlaanderan (The Netherlands), Peter Krebs (Germany), Brian Albright (England) Petra Engelke Tomlinson (England and Germany), Jim Barrett (the United States), Alan and Beverly Vanz, of Vanz Pots (New Zealand), Dean Hastie and Noel Plowman (New Zealand), Mario Remaggio, of Certre Pots (Italy), Dasu Pots (Iowa, United States), Max

Braverman (who works in Seattle, United States), and Michael Hagedorn (United States).

The manufacture of bonsai pots in Europe is a relatively recent development, and some of the earliest European bonsai pots of the late 1940s through to the early 1960s were made by such noted ceramicists as Lucy Rie and Bernard Leach (who learned some of his craft from Japanese master potters). It was the study of ancient Chinese glazes that particularly interested Gordon Duffett, the first professional bonsai potter working in Britain, and it was his influence that inspired many of today's British potters.

The art of Gordon Duffett

For many years now, the makers of bonsai pots have been trying to recapture the ancient glazes of China. Some do it well, others not. The mark of a good pot-maker is not how he or she makes the pot, but whether they create a balanced image that will work with the tree. To explain further, a pot should be a frame for a bonsai and should not distract your attention from a tree. Although a bonsai pot should therefore be unassuming, when you look at it closely, you should be able to read the story that is written in glaze or in the elegance of its design.

I first met Gordon Duffett in 1983, after buying two of his pots at the second British Bonsai Convention. Although they were very heavy, their glaze color was outstanding. (I still have the one that features in photographs 1a, 1b, and 1c. Its gray-and-cream glaze appears to drip off the lower edge). Gordon soon discovered how to make lighter-weight pots with equally excellent glaze colors, however, and before long I had amassed a large collection of them. In fact, Gordon started making pots for me, to my design as well as his, but because his were always better, I usually went along with his suggestions.

1a

1b

1c

I never worried about buying a pot to complement a tree, but instead bought a pot and then found a tree to match it. Many of my early pots, along with most of my bonsai, were stolen from my garden in 1991, and I spent two years searching for the gang that had robbed me of so many years of my work, as well as my collection of Duffett pots. I eventually identified the thieves, but although I recovered most of my trees, the pots were lost, having apparently been thrown off a bridge. I started to collect Gordon's pots once more, however, and some of his traditional and original designs for my collection feature within these pages.

Gordon penned the following words for an exhibition of the work of British and European pot-makers that I organized for the Federation of British Bonsai Societies in 2000. At this exhibition, Gordon sold me many of his early pots, including his first. Gordon rarely makes pots now, and should you ever have the opportunity to own one of his wonderful works of art, don't hesitate to buy it because you'll rarely find anything comparable.

As a collector of bonsai, I have always been interested in making pots for my own trees, particularly as when I first started to collect bonsai there weren't many pots to be had. This interest in making pots has grown, together with that of painting and the visual arts in general. My progression into making pots for other trees is simply a development of this interest.

I graduated from Bristol College of Art in 1977 with a degree in ceramic sculpture. After teaching for a couple of years, I studied for a master's degree in California. In 1982 I started a program of research at Southwark Institute of Art into suitable glazes for bonsai pots based on my interest in the collection of exquisite thirteenth-century Chinese ceramics in the British Museum in London.

It took two years and many hundreds of glaze tests to produce the first couple of satisfactory glazes. I have continually made tests in order to increase and improve the range of colors and textures. Despite that, I still have only five or six good glazes.

I think that it is difficult to pick the right pot for a tree. There are so many choices to be made with regard to the size, shape, color, and surface texture. I can suggest that before buying a pot, the enthusiast takes photographs of the tree and then makes several drawings of pots on paper that can be stuck on the photographs to allow comparisons between the different drawings. This may help you make the right decision as to the best shape and size. The color is a different matter. Refer to good picture books, such as the Gingko Competition books, Kokufu Exhibition annuals. and the various bonsai magazines that often display masterpiece bonsai in excellent containers.

Gordon Duffett. Published by Craig Coussins, designer of the Art of the British Potter, Fobbs Exhibition, 2000, Stratford, England.

The following illustrations cover the beginning of Gordon's life as a bonsai potter up to the present day. Gordon started signing his pots during the early 1980s and dating them (by year) in the mid- to late 1980s, and most of the pots illustrated here are dated and signed.

1 An early semi-cascade, brown, unglazed pot measuring 9 x 4in (22.9 x 10.2cm), 1973. Gordon writes: "I made this pot for an early bonsai in my collection during 1973. It was made by pressing clay into the bottom half of a plastic bucket and adding the rim and feet after the clay had hardened a bit. It was fired to 1940°F (1060°C) and was rather a naïve attempt to replicate the characteristic brown of some Japanese mass-produced pots that I had seen, although the result was not quite as bland. You can still see the shape of the plastic bucket. If I was to make the same pot now, I would glaze the pot with reference to the color of the bark and fruit of the bonsai."

2 An early rectangular, brown-olive, unglazed pot measuring 15 x 9 x 2in (38.1 x 22.9 x 5cm), 1975. Gordon writes: "This pot was made two years later and is the result of some clay body-color tests that I made using metal oxides at Bristol College of Art. The surface color and texture changes make this pot more advanced than the previous example. I created this pot for a Scots pine (*Pinus sylvestris*)."

4 A circular, brown-oxide pot measuring 10 x 2in (25.4 x 5.1cm), 1978.

3 An early green, clay pot measuring 16 x 11 x 5in4 (0.6 x 28 x 12.7cm), 1976.

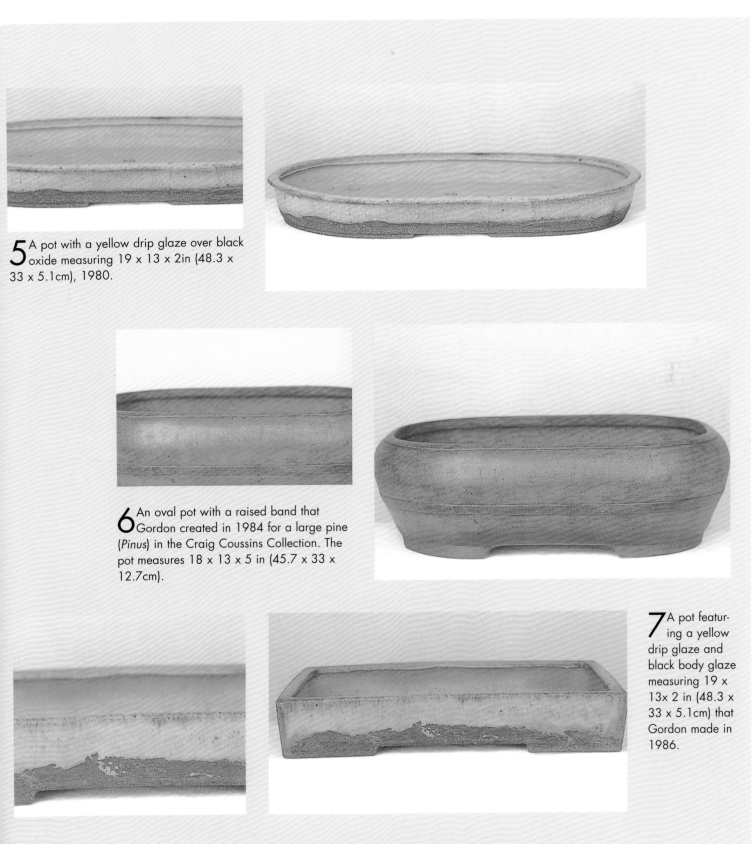

5 A pot with a yellow drip glaze over black oxide measuring 19 x 13 x 2in (48.3 x 33 x 5.1cm), 1980.

6 An oval pot with a raised band that Gordon created in 1984 for a large pine (*Pinus*) in the Craig Coussins Collection. The pot measures 18 x 13 x 5 in (45.7 x 33 x 12.7cm).

7 A pot featuring a yellow drip glaze and black body glaze measuring 19 x 13x 2 in (48.3 x 33 x 5.1cm) that Gordon made in 1986.

8 A rough, dark-brown literati pot with black highlights measuring 8 x 2in (20.3 x 5.1cm) that Gordon created in 1987.

9 A smooth, oval pot with a graded muddy-yellow glaze extending to the pot's black feet. The pot measures 7 x 2in (17.8 x 5.1cm) and was made in 1987.

10 An oval pot with a gray-beige drip glaze and black-oxide body glaze measuring 25 x 15 x 2in (63.5 x 38.1 x 5.1cm) and dating from 1988.

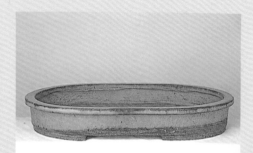

11 A pot with a rough, oxide glaze and slightly flared, shaped walls. Note the black highlights on the top and bottom edges. The pot, which measures 16 x 12 x 3in (40.6 x 30.5 x 7.6cm), was made in 1988.

12 A pot with a gray-black glaze running into black glaze and a turned lip. The pot measures 20 x 13 x 2in (50.8 x 33 x 5.1cm) and was created in 1992.

14 A drum pot and a small, square pot, with a superbly colored glaze dripping into the oxide of the body, made in 1993.

13 A rectangular pot with a fine, russet-red-colored glaze in the middle and dark highlights with a slight sheen on all of the edges. Made in 1992, the pot measures 17 x 12 x 3in (43.2 x 30.5 x 7.6cm).

15 A pot with a russet glaze, incorporating darker shades and flashes of black in some of the central areas. Measuring 24 x 13 x 2in (60.1 x 33 x 5.1cm), the pot was created in 1994.

16 An oval pot featuring a deep-blue glaze incorporating darker-blue specks and shadows. The pot measures 20 x 13 x 2in (50.8 x 33 x 5.1cm) and was created in 1997.

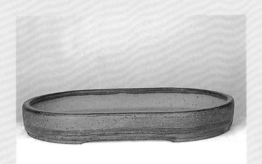

17 A superb cascade pot, with a pink-and-gray glaze over the black and brown oxides of the body. Made in 1995, the pot measures 8 x 4in (20.3 x 10.2cm). Measuring 24 x 13 x 2in (60.1 x 33 x 5.1cm), the pot was created in 1994.

18 A literati pot with variant ridges on the sides, which Gordon calls a "wobbly pot" because it is made off the true with uneven sides in emulation of a natural, organic shape. Gordon has made similar pots measuring up to 22in (55.9cm) in circumference for me. He created this 20in- (56cm-) pot in 1994.

A potter's view

Allan Harriman's English bonsai pottery is called China Mist. A popular speaker at many bonsai clubs, Allan and his wife display their wide selection of hand-made pots at most of the major bonsai shows all over the UK. I have been a fan of Allan's pots ever since he began making them, and he regularly makes large suiban in the old bronze dhoban style for my suiseki.

Designing a pot from a potter's viewpoint, by Allan Harriman (England)

How many bonsai pots do you have on your shelves? If it's a lot, don't worry: most bonsai enthusiasts have quite a collection of pots that were, or were not, purchased for specific trees. And if you purchase a pot for a tree, the decision is usually made when the tree's at home and you're in the shop. Not a good idea! Even if you do happen to have the tree with you at the time of purchase, there is still no magical solution to buying the right one. A handful of guidelines, a bucketful of experience, and a sprinkling of good luck, do, however, lower the chances of getting it wrong.

The following suggestions are useful starting points for the beginner, as well as for the more experienced bonsai-grower, when looking for the right pot for a tree. I must emphasize, however, that these guidelines are my own.

a) The length of a suitable pot is often two-thirds of the tree's height (or width, depending on which is the greater).

b) The depth of a suitable pot often relates to the trunk's diameter when measured just above the roots—the measurements should generally be the same.

c) A more reliable method of ascertaining the correct depth of a pot is to visualize the front area of the pot as measuring one-third of the tree's front area, taking into account the trunk, branches and leaves, but not the spaces. ("Negative speed" is an art term for using spaces between the object's internal structure as a part of the design. "Space" is an easier term to understand.) This is not an easy task, but well worth the effort.

d) Finally, you can obtain a variety of images by cutting out small cardboard shapes of possible pot profiles and holding them against the tree where a pot would be positioned. You can vary the image size by moving the cutouts closer or further away from the tree.

Note that for trees grown in the literati and cascade styles, points a), b), and c) do not apply and that your best chance of success in these instances is using strategy d).

Design number one

In an attempt to demonstrate the importance of the tree–pot relationship, I will start at the very beginning, when the tree, in this case a larch (*Larix*), is restyled, followed by the designing of the pot, the making of the pot and, finally, the uniting of tree and pot.

Restyling the tree

Have you noticed how some trees catch your eye? Whether it is your own tree or someone else's, it either has a certain something or it doesn't. It had been two years since I restyled this larch, transforming it from a quite boring formal upright into an equally boring slanting style. The tree has a decent taper, the branches are in the correct positions, but it lacks that certain something (Figure 1).

FIG. 1

FIG. 2

FIG. 3

It was the large, one-sided root system that had led to the style being changed to a slanting one in the first place, but the tree still didn't look right tilted. So how about tilting the soil? Or creating a little more character by using driftwood to give the illusion of a twin trunk with exposed roots on a sloping bank? (Figure 2).

Having considered these potential adjustments, the solution became clear. I would:

a) tilt the soil level to give the roots a natural look and return the tree to the vertical;

b) create false dead wood within the overly large, exposed roots;

c) connect these roots to a twin trunk made of dead wood.

Having acquired the necessary material for the false trunk and root, the grinder was set to work to create a look resembling natural dead wood. The two elements were then secured into place and their timber treated with lime sulfur. To tone down the effect of the lime sulfur, a little black stain was added and mixed before the solution was applied (Figure 3).

Designing the pot

To achieve a sloping soil level, the pot will have to be a form of crescent or crag, the exact shape of which can be decided by holding cardboard cutouts in front of the tree.

In addition, it will have to give the soil the correct angle, be large enough to contain the roots, and create an understated image of a rocky environment to complement the tree. The pot will also have to be stable (an apparently good design solution will often fall over backward!).

Making the pot

Potters are a secretive lot: it takes a long time to develop a manufacturing method that works every time (well, most of the time). Some of our methods are simply down to common sense, however, and I don't mind sharing these with you.

I make crags upside down on a bag. The clay is placed over a plastic bag covering a bag of soil in order to form a shape. The bag needs to be of the correct size and shape and has to be flexible enough to pull out of the curved pot when the clay has become as hard as leather. The whole operation can be completed in one go (Figure 4).

FIG. 4

FIG. 6

After the drying process has been completed, the pot is biscuit-fired to a temperature of 1832°F (1000°C), after which the glaze or oxide is applied. In this case, a black oxide is sprayed on the pot before it is returned to the kiln for a second firing at 2300°F (1260°C). Figure 5.

In order for it to do its job correctly, the pot must have a drainage hole at its lowest point, feet to make it stable, and plenty of tying-in holes with which to secure the tree in position. Figure 6 shows the tree and pot united.

FIG. 5

Design number two

Some fifty-year-old photographs in my neighbor's possession show that his hedge was already quite mature at that time, and when he finally decided to have it removed, I offered to dispose of it for him.

The bonsai material

FIG. 7

One of the trees that I lifted from the hedge had some bonsai potential. There was a rotted area at the base of an interesting-looking, dead-wood area of the trunk, however, and disguising this would not be easy (Figure 7).

When looking around for material to use in this project, I found a rock that fitted perfectly around the tree, covering the rotted section, and giving the appearance of having been there for years. I therefore decided to style the tree (Figures 8–9).

FIG. 8

FIG. 9

Designing the pot

The task of designing a pot for this rather unusual-looking tree, with a stone sticking out of one side, seemed daunting. After a couple of years, the rock had become part of the equation and had to be taken into consideration when deciding on the correct depth of the pot. I also had to consider the fact that the foliage pads were in an early stages of development and would become much larger (Figure 10).

FIG. 10

I decided on an oval pot two-thirds of the tree's height in length, with a depth that would give a front-of-pot area one-third of the tree and rock's total width.

Because most of the trunk was quite thin in relation to the depth of the pot, glaze would only be applied part of the way down the pot to help prevent the depth of the pot overpowering the thinness of the trunk. The lower part would be left unglazed and would be slightly textured.

When deciding on the color of a glaze, I like to pick out an aspect of the tree's natural coloring, and in this case my options were:
a) the trunk's creamy-yellow color;
b) the gray tones of the dead wood;
c) the rock's sandy brown;
d) the green of the leaves.

If an aspect of the glaze relates to one of these colors, a bond between tree and pot can be established. Alternatively, you could choose a color that contrasts with, rather than reflects, the tree's coloring.

The advantage of making your own bonsai pots is that you can experiment with different options, giving you a choice of more than one. My second choice of pot was round, with a curved profile. The diameter would be less than the oval pot's length, but it would have extra depth to meet the one-third of the tree width criteria. It would be glazed in the same way as the oval pot.

Making the pot

1 The pot being thrown on the wheel.

2 The pot being turned on the wheel.

3 The construction of the clay slabs.

Pots

4 The shaping of the oval pot's profile.

5 Spraying the crescent.

6 Brush-glazing the oval pot.

7 The tree united with the pot.

Postscript

The total amount of time spent undertaking these two projects was four weeks, just before Christmas. Assuming that they have survived the experience, the trees will look very different when spring comes and they start sending out new growth.

Alan Harriman.

The development of penjing pots in China

Craig and I will now look at the development of penjing pots in China, and the photographs that follow include some examples of Chinese pots dating from the fifteenth century to the mid-twentieth century, many of which are part of the Craig Coussins Collection. Such pots, which are collector's items in China, Japan, and Korea in particular, are the source of many modern potters' inspiration.

The growth of interest in suiseki (viewing stones) has brought about the growth in popularity of the suiban, a tray with no holes that is designed to hold a stone, with, or without, water. The dhoban (or doban) was once the container principally used for both tree-scapes and stones, and three examples are also pictured. The antique pots are Craig's.

1 A nineteenth-century Qing Dynasty kowatari, or "old crossing," pot. Measuring about 10 3/4 x 11in (27 x 29cm), and featuring a wide geho-bachi rim, it is an exceptionally well-glazed pot whose moyo (picture glaze) incorporates a beautiful aurora borealis design in shades of blue.

2 An extremely well-proportioned, earthenware Ming Dynasty pot from the late sixteenth century measuring 6in (15.9cm) in height and 10in (25.4cm) in width. Its remarkable blue moyo (picture glaze) shades depict a mountainscape.

3 A fifteenth-century white-glazed earthenware pot.

4 An eighteenth-century pot with a superb patina. This type of pot is very popular for specimen bonsai.

5 A sixteenth-century pot with a yellow glaze.

6 A smoke-glazed seventeenth-century pot.

7 A simple, Japanese earthenware pot measuring 8 x 9in (20.3 x 22.9cm). An image of Mount Fuji appears on one side, and a chrysanthemum on the other. Eighteenth century.

8 Although the style of this hexagonal pot appears very modern, it is, in fact, based on a kimono design. Its geometric shapes are like the traditional kimono coat worn by the Japanese, and it dates from around 1920. Of Chinese or Japanese manufacture, it measures 6in (15.2cm) in width.

9 A pot with rounded corners and a deep patina dating from the late eighteenth century.

10 The form of this handmade, eighteenth-century pot is excellent, and its oval holes are an unusual feature.

11 This shows the underside of the pot in picture 10.

12 A nineteenth-century pot with beautiful feet and deeply incised decorative work on its body.

13 A very rare and beautiful Qing Dynasty kowatari pot that started life as an incense-burner. Although it has been dated to 1750, I believe that it may be older and, although it is unsigned, that it was made for a member of the imperial family or palace. Measuring 15 3/4 x 11 3/4 x 5in (40 x 30 x 13 cm), this fine-quality pot features pearskin nashikawa-ara (surface texture), and shudei-da-en-bachi (width of rim edge), with deep shami-do-sides.

14 A seventeenth-century pot.

15 A seventeenth-century pot.

16 Marked with the maker's seal, this Chinese pot, which measures 13 x 10 x 2in (33 x 25.4 x 6.4cm), dates from the eighteenth century. A magnificent, terra-cotta-colored pot, it flares out well beyond the normal distance, has a deeply incised rim, stands on cloud-shaped feet, and has an excellent patina.

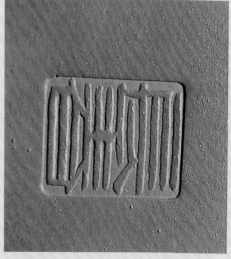

17 The underside of the pot in picture 16.

18 A ceramic pot inset with cloisonné.

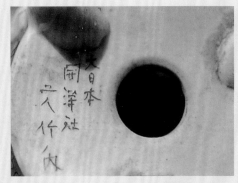

19 A close up of the signature on the underside of the pot in picture 18.

20 Dating from 1800, this wonderful Chukogu Chidai (old crossing) pre-nineteenth century Chinese pot has unusually large feet that form simple half-curves on the outside, but triangles on the inside. With a rich, terracotta-colored water glaze on the body and smoked-black edges, it measures 12 x 4in (30.5 x 10.2cm) and is marked with the maker's seal on the base.

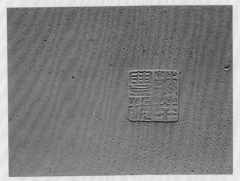

21 A close up of the maker's seal on the base of the pot in picture 20.

22 You will rarely come across a dhoban (doban) today, but this pottery suiban made by Alan Harriman resembles a bronze example. Early suibans were generally lacquered trays.

25 A group of Japanese larch (*Larix kaempferi*) in a handmade Japanese pot, which measures 35in (88.9cm) in length, from the Craig Coussins Collection.

23 The superb color of this Japanese pot is crystallized within the glaze.

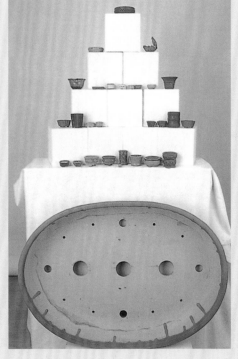

24 The largest pot measures 34in (86.4cm) in length; the rest have been designed for mame or shohin bonsai.

Pots

26 The smallest pot is a handmade receptacle for tiny bonsai.

27 A close-up view reveals its form.

28 Although Ian Baillie makes many different kinds of pot, my favorites are his literari. This is a tiny example, but he also makes very large ones.

29 A handmade miniature Japanese shohin pot.

30 These miniature pots were made by potters from all around the world. The pink one is by Vanz Pots of New Zealand, while the mixed grog pot is by Dasu Pots, which is based in Iowa; it was given to me by Frank Mihalic.

31 A nineteenth-century pot.

32 A superb, very expensive, hand-made pot from Japan. Its water glaze gives it a soft sheen.

33 Another exceptional handmade pot from Japan.

34 An English-made pot in the Chinese style.

35 A miniature pot, one of Gordon Duffett's creations.

36 Pots come in all sizes, as illustrated by this selection of pots created by Alan Harriman.

Tools

Bonsai tools, by the Joshua Roth company

There are two important principles to remember when it comes to bonsai tools. The first is that bonsai tools are specialty tools designed for a specific purpose. Using the right bonsai tool for the task can make the bonsai experience a pleasure rather than a chore. The second is that using a well-maintained tool rather than a neglected tool is just as important as using the right tool. A well-cared-for tool, used properly, will work for you, making your bonsai experience what it should be: a source of enjoyment.

A lot has been written about the importance of caring for your tools—tools of any kind, from everyday garden implements to the utensils used in the most exacting of crafts or professions. Not as much has been written about the importance of using the right tool for a specific purpose, however, so that is where we will start.

Using the right tool for the job

Bonsai is an art, and you owe it to yourself to have the right tools for your art. It is not only important to know your tools' purpose, but also their limitations. So use the appropriate tool for the work to be done and, as with any art, don't forget that the most important tool of all is your imagination!

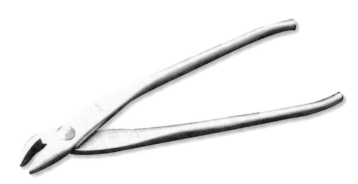

A pair of pliers

It is also important to purchase the highest-quality tools that your budget will allow. In general, the life of the tool relates directly to the hardness of the steel used in its construction, to the manufacturing method employed, and to the attention to detail paid during assembly. The harder the steel, the more difficult it is to manufacture, hence the variations in cost from grade to grade. A true stainless steel, with the cutting edges laminated with a high-carbon compound to extend their sharpness and life, increases the cost, but the result is a tool that really will last a lifetime.

Basic tool requirements

Cutting away the unwanted portions of a tree is crucial to the art of bonsai. The most important tools for this task are shears and pruners. Pruning enables you to shorten a branch or the height of a tree, as well as remove unwanted branches entirely. Shears enable you to thin and defoliate bonsai, but are not meant to cut woody or dead ends of branches. Each of these tools works in a different way: shears cut using a by-pass action, while cutters bite, and the edges of biting tools usually overlap slightly so that they close one over the other, without making contact.

A basic assortment of bonsai tools should include those needed to accomplish basic pruning and shaping tasks, as follows:

- a pair of concave-cutters;
- a pair of shears;
- a pair of leaf trimmers;
- a bonsai rake;
- a pair of bonsai tweezers;
- a saw;
- a pair of wire-cutters.

Concave-cutters

The single most important tool for bonsai use is a pair of concave-cutters. There is no substitute for them because they are designed to cut branches flush to the trunk, resulting in a cut that heals faster and leaves less scarring than if another type of tool were used. Concave-cutters are sold in several sizes, and the most useful to start with is a pair with an overall length of around 8in (20.3cm), a size that has a medium-sized cutting surface, making it a good choice for most cuts.

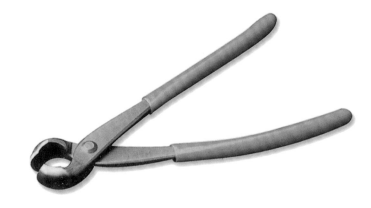

A pair of half-concave-cutters (or half-wen cutters)

There are also special-purpose concave-cutters, such as spherical concave-cutters (also known as knob-cutters). The blades of spherical concave-cutters are more rounded than those of standard concave-cutters and make deeper spherical cuts, which are round, hollow, and heal in the most aesthetically pleasing way, leaving the least-visible wounds. Spherical concave-cutters are used for thick roots or heavy knots and are not a substitute for basic concave-cutters.

For smaller, more delicate bonsai, the Me-Tsumi concave-cutter, because it is a smaller size than the regular concave cutters, permits incredibly fine, close cuts to be made when working on very small foliage, such as that of young bonsai and the new growth of larger trees. Knob-cutters (also known as knot- or wen-cutters) are used in conjunction with concave-cutters when a deeper bite is required to produce a wound that heals over easily, resulting in a more natural look.

Shears

A pair of larfe shears

Shears are the basic tools used for bud-trimming, thinning foliage, and defoliation, all of which are crucial components of the art of bonsai. Although many sizes and shapes of shears are available, you'll find two sufficient to start with.

Bud-trimming shears have a generous opening between the handles, which helps to prevent you from injuring other buds as you are pruning your target ones. These shears are designed to cut at all points of the blade edge, thereby giving you control over what you are cutting by enabling you to cut only those parts that need trimming, leaving the surrounding foliage undamaged.

A pair of 8in (20.3cm) Ashinaga shears with 2in (5cm) blades is a good, basic, by-pass tool for thinning and defoliating bonsai. A pair of shorter Hasami shears is the best type of shear for cutting capillary roots. Its stronger blades are also excellent for light

branch-cutting and general bonsai-trimming, making it a useful pair of combination shears for gardening and cutting flowers, as well as bonsai.

Leaf-trimmers

A pair of miniature leaf-shears used for defoliation

Leaf-trimmers, also known as defoliating shears, are the preferred tool for removing unwanted leaves and buds because they enable the fast and precise removal of foliage. Leaf-trimmers are sold in a variety of sizes and styles, and it's a matter of personal preference whether you buy a pair with straight or angled blades.

Other types of specialty shears designed to accommodate different foliage densities and depths and, most importantly, personal preferences, are also available.

Rakes and tweezers

A soil rake

Rakes and tweezers are also useful tools to include in your basic bonsai tool set. Rakes are used for working the soil during the transplanting process, to remove soil from around the bonsai's roots, as well as to stir up the soil as part of your bonsai's general care. Most bonsai rakes also incorporate a spatula at the other end with which to tamp down the soil around the base of a bonsai.

Bonsai tweezers are used to remove dead leaves, insects, foliage needles, weeds, and other types of fine debris from around the base of the bonsai. They, too, often have a spatula at the other end.

Tools

Saws

A saw is a must for most root-pruning. The advantages of using a saw instead of shears are two-fold. First, using bonsai shears with which to cut into a root ball would damage their fine cutting edges. Second, if you use a saw that cuts on the pull strokes, which I recommend, it prevents the blade from bending, reduces binding, and improves the smoothness of the cut.

A root saw

Root-cutters, root-hooks, and root-picks

Root-cutters, root-hooks, and root-picks are also useful tools for root-pruning. Root-cutters are specifically designed to prune roots during the transplanting and repotting processes. Unlike knob-cutters, which have spherically contoured heads, their wide—usually 1/2in (1.25cm)—cutting blades are straight. Their blades are much stronger, too, making them ideal for cutting the denser, woody fibers that are usually found in roots. In addition, the head of a pair of root-cutters is contoured to provide added clearance.

Root hooks and root picks are used respectively to untangle and separate small- and medium-sized capillary roots during the transplanting and repotting processes.

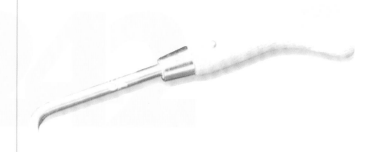

A root hook

Wire-cutters and branch-benders

Wiring, another way in which to alter the shape of branches and trunks, is done either to preserve the bonsai's current shape or to produce a different form. Unlike the wire-cutters found in most tool-boxes in the home, bonsai wire-cutters are specifically designed to cut bonsai wire and have a rounded head to prevent the bark from being damaged, enabling you to get really close to the branch or trunk as the jaws cut the wire symmetrically and cleanly. Basic bonsai wire-cutters are available in many sizes, the thickness of the wire being used dictating the size required.

Branch-benders are used either to curve or straighten branches that are too heavy or awkward to be bent with wire.

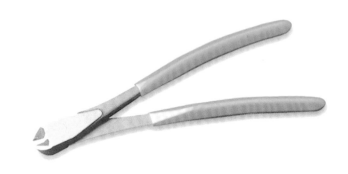

A pair of short-headed wire-cutters

Specialty tools

Jinn pliers are specialty tools that will strip bark and fiber from a tree to create jinn. Their angled head also makes them suitable for working with bonsai wire. Further useful tools for making jinn include a Graving tool set consisting of bark scalpels and chisels designed to remove bark.

Trunk-splitters are designed to split trunks, thereby causing minimal residual damage. The shape of the head and the symmetrical cutting blades provide the clearance and cutting action necessary to achieve clean splits.

A pull saw

Tool care and maintenance

Regular care and maintenance are essential if you want the best performance from your bonsai tools, as well as minimizing the need for repairs or replacements. It's therefore important to observe the following care and maintenance measures.

- Always store your tools inside, preferably in a pocketed tool roll that protects them from each other.

- Do not drop your tools.

- Don't twist or wrench shears or cutters while cutting because this will throw their blades out of alignment and ruin the tool.

- After each use, clean your tools with soap and water or rubbing alcohol and remove any resistant sap with a little turpentine.

- After cleaning them, always dry your tools and lubricate them lightly with a good-quality, rust-preventative lubricant like Tri-Flow™ or WD40™ (which does not attract dust and dirt).

- Remove any rust or minor pitting with a rust-eraser, such as Sandflex™ by Klingspor™ or wet-and-dry sandpaper (can be used wet or dry). Grit is embedded throughout the sandflex™ rubber-compound block, and continued use exposes new grit. The block is self-cleaning, easy to use, and can also be shaped to special contours. Rust-erasers can also remove water salts and stains from the edges of bonsai pots.

- Keep cutting edges free of nicks.

- Before cutting branches or roots, carefully remove any small pieces of gravel or dirt that may be clinging to them.

- Sharpen cutting edges only if necessary and if you know what you are doing.

- Remember that by-pass blades like shears should be sharpened in a different manner to blades that meet, such as cutters. Read the instructions given on each set of shears.

- Cutters and shears have different beveled angles, and you must maintain the original bevel and angle of the tool if it is to work properly when you have finished sharpening it.

- When sharpening knob-cutters or concave-cutting tools, do not remove their overbite. After they have been sharpened, concave-cutters may need adjusting by filing the stop pin to ensure that they close properly.

- Remember that if they are properly cared for, good-quality bonsai tools will hold their cutting edge for a very long time.

Soil scoops

A mini-pencil blowtorch with which to bend dried jinn

A pair of tweezers

A pair of clamps

Carving tools and bits

Today's bonsai artists use power tools to remove wood quickly from bonsai (see the section on carving trees, page 202), and as we develop our skills, so specialist manufacturers the world over, such as William Vlaanderan's Samurai Tools in the Netherlands, are meeting our demand for the bits that we need for our routers and grinders. The following photographs illustrate some of the router bits that I use.

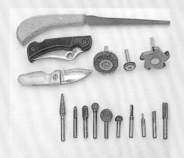

1 Using a Dremel™, or mini-router, with fine bits will result in very detailed carving.

2 Angle-cutters and routers will quickly remove wood from larger trees.

3 I consider the Samurai cutter to be the best cutting blade on the market.

4 Samurai Tools' mini-cutters are available with 3mm (around 2/16in) and 6mm Shanks.

5 The Samurai TornadoT™ cutter is my preferred size for most carving work.

6 These three bits, which are manufactured by Samurai Tools, cover most of my carving needs.

7 Flapper heads can be attached to router machines, and this carbide wheel is a very good cutter and bark-remover.

8 Remember to protect yourself whenever you use power tools. Wood dust contains carcinogens, so wear a mask, along with a pair of goggles to protect your eyes.

The art of the viewing stone

Suiseki, as it is known in Japan, North America, and Europe, has many other names in the Far East—gongshi ("fantastic rock shapes") in China, "long-life rocks," in Korea and suisok in Indonesia—all of which have a long association with bonsai and penjing. In her excellent work, *The spirit of gongshi*, Kemin Hu, who is a world renowned expert on Viewing and Scholars Stones, quoted the following poem by the great Tang Dynasty poet Bai Juyi (A.D. 722–846). The poem is one of the earliest-recorded celebrations of the imagery in a rock.

Then I turned toward my two rocks asking
if they would stay with me when I am old.
They could not speak yet seemed to say
that they would remain my faithful friends.

Bai Juyi lived in Suzhou, in China's Jiangsu Province, near Lake Taihu, where many famous, deeply eroded limestone rocks are found.

Notable viewing-stone collections

Notable viewing-stone collections can be seen in many places around the world. In the United States, the Boston Museum of Fine Arts has a particularly good collection, which was started nearly ninety years ago, and a fine stone stands outside the museum. The Penjing and Suiseki Pavilion in Washington, DC, also includes the National Bonsai Collection, while the Golden State Bonsai Collection can be seen in San Francisco. Among other notable Western collections can be counted the Penjing and Bonsai Exhibit in the Montreal Botanic Gardens. Some excellent gongshi stones can be viewed in China, including collections at the Imperial Garden and Summer Palace in Beijing, Yuyuan Garden and the Stubborn Rock House in the Guqi

Gardens in Shanghai, Zhan Garden in Nanjing, Tinglin Park in Kunshan, Jiangnan Famous Stone Garden in Hangzhou, and Liuyuan Garden in Suzhou. Many more collections can be viewed on the Internet.

An introduction to viewing stones

Bonsai or penjing and viewing stones, suiseki or gongshi, are inextricably linked. The appreciation of stone landscapes began in China and Korea nearly two thousand years ago, part of the culture of appreciation of miniature trees, with or without stones. An appreciation of the stones in their own right evolved, along with distinctions between Chinese, South East Asian, and Japanese appreciations of such images.

European and North American interests took their own paths, and I have therefore asked Felix Rivera, one of the United States' most respected authorities on viewing stones, to give you an introduction to the modern philosophy of suiseki.

Pictured in this section are suiseki from Felix Rivera's collection, all of which were collected in California, with the exception of that pictured on page 249 (Ligurian Stone), which he collected in the Italian Alps. Also featured here, as well as throughout *Bonsai school*, are some Chinese stones, both traditional and contemporary, that have never been seen in the West before. These were sent to me by some of the most important Asian collectors through my friend Liu Jian Jun.

Suiseki can reflect mountainscapes like these in miniature.

A view of the Dolomites in Italy. Many suiseki can look like such an image.

Unraveling the secret worlds within stone, by Felix Rivera (United States)

Suiseki are small stones that have naturally weathered into aesthetically pleasing shapes. Many suiseki suggest mountains, islands, and waterfalls; others resemble human or animal figures or are prized for their colorful or abstract textures. Collected in the wild, on mountains and in streambeds, and then displayed in a natural state, these stones are objects of great beauty. They are also sophisticated tools for inner reflection that stir an appreciation for the awesome power of the universe in all who see them. The Japanese have gathered suiseki for many centuries, but the art has only recently become popular in the West, especially among bonsai-growers.

Suiseki are dark in color, with an elegant patina symbolizing the timelessness of the art. Their pristine condition, universal appeal, and suggestiveness contribute to the appreciation of suiseki as works of art. The beauty and evocative powers of suiseki enable viewers to stimulate their own memories of past events and places; they create emotional connections and serve as a medium for relaxation. For some collectors, the quest for suiseki is akin to a spiritual or mystical experience.

The aesthetics of suiseki

The most important variable in the appreciation of suiseki is that of their beauty. Their attractiveness comes about from a grouping of elements unique to the natural world that have come together, unmodified, in a manner deemed beautiful by the standards of art. Suiseki imitate nature in their content, proportion, shape, color, and texture. The better a suiseki's intrinsic qualities, the more powerful its evocative strength and beauty.

A suiseki is millions of years old. It has arrived at its present shape through the inexorable forces of nature. Captured in its static form are thus the dynamics of time, heat, cold, and weathering. Ironically, the more eroded and battered the stone, and the longer it has been engaged by the elements, the more it is assured of becoming an object of artistic appreciation.

A suiseki may be viewed quite simply as a pretty stone with a nice shape or it may be viewed at the various levels of complexity that embrace art, philosophy, or mineralogy. It can also serve as a metaphor for the connection between one's private world and the universe. These levels of enjoyment and appreciation make the appreciation of suiseki not merely an art form, but a means by which field collectors can achieve personal satisfaction and peace.

Collecting suiseki

There are a several techniques that a collector can use to increase the chances of finding good-quality material suitable for suiseki. Careful preparation leads to sites with potential stone and mineral availability and thus to successful collecting. There is more than luck and preparation involved here, in my opinion, and the coming together of a stone and field collector can indeed be akin to a spiritual experience.

The Japanese call the collecting site the "kawa dojo" (roughly translated, "the classroom of the riverbank"). As they study the endless sea of rocks before them, field collectors are able to discover potential suiseki by matching rocks against their mental images of both natural landscapes and those good-quality stones in their own collections that they have built into landscapes over the years.

Metaphors in stone

The art of suiseki begins with the collection of stones in nature and culminates in a new sense of beauty and an emotional and spiritual relationship between the field collector and the stone. Suiseki's charm and attraction as a hobby and, indeed, as a way of life, lies in its elegant simplicity: a stone in its natural state is admired for its unique shape, color, and mineral properties or for the way in which it provokes memories of events and times past. A well-proportioned suiseki satisfies the eye, yet inspires awe; through the process of scaling, it can reproduce a famous mountain or island in miniature. Suiseki can also be treasured as spiritual and philosophical constructs, making them metaphors in stone that help us to connect with, and understand, those things that we value in life.

Yosemite

A suiseki measuring 15 x 12 x 6in (38.1 x 30.5 x 15.2cm).

A suiseki measuring 12 x 8 x 7in (30.5 x 20.3 x 17.8cm).

A suiseki measuring 19 x 9 x 7in (48.3 x 22.9 x 17.8cm).

A suiseki measuring 11 x 6 x 3in (27.9 x 15.2 x 7.6cm).

A suiseki measuring 14 x 9 x 4in (35.6 x 22.9 x 10.2cm).

A suiseki measuring 23 x 8 x 5in (58.4 x 20.3 x 12.7cm).

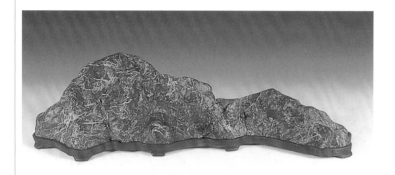

A suiseki measuring 19 x 5 x 8in (48.3 x 12.7 x 20.3cm).

A suiseki measuring 11 x 7 x 11in (27.9 x 17.8 x 27.9cm).

A suiseki measuring 11 x 3 x 3in (27.9 x 7.6 x 7.6cm).

A suiseki measuring 18 x 8 x 7in (45.7 x 20.3 x 17.8cm).

A suiseki of Ligurian stone measuring 21 x 9 x 4in (53.3 x 22.9 x 10.1cm).

A suiseki measuring 6 x 6 x 6in (15.2 x 15.2 x 15.2cm).

A suiseki measuring 11 x 7 x 2in2 (7.9 x 17.8 x 5cm).

A suiseki measuring 25 x 8 x 8in (63.5 x 20.3 x 20.3cm)

A suiseki of Ligurian stone measuring 21 x 9 x 4in (53.3 x 22.9 x 10.1cm).

A suiseki measuring 20 x 1 x 9in (50.8 x 2.5 x 22.9cm).

The art of the viewing stone

1 These natural rocks in northern Spain resemble a Chinese landscape and embody the kind of image that bonsai artists aim to recreate.

2 This rock planting, which I created on a limestone rock measuring 32in (81.3cm) in width, is intended to suggest trees growing on the edge of a canyon.

3 A Korean suisok, with the image of a glacier running through its center.

4 Collected in England, this suiseki suggests a snow-capped mountain.

5 A Japanese furuyashi stone. These stones are found in a remote part of Japan and are very mountainous in shape.

6 This stone was collected in the United States, from California's Eel river.

7 The peaks of the Gweilin (Guilin) region of China are inspirations for both suiseki and saikei (rock planting).

8 A very tall stone from Lake Taihu.

9 Stone collected from Lake Taihu features in many Chinese gardens, such as this one near Lake Taihu.

A final word

When studying bonsai, be it by reading books like this or working with bonsai teachers, you will need a degree of patience, as well as enthusiasm. In this vein, I would like to borrow my final words from another authority, Professor Hew Choy Sin, of the National University of Singapore, who, on opening the Sixth Penjing and Stone Exhibition in Singapore, said the following words. I was moved by the purity of the professor's reflection:

"Any form of art is the crystallization of human culture. Man can not live without art. Penjing is a highly technical knowledge combining horticulture, art, literature, and human cultivation into a creative art form. It's a silent poem and a three-dimensional painting which brings and adds charm to our life."

Index

Credits and acknowledgments

Photography credits
Robert Atkinson/Craig Coussins: 212-214
Dan Barton: pp3, 198
pat breen: pp162-163, 177, 193, 194, 200t, 200br, 201
lew Buller: pp211, 24tl, 40, 41
Craig/Svetlana Coussins pp12, 17r, 13, 15, 16, 17, 19, 20b, 22bl, 23br, 24r, 24bl, 25t, 32b, 34b, 36t, 64, 65, 66, 67, 68, 71, 74, 75, 76, 77bl, 78, 82tr, 87, 88, 102-107, 109-111, 113, 115, 116tm, 116l, 116r, 116b, 116br, 117, 118m, 118br, 119l, 120l, 126-161, 164-166, 170-172, 175-176, 178, 186-188, 195, 199, 200bl, 215-217, 225-228, 231-236, 237t, 237, 238-244, 250
FOBBS: 38, 39, 72, 73, 77t, 77br, 116tr, 116m, 116bm, 118t, 118bl, 119r, 120r, 121-125
Reiner Goebel: pp218-223
Frank Mihalic: pp173-174
Dinh Nguyet-Mai: 179-181
Michael Persiano: 203-205
Felix Rivera: pp245-249
Koos Le Roux: pp182-185
James Russell: pp14, 18, 20t, 23t, 25b, 32t, 32l, 32r, 33t, 34t, 186tl
Bob Shimon: pp196-197
Tony Tickle: pp168-169
William Valavanis: pp6, 7, 71, 82bl, 83, 206-211, 229
Duncan Wiles: pp189, 190-192
Po Man Wu: pp11r, 25tr, 26-31, 32br, 33ml, 35, 36b, 42-47, 69, 91, 171, 211
Yerbury Studios: pp1, 8, 9r, 10, 111, 21r, 22tl, 22r, 114, 237m
(where t=top, b=bottom, l=left, r=right, m=middle)

I would like to thank the following people:
The committee of the Federation of british Bonsai Societies (FOBBS) for their outstanding help in making available the library of images from FOBBS conventions over the past few years. John North, Kathy Shaner and the committee of the Golden State Bonsai Federation Collection North, based in San Francisco, for allowing me access to the collection and taking photographs of gardens and scenes.
My grateful thanks, too, to the many bonsai artists and friends who have supported me. They include the following individuals.
Lit Van Phan and Lew Buller. Lit's section on Hon Non Bo (see pages 179 to 181) is based on their book, *Mountains in the sea: The Vietnamese miniature landscape art of Hon Non Bo*, Timber Press, Portland, Oregon, 2001. My thanks to both Lit and Lew for supplying the images to accompany this section.
Po Man Wu, of the famous Man Lung Penjing, the collection of the late Yee-Sun Wu, for his wonderful help in bringing Chinese penjing artists to the attention of us all. We are indebted to the following Chinese publications for their help to Man Lung Penjing; Zhongguo Huahui Penjing .(2) *Flowers Trees Potted Landscape* (Penjing Shangshi). Patrick J Breen, for the Metasequoia photographs (from Oregon State University, Department of Horticulture, Agriculture, and Life Sciences, 4017 Corvallis, OR 97331, USA) that appear in the section on giant redwoods (see pages 195 to 201).

Credits and Acknowledgements

Liu Jian Jun, for sharing his wonderful photographs of viewing stones from China
Gary W Field, of the Angelgrove Tree Seed Company trees-seeds.com
Frank Mihalic and his father, Tony Mihalic. The Mihalics own and operate Wildwood Gardens, in Chardon, Ohio, USA (wildwoodgardens.com) where I have had the pleasure of working.
Joe Day, for his kindness, advice and help with *Bonsai school*.
Rob Moak, for working with me and for his extremely helpful suggestions.
William Valavanis, who also sent me some photographs of his own wonderful bonsai creations from the William Valavanis Collection in Rochester, New York, USA
Thuenis Roos, Jessie Edwards, and Duncan Wiles.
Reg Bolton, the chairman of the Federation of British Bonsai Societies.
Felix Rivera, for the use of some of the stones illustrated in his own book, *Suiseki and Miniature Landscapes*.
José I Ileó Faura and his Rooter Pot™ (see pages 106 to 107) (rooter-pot.com)
William Vlaanderan, of Samurai Tools, in the Netherlands, whose website can be found at: www.samurai.nl
Valerio Gianotti, for spending a week with me and for working very hard with his assistant, Enrico Stracca.
Salvatore Liporace.
Gary Marchal and his Cajun bonsai.
Tony Tickle, for his article on making a raft-style bonsai (see pages 167 to 169).
Robert Baran, for his help with the history of bonsai and penjing (see pages 26 to 39). (Robert J. Baran would like to acknowledge the two principal references for his articles on Japanese bonsai and Chinese penjing: *Chinese penjing, miniature trees and landscapes*, by Yunhua Hu (Timber Press, Portland, Oregon, 1987, and Wan Li Books Co Ltd, Hong Kong) and *The living art of bonsai*, by Amy Liang (Sterling Publishing Co Inc, New York, 1992).
Karen Zaller, Tony Sarraceno, Gloria Dugger, the Kopenen family, George Straw, Lance Williamson, Maria Theresa Volunterio, David Prescott, Robert Atkinson, Joy Williams, Kath and Malcolm Hughes, Robert Porch, Dan Barton, Peter Tapper, Simon Misdale, and last, but certainly not least, Alex Ferry, who looks after my trees when I am away, helps me to lift the really big 'uns and makes some kind of sense out of my gardens.
If I have forgotten anyone in my drive to finish this book, please forgive me, let me know and I will make a full apology on my website.
One final mention, and the most important for peace and harmony in my own life: I wish to pay homage to my wife, Svetlana, who sustains my mind, heart and soul. Thank you for having been there when I needed you. You are my best friend and my muse, my reason to write, live and my reason to love. "Ya lubli yu tebea maya zaitchka."

Recommended bonsai magazines

There follows a list of recommended, extremely high-quality, English-language bonsai magazines that were available at the time of writing. A serious student of bonsai should subscribe to all three, as well as to the Internet magazine mentioned below. It's a small investment to make in return for so much wonderful information. Other bonsai magazines may also be published in your country.

International Bonsai Magazine, published by William Valavanis, Rochester, New York. This contains Oriental and North American stylings. For more information, visit internationalbonsai.com

Bonsai Today, available in North America, the UK and other English-speaking countries. The material featured is from Japan. The magazine is published in other countries under different names. For more information, visit www.stonelantern.com

Bonsai in Europe, published by Farand Bloch. This high-quality magazine covers European bonsai stylings. For more information, visit www.bonsaimagazine.com

One or two Internet bonsai magazines are currently available,
1. presented by Frank Mihalic: wildwoodgardens.com
2.. DaichiBonsai.com

Detailed information on many of the artists and people involved in bringing you *Bonsai school* are on my Links Pages at bonsaiinformation.co.uk